TELEVI

SCREE

From Conce

Fourth Edition

TELEVISION AND SCREEN WRITING

From Concept to Contract

Fourth Edition

Richard A. Blum

FOCAL PRESS
Boston • Oxford • Auckland • Johannesburg • Melbourne • New Delhi

–Heinemann.

∞ Recognizing the importance of preserving what has been written, Butterworth–
Heinemann prints its books on acid-free paper whenever possible.

Butterworth–Heinemann supports the efforts of American Forests and the Global ReLeaf
program in its campaign for the betterment of trees, forests, and our environment.

Library of Congress Cataloging-in-Publication Data

Blum, Richard A..
    Television and screen writing: from concept to contract / by
Richard A. Blum. –4th ed.
        p.cm.
    Includes bibliographical references and index.
    ISBN 0-240-80397-3 (alk. Paper)
    1. Television authorship. 2. Motion picture authorship I. Title.

PN1992.7 .B58 2000
808.2'5—dc21
00-058735

British Library Cataloguing-in-Publication Data
A catalogue record for this book is available from the British Library.

The publisher offers special discounts on bulk orders of this book.
For information, please contact:
Manager of Special Sales
Butterworth–Heinemann
225 Wildwood Avenue
Woburn, MA 01801-2041
Tel: 781-904-2500
Fax: 781-904-2620

For information on all Focal Press publications available, contact our World Wide Web
home page at: http://www.focalpress.com.

10 9 8 7 6 5 4 3 2 1
Printed in the United States of America

FOR ILENE, JENNIFER, AND JASON

Contents

PART FIVE: TELEVISION SCRIPTS

Acknowledgments

I was pleased to learn that the second and third editions of this book have become classics in the field. They have been used widely at universities, professional workshops, and studio story conferences, and by television and film writers nationwide. I am grateful to all the readers, writers, teachers, and users of this book, and it is due to their interest and enthusiasm that this fourth revised edition is possible.

There have been some significant changes in the industry and I have tried to incorporate them into this volume. I encountered many people who provided valuable resources and offered practical suggestions for this book. For the latest creative trends, formats, techniques, and marketplace insights, I received much help from studios, production companies, the Writers Guild of America, trade publications, and specific Websites. Please see specific names and acknowledgments below.

At Focal Press, my thanks to publisher Marie Lee for strongly recommending I do this fourth edition. And thanks to Terri Jadick, my editor, for her reliable knowledge and guidance.

My University of Central Florida screenwriting student assistant, Paul Fields painstakingly reviewed and updated information in the figures, bibliography and appendixes. This edition would not have been completed without him. Colleagues at the University of Central Florida, among other universities, have shared their professional insights and values. My gratitude to you all.

I would like to thank my family for bearing with me, once again, in the preparation of this book. I am particularly grateful to my wife, Ilene, for her understanding and patience over these many months. She provided many helpful ideas and personal support at every stage. Words cannot express how much I appreciate that. And thanks, too, to my children,

Jennifer and Jason, who showed constant interest in the progress of this book. I appreciate their endless support.

My writing students served as the initial impetus for this book. The questions asked, issues discussed, projects written, and experiences shared helped codify the concerns of talented new writers. I hope this edition fulfills some of their needs, and yours, in the pursuit of many films and television writing credits.

Friends and colleagues offered a strong network of support.

Richard D. Lindheim provided professional advice and granted permission to use script samples from: "Frasier," episode entitled "Hot Pursuit," first draft written by Charlie Hauck. All rights reserved; "Becker," episode entitled "One Angry Man," from a first draft script by Dan Wilcox. All rights reserved; "Star Trek: Voyager," shooting script entitled "Life Line," story by John Bruno and Robert Picardo, Teleplay by Robert Doherty and Raf Green. All rights reserved. He also granted permission to reprint excerpts from our previous books, *Inside Television Producing* (Focal Press, 1991) and *Primetime: Network Television Programming* (Focal Press, 1987), which are out of print. He is Executive Director for the Institute for Creative Technologies at the University of Southern California and Consultant for Paramount TV Group. We expect to co-author a new book entitled *Law & Order: The Official Inside Story*.

Dr. Frank Tavares suggested it was time to do a new edition for the new millennium and had many sound ideas. I appreciate his reliable feedback. He also granted permission to reprint story and screenplay excerpts from "The Elton Project" © and from "The Beltway Bandits." All rights reserved.

Software program Final Draft, Inc. granted permission to utilize all format samples, which are part of its software program. All rights reserved.

Screenwriting software program, ScriptThing, Inc., granted permission to reprint the Sample Multimedia Script with permission of Script Perfection Enterprises. All rights reserved.

Hollywood Scriptwriter: The Trade Paper for Screenwriters granted permission to reprint "Writing Effective Query Letters," by Kerry Cox. All rights reserved.

Dr. Gregory A Rogers, granted permission to reprint story and screenplay excerpts from "MODE VIII"© screenplay by Rick Blum, based on the novel by Gregory A. Rogers. All rights reserved.

Done Deal, at this Website: http://www.scriptsales.com/ granted permission to reprint "Loglines for Current Script and Pitch Sales," "Television Deals - Project Sold and Setup," "A Sample Release Form," "Major Studios and Production Companies," and "Television Production Companies." All rights reserved.

InHollywood.com at this Website: http://www.inhollywood.com, Jason Agard, Webmaster, granted permission to reprint "Script Sales by Studio - 1999," "Script Sales by Genre - 1999," and "Script Sales by Source Material - 1999." All rights reserved.

Moviebytes.com at this Website: http://www.moviebytes.com/ granted permission to reprint the "Selected Screenwriting Contest List." All rights reserved.

Dan Wilcox, co-writer of "The Wind Chill Factor," granted permission to reprint excerpts. All rights reserved.

"The WGAw Agency List," "Portions of the WGA 1998 Theatrical and Television Basic Agreement Theatrical Compensation," and the "WGAw Theatrical Short-Form contract (for employees)" are reprinted with the permission of the Writers Guild of America, west, Inc. They are also available at the WGA Website at: http://www.wga.org/. All rights reserved.

The "Interactive Program Contract" and the "Informational Program Contract" are reprinted with permission of the Writers Guild of America west, Department of Industry Alliances. All rights reserved.

1

Introduction

When I was asked to revise the fourth edition of *Television and Screen Writing: From Concept to Contract* for the new millennium, I was reminded that it was one of the best-selling books in the field and a classic resource for students and professionals. I knew that this revision was an important opportunity to include the most up-to-date resources and practical information for screenwriters and television writers in the twenty-first century and beyond. I also wanted to make the book more accessible for screenwriters and television writers, by focusing first on screenwriting techniques and then on television writing techniques.

No producer, executive, or agent will pick up a script unless it's in the proper format. Not all worthy projects will be produced—in fact, most scripts won't even be read—but if the project is well-written in concept, style, and format, then it stands a much better chance of being evaluated. Technique and format are essential for writers who seriously intend to enter the mainstream of the profession.

After working in the industry and analyzing industry requirements, I've concluded that writing for motion pictures and the small screen share these needs: the development of producible stories, appealing and castable characters, credible dialogue, expert structure, and skillful visualization. This book shows how to fulfill each of these needs for theatrical motion pictures, the sitcom series, one-hour dramatic series, long-form television, soaps, talk shows, variety, animation, interactive and new media, and non-fiction entertainment.

This book gives you specific techniques for writing high-quality and producible scripts. It reveals the secret of creating a driving force for characters in the premise and demonstrates how that is the core of all successful motion picture and television scripts. It discloses how to become a creative and marketable writer in every professional arena, including for major studios, production companies, networks, cable and pay TV, interactive programs, screenwriting contests, and national and state funding agencies.

One of the most important skills for writers is to learn how to develop *spec* scripts ("speculative" means you don't get paid for it). That script serves as a consummate sample of your ability to write for film and television. It markets you as a professional to agents and producers.

In motion pictures, the spec script serves a twofold function. First, if you get a lot of interest and create a "buzz" on a script, then it may generate that rare but headlined million-dollar spec script sale. In 1999, two of my students, Chris Skinner and Brad Keene, sold their first spec screenplay, "Gravediggers," to Artisan Entertainment for $200,000. The project script is a horror film and generated a lot of interest. The screenwriters got exclusive representation by the William Morris Agency. On the basis of that "buzz," they were invited to set up a few pitches to various studios. A new deal might be on the horizon for them.

Artisan is also the same company that purchased the rights from five former University of Central Florida students, including Daniel Myrick, Eduardo Sanchez, Robin Cowie, and Michael Monello, for "The Blair Witch Project." It cost around $35,000 to produce. In its first two weeks of general release, it earned more than $50 million in profits.

That same year, 1999, on the basis of his spec script, a former student, Duane Adler, was hired to write a screenplay titled "Save the Last Dance" for Paramount and the Cort/Madden Company. Robert Cort and David Madden are the producers. It is an interracial love story about a 17-year-old white girl and an 18-year-old African American boy, a dance movie in the tone of "Saturday Night Fever." It took three years for the project to reach production. At that point, he was officially hired to write another project, and this one is an ensemble, coming-of-age story in the tone of "American Graffiti" and "Rebel Without a Cause."

Another former student, Malcolm Johnson, whose spec script won an African American screenplay competition, just landed an assignment for Warner Brothers, who are doing a remake of the 1970s film "Superfly."

Many others optioned their feature screenplays to the major studios and production companies, including every genre. In fact, most spec scripts are optioned, rather than sold outright.

The second purpose of a spec script is to have your agent submit your script as a sample of your work to a producer who is actively in preproduction. That producer may hire you to "fix" a screenplay in rewrite. That has also happened to my students.

New television writers can shine with a spec script showing an understanding of the existing story structure and character relationships in a current series. Freelancers who deliver producible scripts often find themselves hired as staff writers. If they're successful on staff, then they move up the ladder to become *show runners* (writers-producers). Show runners are worth their weight in gold, earning millions per series.

In terms of developing new series, over the years the costs of pilot and series production have escalated wildly, and networks, cable, and pay TV fought for survival in a raw competition for viewers. As a result, networks are much less likely to want to launch a new show, especially if they do not know the writer. In the late 1990s, however, a new phenomenon called "put" pilots occurred, in which the developers are guaranteed a slot in the competitive schedule. So, there is a section on how to develop new series in this latest revised edition.

There is something very gratifying about developing new motion picture and television projects. Perhaps it relates to the writer's eternal fantasy of creating something that will have an impact on an audience. Think of the frustration you feel seeing a movie with characters that are wooden or a plot that is a bomb. Think of the television viewer, who is bombarded with banality every night. In a real way, this book is about how you can affect the quality of that barrage. Knowing the ground rules for success can help you improve the quality of what millions of viewers see. It's a worthy fantasy to pursue.

The fact is that the writer who stands the best chance of making it is one with industry awareness and contacts, coupled with talent, technique, and indomitable perseverance. If you're willing to confront incredible odds with highly professional scripts, then your perseverance might pay off. The industry consumes thousands of stories and scripts every season. It requires a horde of talented writers to keep the home fires burning and to draw audiences to see a box office smash.

This book can provide you with certain writing techniques, but only you can provide the essential ingredients of talent and creativity. Once you know the format, the demonstration of imagination and style is up to you. Why not put them to work and see what happens?

Part One details how to create marketable premises for motion pictures and TV. It explains how to create a driving force for characters in the premise and analyzes successful motion picture premises, including high concepts, loglines for current script and pitch sales, successful independent film loglines, and other successful motion pictures. The challenge of adaptation is also explored. This section also scrutinizes all aspects of television, including loglines from successful sitcoms and dramatic series. It covers developing projects for television films and movies of the week, as well as animation, interactive and new media, and nonfiction entertainment.

Part Two analyzes the creative process of story development. It shows how to develop a marketable story. Chapter 3 examines genres and themes, and plot patterns that are most recognizable in film and television. Chapter 4 explores how to write the story. It explains where to begin: how to choose the story area and the lead character, and how to advance the story effectively. There is a discussion of strategies for developing convincing treatments and step outlines, with a sample narrative treatment and sample step outline, as well as storylines for television. Chapter 5 examines dramatic elements and act structure in motion pictures and television. It deals with the issues of dramatic elements in a story, classical three-act structure, structure in motion pictures, plotting audience interest in your story, and sample audience interest curves.

Part Three is centered on character development and dialogue. Chapter 6 details the most effective devices for developing castable characters. It also demonstrates how "Method" acting techniques can be used to create dimensional characters in the script, as "The Method Writer." This chapter illustrates how character arcs are used to effectively build characterization in film and television. It also discusses the importance of setups and payoffs for lead characters. Chapter 7 reveals how to write realistic dialogue. It unravels the top-ten worst dialogue problems and solutions—how dialogue problems can be identified and corrected in the script phase of writing.

Part Four is centered exclusively on motion picture screenplay format. It unravels all of the techniques of spec screenplay format, including details about formatting a screenplay and how to prepare it professionally. This chapter also examines the latest screenwriting format software and software for script development. Chapter 9 details how to write effective scenes in screenplays. It offers eight pitfalls in scene descriptions, and how to solve them. It also highlights the importance of writing effective opening scenes and provides samples from screenplays. Chapter 10 is short but important because it provides a checklist for script revision and tips on how to apply the final polish to your screenplay.

Part Five deals exclusively with television scripts. It unravels the specific techniques of television sitcom writing. Chapter 11 details TV sitcom format and offers vital professional format samples from current hit sitcom series, including "Frasier," "Friends," and "Ally McBeal." It also provides a sample cast and set list from "Frasier" and a sample tentative production schedule from "Becker." Chapter 12 analyzes how to write professional scenes in sitcoms. It demonstrates the significance of sitcom characters and dialogue, and it provides professional script samples and analysis of scenes from "Frasier" and "Becker."

Chapter 13, which is new for this edition, encompasses the latest trends in animation, interactive and new media, and nonfiction entertainment. It provides animation script format professional samples from current animated series, including "King of the Hill," "The Simpsons," and "South Park." This chapter also deals with interactive and new media, and presents a sample for multimedia script format. It also offers samples of the latest interactive and informational program contracts.

Chapter 14 examines television drama format. It analyzes spec TV drama script structure and provides essential professional format samples from current hit drama series, including "ER," "Law & Order," "NYPD Blue," "Star Trek: Voyager" and "The X-Files." Chapter 15 examines how to write professional scenes in TV drama. It analyzes action, characters, and dialogue in TV drama. It also provides vital professional samples from "Star Trek: Voyager."

Chapter 16, which is another new addition for this edition, encompasses soaps, talk shows, and variety. It covers soap opera writing format and offers professional format samples from current soaps, including "Days of Our Lives," and "General Hospital." It also offers a sample song segment from a late-night television talk show.

Chapter 17 details how to create new television series. It examines how TV series concepts are developed and the impact of "put" pilots. It differentiates series concepts, presentations, and series bibles. It demonstrates how to create marketable television series concepts, explains what makes an effective TV series concept, offers a sample concept from "Coach," and details how to write original TV series presentations. The art of *pitching* ideas—and personal ingredients necessary for successful pitching—is also revealed in this section.

Part Six details every aspect of marketing and selling your script. The odds against selling a new project are staggering, but without knowledge of the marketplace, there's no glimmer of hope for success. This section provides the answers every writer should have to key questions, as well as a fully detailed examination of the marketplace and distinct strategies for marketing spec scripts.

Chapter 18 examines how to sell your motion picture screenplay— what you should know before marketing, how to register and copyright your script, joining the Writers Guild of America (WGA), the release form, writing query letters, the synopsis, how to prepare your script for submission, submission status reports, and how to get an agent. This chapter also helps you analyze the marketplace, with information on major studios and production companies, script sales by studio in 1999, spec screenplay trends, sources for top grossing films in 1998, spec screenplay trends in 1999, script sales by genre for 1999, script sales by source material for 1999, the million-dollar spec script, pitching, development trends in theatrical motion pictures for 1999–2000, and sample going rates for "star" screenwriters for 1999–2000. It also includes business deals and contracts for spec screenplays, including the Writers' Theatrical Short-Form Contract, screen credits and arbitration, and a closing section on writing violence in films.

Chapter 19, also new for this edition, details how to sell your television script—what you should know before marketing, how to register and copyright your script, and how to get an agent. This chapter helps you analyze the marketplace, with marketing trends in television and the television writers' marketplace. It includes information on writing professionally for television, pitching TV series concepts, long-form television, business deals and contracts in television, and credits and arbitration.

Chapter 20, the final chapter, investigates national funding sources (CPB, PBS, NEA, NEH) and state funding sources, as well as private foundations and corporate sources. It explains how to write grant proposals and how projects are evaluated.

The *Appendixes* offer a wide range of contacts for you to explore and contain the most up-to-date resources. *Appendix A*, located at the back of this book, includes Portions of the WGA 1998 Theatrical and Television Basic Agreement Schedule of Minimums. Our companion website, available at www.focalpress.com/companions, offers information and links to major studios and production companies, television production companies, state film/television commissions, state arts and humanities agencies, and professional unions and associations. Also available on the website is an *Annotated Bibliography* for further reference.

Just as an actor learns basic techniques to create effectively, so the screenwriter and TV writer must learn techniques of writing, from the germination of an idea to the revision of a final draft. If the stress on format seems a bit dogmatic at times, please remember that competition is incredibly stiff, and a professional-looking script can help you past that first major hurdle—getting the project read.

PART ONE

CREATING MARKETABLE PREMISES FOR MOTION PICTURES AND TV

2

How to Create Marketable Premises for Motion Pictures and TV

The Importance of a Producible Plot and Castable Characters

I had the pleasure of studying screenwriting with the legendary Irwin R. Blacker at USC (the University of Southern California). He taught screenwriters the importance of using Aristotelian Greek dramatic theory as applied to screenwriting. He forced screenwriters to know Aristotle's theories inside out and to think of a screenplay as a blueprint for making a film, with the same constructs classical playwrights used to appeal to audiences, including the three-act structure, and the importance of plot, conflict, character, exposition, and dialogue in well-written scripts. Irwin Blacker's lectures were published posthumously in a valuable guidebook for writers entitled *The Elements of Screenwriting*.

USC screenwriting students learned the craft of dramatic storytelling well. Among them were George Lucas (STAR WARS), Willard Huyck, Gloria Katz, John Milius (AMERICAN GRAFFITI), Francis Ford Coppola, Robert Zemeckis and Bob Gale (BACK TO THE FUTURE), Dan O'Bannon (ALIEN), David S. Ward (THE STING), and John Singleton (BOYZ N THE HOOD).

Successful screenwriters and teachers may have different personal approaches, but they agree that marketable scripts should be written with a clear structure. Richard Walter, head of the UCLA graduate screenwriting program, uses a classic three-act structure. So does his UCLA colleague, Lew Hunter. Linda Seger has eight sections within three acts. Linda J. Cowgill uses the Aristotelian concepts to analyze dramatic structure. Syd Field has a three-act paradigm. Robert McKee uses a five-part narrative. John Truby sets out his seven major steps.

Prolific screenwriter William Goldman (BUTCH CASSIDY AND THE SUNDANCE KID, MARATHON MAN, MISERY, ALL THE PRESIDENT'S MEN, THE PRINCESS BRIDE, and A BRIDGE TOO FAR) and author of the tell-all book *Adventures in the Screen Trade: A Personal View of Hollywood and Screenwriting* and the sequel *Which Lie Did I Tell: More Adventures in the Screen Trade* is noted for two of the most famous phrases in screenwriting: "Screenplays are structure" and "Nobody knows anything."

As Goldman suggests, a screenplay can't be produced without input from producers, studios, actors, and directors. For a script to be marketable, it must have strong and flattering star roles; otherwise, no one will want to play the parts. Big stars will only agree to do a film if they get all of the good lines and all of the memorable moments in the script. Even if you write independent films, you will have to write a story and script that will be produced, directed, and marketed correctly. Here is how.

How to Create Quality Premises for Spec Scripts That Will Be Producible and Marketable

One of the most important skills for writers is to learn how to develop professional "spec" scripts that will be appealing to producers and serve as qualitative samples of your work. *Spec* script mean "speculative"—you don't get paid for it. That screenplay serves as a consummate sample of your ability to write for film and television. It markets you as a professional to agents and producers. If you're very lucky, the screenplay will sell for a fortune.

New television writers can shine with a spec script showing an understanding of the existing story structure and character relationships in a current series. Freelancers who deliver producible scripts often find themselves hired as staff writers. If they're successful on staff, then they move up the ladder to become *show runners* (writers who also produce). Show runners are worth their weight in gold, earning millions per series.

My approach is based on Aristotelian theory and is professionally realistic. Screenwriters need to create quality stories and scripts that will be producible and marketable, or no one—director, actor, producer, studio executive—will take them seriously. After working in the industry and analyzing industry needs, I've established the following working principles to help achieve that goal for your spec script:

- The premise has to be unique and focused, so it can be pitched in a *logline*. A logline is the sentence or two that tells the film's story, like a *TV Guide* blurb.
- The genre must be clear and consistent. The spine of the story must be clear, and the driving force of the story has to be credible to push your characters into action.

- The characters have to be strongly motivated and susceptible to give them appeal and castability.
- The story has to offer conflicts and twists for your characters to overcome.
- Your writing style must reflect an understanding of production pragmatics.

Creating the Driving Force for Characters in the Premise

The easiest way to set up a crisis in the story is to create a driving force for your main characters. Put them in a situation in which they need to achieve an important goal. Any obstacle you throw in the way becomes a significant conflict to be resolved. They must overcome those problems with ingenuity and successfully deal with new story twists.

Whichever genre you write for, you can use the same principles to analyze the effectiveness of the premise. For example, let's examine sample loglines for motion picture premises, then television.

Motion Picture Loglines

In features, the logline has to be told in a carefully crafted sentence or two, suggesting how characters deal with the driving forces of the story. You can find film loglines in the local papers, in motion picture catalogues, or in movie guides. You can also find film synopsis on Websites like Moviebytes at www.moviebytes.com or CinemaMedia at www.cinemedia.org.

A most relevant Website called Done Deal (www.scriptsales.com) lists all of the current loglines for scripts and pitches sold each quarter and each year. Read the loglines for all scripts and pitches sold carefully. They will give you an idea of the kind of marketable loglines you need to write. *The Spec Screenplay Sales Directory, 1991–1999* offers a comprehensive listing of loglines for scripts and pitches sold, as well as contact production companies. It is available online at www.hollywoodlitsales.com.

High Concepts

A film has a much better shot at being developed if it can be pitched as a high concept. In a *high concept*, the premise can be told in a sentence or two with a unique twist for casting and special marketing appeal. It's all story-driven. For example: What happens if dinosaurs go wild in a modern theme park? What if a comet is heading toward the United States? What if extraterrestrials land and want to destroy the world? What if astronauts are forced to abort a critical mission in the ocean during a hurricane?

Where did the high concept come from? Robert Kosberg, the "pitch king," says: "It seems to have started with Barry Diller and Michael Eisner and other executives who were at ABC doing television movies and they realized that 40 million people were tuning in to watch TV movies on any given night, based on one or two sentences that were written in *TV Guide* that boiled down the entire plot. . . . For instance, the movie 'Splash' is a man meets a woman and the woman turns out to be a mermaid. That's a very high concept because that plot drives the whole movie."[1]

Kosberg reminds writers that "the really great high concept stories are the ones that the minute you hear the idea expressed, you know it because one scene inevitably flows from the one before." [2]

Successful Loglines for Current Screenplay and Pitch Sales

To stay on top of current loglines for scripts and pitches sold, go to the Done Deal Website at www.scriptsales.com. The following is a sample of the script and pitch sales for January 2000. It is reprinted with permission of Done Deal.

TITLE: STEVE WAS HERE

Logline: Centers around a financially depressed desert town that decides to stage a fake UFO landing in order to generate tourism and reap the benefits much like Roswell does. But the townsfolk find they are in for more surprises than they ever imagined.

Writer: Norman Steinberg

Agent: ICM's Mike Eisner

Buyer: Centropolis Entertainment

Price: Six Figures

Genre: Science Fiction/Comedy

Logged: 1/20/00

More: Jonathan Frakes will direct this pic that Centropolis purchased from their discretionary fund. Story was developed by Steinberg and Michael Hertzberg. Frakes will produce, along with partner Lisa Olin and Hertzberg, with Centropolis partners Dean Devlin and Roland Emmerich exec producing.

TITLE: THE GUARDIANS—BOOK ONE: THE UNBOUND

Logline: Story about an 18-year-old superhero named John Porter who discovers that he has the power to defeat an evil organization planning on taking over the world.

Writer: Larry Shultz and Dave Smeds (authors)

Agent: n/a

Buyer: Warner Bros.

Price: Small $$$ upfront, but a significant backend to the creators

Genre: Super-Hero/Action

Logged: 1/15/00

More: Studio optioned this unpublished manuscript, created by Stan Lee and Larry Shultz, and is thinking about it as a possible franchise pic. Manuscript was written by Shultz and Dave Smeds and is the first novel in a series.

TITLE: DEMOLITION ANGEL

Logline: Centers on a female bomb squad detective and a male ATF agent who are tracking down a serial bomber.

Writer: Robert Crais

Agent: Broder-Kurland-Webb-Uffner's Tricia Davey, Emile Gladstone, and Norman Kurland

Buyer: Columbia Pictures

Price: $525,000 against $1 million

Genre: Thriller

Logged: 1/14/00

More: To be adapted from Crais' upcoming novel due out this May, published by Ballantine. Pic will be produced by Laurence Mark, who made a preemptive bid on this acquisition.

TITLE: BLACK ICE

Logline: Centers around LAPD homicide detective who finds his partner dead of suicide in a sleazy LA hotel. As he investigates, he discovers not only that it may not have been suicide, but it may not have even been his partner.

Writer: Scott Rosenberg

Agent: Barbara Dreyfus/ ICM

Buyer: Columbia

Price: $1.3 million with undisclosed backend points for Rosenberg

Genre: Detective Drama

Logged: 1/11/00

More: Rosenberg will rewrite his own original 1992 adaptation of Michael Connelly's novel. This is a joint production between Columbia and Paramount. Col will submit all creative elements to Paramount for approval, with the studios splitting both the domestic and foreign grosses equally if all the elements are agreed upon. Should Paramount not accept their proposal, Col can go at it alone, or with another partner. Rumors have it that Oliver Stone, John Frankenheimer, and Steven Soderbergh are on the studio's wish list for directors. Mace Neufeld will produce.

TITLE: THE BRIGADE

Logline: True story of a group of Palestinian Jews who were trained by the British and made into a battle brigade that fought the Nazis in WWII. Later, they began importing Jewish refugees into the Middle East in what would later become Israel.

Writer: Howard Blum (author of book)

Agent: CAA's Robert Bookman repped author

Buyer: Miramax

Price: Mid-six figures

Genre: Drama

Logged: 1/7/00

More: To be adapted from Blum's soon-to-be-published novel. Nick Wechsler and Keith Addis will produce.

Disclaimer: All data provided by Done Deal is provided on an "as-is" basis, and any or all warranties of any kind or character whatsoever, whether express or implied, including, without limitation, any warranty of merchantability or fitness for a particular purpose, are hereby expressly disclaimed. Done Deal does not guarantee or warrant the sequence, accuracy, timeliness, or completeness of any such data/material. Done Deal shall not be responsible or liable to any person or entity whomsoever for injury, claim, liability or other cause of any kind or character whatsoever based upon or resulting from any data/material provided.

As you can see, in successful premises, the lead characters are integrally related to the plotting, which must be credibly motivated and dimensionally conceived.

Successful Independent Film Loglines

Independent films or genre-mixing films need the same kind of setup in the loglines. Here are premises from several successful independent films.

AMERICAN BEAUTY

A magazine professional takes a self-improvement course to extremes in this black comedy when he quits his job and starts to pump iron, buys a hot car, and gets a job in a fast-food joint to impress a young girl. He has a high-powered, real-estate–selling wife.

The screenplay by Alan Ball won awards and acclaim, including the 2000 Best Screenplay Award from the Academy of Motion Picture Arts and Sciences and the Golden Globe Awards. The film is about Lester Burnham (Kevin Spacey), a 42-year-old husband and father who suffers midlife crisis and suburban angst. In an interview, Ball reveals different inspirations for the screenplay: "I was very fascinated by the Amy Fisher trial. I felt there was a real story underneath the media hype that I'm sure, in a way, was more fascinating and way more tragic then any that we can see from just the media coverage. In the first draft of "American Beauty," there's a big media trial in which Ricky and Jane are being tried for Lester's murder because the videotape finds its way into the hands of the police. And then I had an encounter with a plastic bag one day in front of the World Trade Center. Also, I've had many jobs that I just detested, working for people that I had absolutely no respect for. A lot of Lester's story came from direct personal experience. I grew up in a household with a somewhat troubled father figure and a somewhat shut-down mother figure, so Ricky's household certainly resembles mine in ways." [3]

He revised the script constantly, up to ten times, but there was no structural change. The mixing of the genres was purposeful, to offer "different tones" in the script. As Ball explains, "I always think when you're able to really mix drama and comedy, it makes both of them stronger. If you've just seen a really funny scene, and then something heart breaking happens, it's got more impact and vice versa."[4]

THE SIXTH SENSE

A celebrated child psychologist, who's healed from a gunshot injury, is driven to treat his first patient, a boy who sees ghosts. The psychologist (Bruce Willis) is the only one who can help the boy.

Written by M. Night Shyamalan, the screenplay won enormous acclaim and huge box office financial successes. The film was a ghost story with a unique "twist" at the end: We learn that the psychologist himself was killed at the beginning of the film. The child was seeing him. Shyamalan recalls the process of writing the story and screenplay drafts: "I kill anything that resembles anything I've ever seen before. Even if it's great, if it smells like piracy, or copying . . . it's dead. . . . The first draft of 'The Sixth Sense' was a serial killer movie. The film script that was sold was the tenth draft. The first draft was a very powerful movie about a kid who saw the victims of a serial killer, and the hunt for this serial killer. But it kept changing; bit by bit, the parts with the ghosts became more and more unique. I've never seen that expressed before, and then the serial killer parts—which were good—I'd seen before . . . I said, 'that's not even part of this movie anymore.'"[5]

As for his process of writing, he outlines the story and revises it constantly.

"I spend months outlining. And by months I mean, I outline it, and that's all I do . . . the outline changes, and then eventually you have to commit. You're reading the outline and go, 'Yeah, I am going to be able to commit the next two years of my life to this.'"[6]

Asked about his strategy of writing a marketable story, Shyamalan responds:

"I've written so many films and some of them are impossible to market. I try to write very different so that they don't feel like other movies. That's a great thing and a bad thing. . . . The studio doesn't know what it is, doesn't know which audience is for it."[7]

Discussing the specifics of his deal, he reveals: "It was the first time ever that a spec screenplay had been green-lit without a rewrite . . . The deal ended up being $2.5 million up-front versus $500,000 deferred. So it was $3 million total for writing and directing services."[8] He had cast approval and technical approvals if the budget was under $10 million. The film was the twelfth highest domestic grossing film of all-time.

THREE KINGS

Special Forces soldiers hunt for a cache of hidden gold bullion in post–Gulf War Iraq.

This comedy-drama was written and directed by David O. Russell, from a story by John Riddle. Special Forces Captain Archie Gates (George Clooney) joins forces with GIs Army Sergeant Troy Barlow (Mark Wahlberg), staff Sergeant Chief Elgin (Ice Cube), and Private Conrad Vig I (Spike Jones) to find the gold bullion snatched from Kuwait by Saddam's army, located on a map they found.

Captain Archie Gates has a strong personal driving force. He's about to retire in two weeks and sees a quick way to make life much better for himself and the others. Working on their vulnerabilities, he convinces them to join together to find the gold bullion and better their lives. They search for the gold in a desert village but encounter confusing situations and twists right up to their final destination. At the end, the Americans are welcomed with open arms by Iraqi civilians, who believe that President Bush is going to back their efforts to overthrow Saddam with U.S. support. The Special Forces treat them brusquely in their single pursuit of the gold bullion, but the Americans need the help of locals to find and carry the bullion. In a confrontation with the Iraqi soldiers, Gates and Elgin are forced to fire on the

Iraqi soldiers who are about to shoot civilians. The Americans flee, but one of them, Barlow, is captured and tortured. Through story twists, his position is revealed by calling on a U.S. cell phone. Now the driving force is set up for the other American soldiers to find him and save him at all costs.

In an interview in *Written By,* screenwriter David O. Russell reveals that "the film that I just made challenges people's perceptions of the way war ended, and the way the guys in the American Army fell, of who the Iraqi Arabs are, and what violence is. It also had more conventional aspects to it, like action and movie stars."[9]

The *Written By* interviewer points out that the film never lets you forget that the people being shot were human beings. Russell's response: "Well, it's provocative, and it's not going to make $100 million domestically because it is harsh in many ways and not easy. . . . This was a good year. Warner Bros. made my movie, which I think was surprising to a lot of people. It raised a lot of eyebrows. And there were high-up executives at Warner Bros. who tried to pull the plug on it when we were in pre-production. It had red flags all over it for them. Politically, stylistic and, it just seemed to violate their whole play book for movie making. It didn't fit into any of those easy categories."[10]

THE BLAIR WITCH PROJECT

In this horror mock documentary, three student filmmakers disappear while investigating the legend of a witch in Maryland.

Five former University of Central Florida students created this mock horror documentary, including Dan Myrick, Eduardo Sanchez, Gregg Hale, and Mike Monello. Myrick and co-writer/director Ed Sanchez demonstrated that screenwriting can sometimes be different than a standard 120-page script. They started with this spooky premise: "What if three filmmakers vanished in a Maryland forest while shooting a documentary about a witch who, according to local folklore, has haunted the area and committed periodic murders for more than 200 years? What if their footage turned up, but not their bodies?"[11]

They created a story outline about the documentary crew's adventure in the haunted woods, and they hired three actors to improvise within this outline. The actors camped out in the woods for eight days, and at each location, with baskets of food rations, were handed directorial notes from Myrick and Sanchez. They watched dailies footage with producer Gregg Hale before writing the next day's corrections. Myrick and Sanchez shaped and refined their story by editing the footage into a pseudo-documentary.

After months of outlining and writing, the final shooting script was a 35-page outline. According to Ed Sanchez, "Dan and I came up with a really detailed outline about a year before we shot it, and outlined hour-by-hour of what was going to happen. Then we broke down that outline into scenes, and then we kind of broke that down further and said, 'how are we going to get people to do this?' A lot of things changed as we developed the outline."[12]

Their low-cost independent film, estimated to be around a $35,000 budget, was purchased for $1.5 million by Artisan Entertainment after its screening at the 1999 Sundance Film Festival. With only marketing carefully orchestrated on their Website—and despite derision from other distributors—the film broke all box office records. In its first two-week general release, it earned more than $50 million. By the end of 1999, the film garnered a $140 million domestic payday. It has changed the way independent filmmaking is perceived.

THE CRYING GAME

A romantic thriller set in Northern Ireland. A sensitive IRA terrorist, Fergus, befriends a British hostage he's been ordered to execute. After the soldier is killed, Fergus flees to London and becomes intimately involved with the soldier's femme fatale lover Dil. Fergus discovers Dil's secret—he is really a transvestite. Fergus must deal with that relationship, forcing him to question his political alliances and his life choices.

The script by Neil Jordan was nominated by the Motion Picture Academy for Best Original Screenplay and by the Writers Guild of America for Best Screenplay Written Directly for the Screen (1993). But the premise was actually considered too political and too "unappealing" for audiences. It was perceived as an art film with little prospect for box office appeal. When it was first scripted, no studio or independent producer wanted anything to do with THE CRYING GAME.

As revealed in an article in *Variety,* Neil Jordan originally wrote the script in 1983, calling it THE SOLDIER'S WIFE. The story was about an IRA member who winds up romantically involved with the wife of a soldier he held hostage. Because it was so heavily political and character-driven, no one wanted to finance it. As Neil Jordan recalled, the story was "unformed and incomplete." Eventually, he added the twist of a transvestite lover and the story took off.[13]

But the major studios still turned it down. An early version of the film was screened at Cannes, and the studios felt it would not make a profit.

Financially troubled Miramax put up $1.5 million and screened it at film festivals in New York, Toronto, and Telluride. At the screening, audiences were urged by Neil Jordan and Miramax not to reveal the plot twist secret.

That was the marketing ploy that worked. The marketing pitch was meant to play down the story's political elements and play up the film's premise as "the movie everyone is talking about, but no one is giving away the secrets." They sold it as an action thriller with a big secret. It debuted domestically in November 1992 and earned nearly $40 million in domestic box office gross by March 1993.[14]

That kind of hype usually surrounds films like PSYCHO and reminds me of the marketing genius of filmmaker William Castle (ROSEMARY'S BABY). I was his associate on the television series based on ROSEMARY'S BABY ("Ghost Story" and "Circle of Fear"). In his heyday, horror film producer William Castle had audiences sign releases that they would not hold the studio liable if they saw the film and had a heart attack. They lined up around the block to see what the fuss was all about.

Loglines From Other Successful Motion Pictures

These are loglines from other successful motion pictures. Think about how the edges of the characters push the story action. Try to do the same when you look at films.

JURASSIC PARK

Two paleontologists, two kids, a hippie mathematician, and an old billionaire developer get trapped in a high-tech theme park 120 miles off Costa Rica with a horde of hungry prehistoric dinosaurs.

This is a classic survival story written by Michael Crichton in his book and screenplay. He set up an extraordinary universe for the story. In this meeting of man and dinosaurs for the first time in 65 million years, whatever can go wrong will go wrong. The driving force is set in motion when billionaire developer John Hammond (Sir Richard Attenborough) egotistically invites a select group to be the first to tour the park—before it's ready to open. The complications take off when the guests arrive, including Dr. Alan Grant (Sam Neill), his colleague and love interest Ellie Sattler (Laura Dern), and two insufferable preteen kids. They are all awestruck at what they see.

But the first twist occurs when a character motivated by greed interferes with the plans. A computer hack, Dennis Nedry (Wayne Knight), knocks out the security system so he can steal valuable vials of mosquito blood. The second twist occurs when an unexpected storm approaches and the "nonaggressively bred" dinosaurs become hungry and violent. As the crisis unfolds, each of the characters, including the two kids, has to survive in the enemy territory of the stampeding dinosaurs. At the climax, the kids, of course, survive on their own virtues.

When his book, *Jurassic Park*, was first submitted to producers, Michael Crichton's agency, CAA (Creative Artists Agency), bypassed the usual auction process. They submitted it to six studios and a few top filmmakers, including Steven Spielberg, with a firm price tag of $2 million for the book. According to *Variety*, $500,000 would go toward a first-draft screenplay written by Michael Crichton. Every studio agreed to the terms, but Crichton chose to develop the script with Steven Spielberg.[15] Crichton knew that Spielberg was a master of storytelling and special effects—an essential element in making the film's dinosaurs "real."

When the film opened, amidst a global marketing blitz by MCA/Universal (which is where Steven Spielberg was headquartered), the film shattered all box office records. In its opening weekend, Jurassic Park pulled in more than $50 million in ticket sales, making it the biggest opening weekend in box office history. In 1993, the film grossed $338,929,640, more than any other film.

HOME ALONE

Kevin, a geeky eight-year-old, is accidentally left home alone by his family, who flew to Paris for Christmas.

In this screenplay by John Hughes, the driving force of the story occurs when Kevin (Macauley Culkin) is left alone and has to deal with his own insecurities—and two burglars. At the beginning, he enjoys the unanticipated treat by indulging in junk food and videos. Then he finds that he must deal with harsh reality—two burglars, Harry (Joe Pesci) and Marv (Daniel Stern), prowling the emptied house during the holiday season. He's compelled to save his home from the intruders. He sets up clever diversion tactics and booby traps. Those actions set up sight gags for the burglars, who have little dialogue but provide funny moments for the audience. By the resolution, Kevin has made a motivated transformation but wishes for his family back in time for Christmas. Because it is a holiday movie and a fantasy genre, that's exactly what happens.

The film was relatively inexpensive to produce, costing $18 million, and earned nearly three times that at the box office. The character was so well-liked and the premise so successful that it was a natural for a sequel, HOME ALONE II: LOST IN NEW YORK. In that premise, Kevin takes the wrong plane to New York and must fend for himself while his family vacations in Florida. He sets himself up in a fancy suite at the Plaza and deals head-on with the two bandits, who also arrive in New York.

MY COUSIN VINNY

Vinny, a Brooklyn attorney who just passed the bar exam, is asked to defend his cousin Bill and his college friend, Stan, who are being tried in a small town in Alabama for a murder they didn't commit. With his sexy girlfriend, Mona Lisa, he sets the conventional local court system on its ear with his unorthodox methods.

This is a high-concept comedy by Dale Launer: What happens when a Brooklyn lawyer who just passed the bar goes to Alabama to defend his cousin on murder charges? The driving force of the story is set up by the arrest of Bill (Ralph Macchio) and Stan (Mitchell Whitfeld), who accidentally shoplift a can of tuna and mistakenly confess to a murder charge. They call Vinny (Joe Pesci) to help. Vinny arrives in his pink Eldorado with his sexy girlfriend Mona Lito Lisa (Marisa Tomei). In the script, everybody else despises Vinny and Mona in town, including the judge (Fred Gwynne), who cites Vinny for contempt at every turn. Vinny and Mona Lisa are driven to help at all costs, and to prove themselves to be intelligent and imposing combatants. At the resolution, they win the case and free Bill and Stan.

BASIC INSTINCT

A psychological cat-and-mouse game is played by a bisexual writer (Catherine) and a San Francisco homicide detective (Nick) who is investigating the ice-pick murder of her male lover. Because a rock singer was also killed with an ice pick in the prime suspect's current best-seller, finding the murderer takes greater urgency.

In the screenplay by Joe Eszterhas, the story's driving force is Nick's passion for the sexual bait thrown by dangerous and sensual Catherine. He's after the murderer. She is revealed through story twists to be a bisexual ice-pick murderer. Nick's life is on the line, but he craves her.

The script for BASIC INSTINCT earned Eszterhas an enormous screen-writing fee of $3 million. The characters were highly castable, appealing to box office megastars Michael Douglas (Nick) and Sharon Stone (Catherine). The film drew protests from gay and lesbian groups, who objected to the depiction of a bisexual murderer in the lead role. Still, it grossed more than $350 million globally.

Joe Eszterhas, writer of SLIVER, FLASHDANCE, and JAGGED EDGE, has sold several story ideas that earned him more than $10 million over the next two years, including a $3.4 million script about mobster John Gotti. Interviewed in *Time*, Eszterhas is depicted as a feisty screenwriter who fights vigorously to keep the controversial elements and intense atmosphere in his scripts: "I've always believed in fighting for my work. . . . I've taken great pride in being a writer, and I demanded a certain kind of treatment. When I haven't been treated that way, I've either fought back very hard or I've walked."[16]

UNFORGIVEN

William Munny, a retired outlaw who is now a farmer, takes up his gun again and rides with old pal Ned Logan and youthful Schofield Kid because he needs the reward money. The bounty hunters face brutal law enforcement opposition from Sheriff Little Bill Daggett.

This is a Western, but with a classy dimension and castable characters. The script, by David Webb Peoples, was nominated by the Motion Picture Academy for Best Original Screenplay and by the Writers Guild of America for Best Screenplay Written Directly for the Screen (1993).

At the outset, we are introduced to Munny (Clint Eastwood), a legendary ex-gunfighter who admits he's been "lucky when it comes to killing peo-ple." We get to know him as a widower who barely makes a living as a pig farmer to support himself and his two kids. That's the susceptibility that makes him likable for the audience.

The driving force of the story is set up when the hothead young gun-slinger Schofield (Jaimz Woolvett) lures Will to join him on a bounty hunt. He needs the money, and the motivation is set up for one last ride. Will pulls in his old partner Ned (Morgan Freeman), and they all set off for the bounty hunt in Wyoming. The story creates a powerful antagonist in the character of the sheriff (Gene Hackman), who is viscerally opposed to bounty hunters in his county. So the characters of Will and the sheriff are driven, by their natures, to a bloody showdown in the climax.

Adaptations

With an increased marketplace for features based on a novel or play, the process of adapting literary works has become an important skill for many writers. In a novel, an author can spend a great deal of time on character development, exposition, and the free association of time and place. In a motion picture script, that same story must be told in a 120-minute structure. That means streamlining the plot and characters from the book.

A screenwriter must be an artistic surgeon, with a very fine and sensitive touch, knowing what must go and what must stay. Ideally, the adaptation should remain faithful to the original work, conveying the same feeling, atmosphere, plot, and characterization, even though scenes, characters, and conflicts have been modified. The final project must be producible and castable.

Adapting novels is very complex, cumbersome, and requires enormous endurance to bring it to the screen. Yet, *Variety* observes: "Filmmakers persist in morphing novels into movies as current marquees."[17]

Analyzing how many adaptations served as the source for the Academy of Motion Picture Arts and Sciences' Best Picture Award, *Variety* found that, "of the 71 best pic winners, 30 have been based on novels." Novels accounted for 42 percent of films' awards.[18]

Anthony Minghella, writer-director of THE TALENTED MR. RIPLEY, acknowledges that, "People think adaptations are mischievous and trespassing and trample all over the source material."[19] Scott Hicks, co-writer-director of SNOW FALLING ON CEDARS attests that: "The dictates of the novel and cinema are different. You're dealing with a medium of emotion not intellect."[20] Lawrence Bender, co-producer of ANNA AND THE KING suggests that, "It doesn't matter what you have as far as authenticity goes; the story has to work."[21]

John Irving, who adapted the screenplay for his THE CIDER HOUSE RULES, insists, "If someone had forewarned me that it was going to take four directors and 14 years, and that there would be two novels I wouldn't write as a result of writing that screenplay . . . well, I probably would have declined to write it."[22] He took a blue pencil to the characters in his novel: "I believed that the characters had to have the same emotional effect on an audience as they had on readers."

In an interview with *Written By*, John Irving openly discusses the frustration and perseverance necessary to see his vision through. "I think people presume that the abortion subject, the delicacy or difficulty of that issue, was why it took so long to make this film, and that is simply not true. Why it has taken so long to make this film is that, from the beginning, I said, 'I have director approval, cast approval, script approval.'"[23]

When asked if he thinks the outcome made the 13 years of toil worth it, he states: "My wife and agent point out to me that 13 years is probably two novels. There's at least one novel, probably two novels, I would have written that I didn't write because of how many times I was working on that script. I'll never get those [novels] back. But I think that's a function of being my age. If I were in my 30s, I wouldn't think twice about that. But I'm 57 and you begin to think, 'Well, how many more novels are you going to write, anyway?' You start counting. And so that's the one negative I feel: I can never get back those books I didn't write. I was doing this. I do favor the novel more than the film."[24]

As for new writers adapting published works, it will be no more than an exercise in futility if acquisition rights are not obtained in advance. Producers, major studios, and production companies are in a constant competitive bidding war for new material, and they have enormous financial resources behind them. Chances are very slim that they'll miss a newly published piece, and even slimmer that a newcomer will outbid them.

In the face of that discouraging reality, a determined writer might still dig up an old paperback or newspaper headline that has outstanding casting and marketing potential. If you do find a project that seems suited for adaptation, investigate the legal situation thoroughly. Contact an attorney to clear the names, events, and titles. Contact the publisher, or the attorney for the estate, to be certain that the rights are available. If you're lucky, you might get the rights by offering them participation in profits.

The actual form of adapted works is the same as for any well-written screenplay. It conveys the appropriate atmosphere, characterization, and dramatic integrity of the published novel or story. Do a treatment first to get a handle on the dramatic structure for the script.

Television Loglines

In a television series, a premise must be so clear that it can be told in a logline. As we've seen, the logline is one or two sentences that describe the story. It looks like a *TV Guide* blurb of any episode for that series. You can find current loglines in your local paper, in the television section, or even at a network or television series Website. When you write your logline, try to get it as close to the real thing as possible. Have the characters driven by motivations and conflicts appropriate for the series. It must sound like the kind of story area that fits into the franchise of the series. The franchise is where the story conflict springs from.

In a *character-driven series*, the premise is focused on lead characters and relationships. Think of the character-centered crises in these half-hour comedy television series: "Frasier," "Friends," "Malcolm in the Middle," "Everybody Loves Raymond," "3rd Rock From the Sun," "The Practice," "Becker," "The Simpsons," "That '70s Show," "Coach," "Veronica's Closet," "The Drew Carey Show," "Sex and the City," "Murphy Brown," and syndicated hits such as "Cheers." The one-hour comedy series "Ally McBeal" is character-driven, as is the spin-off half-hour series "Ally."

In a *story-driven series,* the premise is centered on action driven by the circumstances faced by the leads. Think of story-driven episodes in one-hour dramatic series such as "Law & Order," "Law & Order: SVU," "NYPD Blue," "ER," "Chicago Hope," and "Star Trek: Voyager." When writing an episode, focus on the key leads—with all the right actions, reactions, and story twists appropriate for the series.

Your logline tells the "A" story, which is the main storyline featuring the lead characters, and a "B" story, if there is one, which outlines a subplot for other leads. Sometimes, there may be time to tell a "C" story, which is a subplot involving other characters in the show.

If you are uncertain about the show's structure, you can analyze the loglines from your *TV Guide* or local newspaper. Those are good resources for analyzing the story areas that have already been produced. Also, try to videotape as many episodes as you can so you can analyze the story and act structure from produced episodes.

Sample Loglines from Successful Comedy and Drama TV Series

These are sample loglines from successful comedy and drama series. Note the strongly developed characters and conflicts for the leads. Think about how the loglines identify the driving force for the characters in each story. And notice how there is a clear setup and payoff in each story for the lead characters.

Comedy Series

"FRASIER"

"A" story: Frasier is convinced by Roz to go to an Annual Broadcasters Convention, which will turn into a sure sexual conquest for them both. "B" story: Martin is recruited by Donny to do a stakeout for $500 to take pictures of a dumpster rental king having an affair.

The lead characters are appropriately set up. The "A" story sets up Frasier, who is convinced by Roz to go to the Annual Broadcasters Convention. She assures him that they will both score conquests because the conference turns into a bacchanal every year. It plays off Frasier's self-admiration, and the driving force is quickly set up. But the place is packed, and Frasier can't get a room. At the end of Act One, Frasier has no choice but to stay with Roz because the whole island is booked. She's afraid that he may cramp her style. But Frasier reassures her that they are two attractive people on the prowl at a conference, which turns into sure sex each year. Neither will be in the room overnight.

In the next act, we learn that they both were turned down, and they must stay in their hotel room, drunk, alone, and horny. They drink, and comic sparks are forced to fly. In the end of Act Two in the hotel room, the sexual tension builds and pays off. Frasier is in his pajamas, Roz has slipped off her robe, and he opens a bottle of expensive champagne, having fun, ready for a fling. At the tag, the show's producer bursts in, without a room, and begs to stay with his friends.

In the "B" story, Donny convinces Martin to do a stakeout in a van. Martin will get $500 if he can get pictures of a dumpster rental king having an affair. In the security van, we see the pseudo-professionalism of Martin, and the guilt-ridden Niles, who comes into the security van with soup, after talking down Martin's security work. An obsessive Niles almost destroys the cover when he talks to the perpetrator and offers free psychoanalytic advice from the van. At the end, they snap the picture of the adulterer.

That logline is from a "Frasier" script entitled "Hot Pursuit," written by Charlie Hauck. To see how the scenes are structured and written, see the "Frasier" script samples in Chapter 12.

"A" story: Niles lands a job as art critic of a magazine, and Frasier's jealousy leads him to cozy up to the station owner's annoying daughter in the hopes of getting a new show focusing on the arts.

In this "A" story, Frasier is predictably jealous of his brother, Niles, who has a new job as an art critic. The setup is clear, as is the payoff. Frasier's driving force is to do anything to top his brother, and that includes cozying up to the annoying daughter of the station owners.

"BECKER"

"A" story: John is called to jury duty, and so is Linda. "B" story: At the diner, Margaret complains about Reggie's coffee and tries to make it better. Bob tries to get Jake a seeing-eye dog.

In the "A" story, the setup and driving force for John is when Linda is called to jury duty. He proudly tells her how he escaped from serving. She tells the jury selection committee about how he escaped jury duty. John is called to serve again. She is accepted. He is dismissed because he's too smart. He's jealous of Linda and angry at the jury system. Finally, he "outsmarts" them and is called to duty. He finds himself in competition with a gushing Linda, who is elected jury Foreman. The payoff is executed with the deft, dark, quick wit of John, playing against Linda's complete naivete. John fancies himself to be jury leader of the "12 Angry Men," but everyone agrees with him.

The "B" story in the diner is set up for Margaret, trying to make Reggie's coffee better with chicory. At the end it pays off with more customers. The setup for Bob and Jake is very funny. Bob tries to give Jake, a blind man, a seeing-eye dog. In the payoff, we discover the dog has flatulence problems and has to be returned to whoever owned it.

That logline is from a "Becker" script entitled "One Angry Man," written by Dan Wilcox. To see how the scenes are actually written, see the "Becker" script samples in Chapter 12.

"ALLY McBEAL"

"A" story: Ally is guilt-ridden about her encounter with Billy. "B" story: Cage is working on a case in which they represent the plaintiff, a bookstore owner who lost her business after a conservative State Senator running for re-election targets her establishment as an outlet for pornography.

In the "A" story, the setup and driving force is Ally's guilt about her encounter with Billy. She is compelled to see her therapist, Dr. Tracy Clark, where she unravels new personal revelations. Ally stresses over her relationship with Georgia. Should she confess all to her, or keep her dirty little secret? Everything tells her to hold back, but she wonders if she'll find comfort and forgiveness if she confides in Georgia. The payoffs are funny and quirky. In the "B" story, Cage is set up to represent a bookstore owner who lost her business after it carried pornography.

"A" story: Word that Billy and Ally came perilously close to an adulterous affair is spreading through the law firm.

In the story, the setup is the rumor about Billy and Ally. Georgia throws Ally icy stares and cold shoulders. The payoff is the explosive conflict between the two women.

"3RD ROCK FROM THE SUN"

"A" story: Dick learns that Mary once had a fling with Dr. Strudwick and determines that he must retaliate, but he has to convince Mrs. Strudwick to take part in his plan.

In the story, the setup and driving force is when Dick learns that Mary once had a fling with Dr. Strudwick. In a jealous payoff, he will do anything to retaliate, but he must first convince Mrs. Strudwick to cooperate with him.

"A" story: After seeing Mary and Tina drooling over a photo of Harrison Ford, Dick looks into the possibility of undergoing plastic surgery.

In the story, the setup is Dick's jealousy over seeing Mary and Tina drool over the photo of Harrison Ford. The payoff is his going to a plastic surgeon. The surgeon assesses his features and pronounces them perfect. Dick's outlook is immediately changed.

"FRIENDS"

"A" story: Ross bleaches his teeth for a date with Monica's co-worker. The only problem is that they now glow in the dark. "B" story: Chandler convinces Joey that Janine is trying to take over his apartment. "C" story: Phoebe makes out with the copy guy at Rachel's office. Rachel spreads rumors about Phoebe.

In the "A" story, the setup is Ross trying to impress Monica's co-worker for his date. The payoff is when he bleaches his teeth—and they glow in the dark. In the "B" story, the setup is how Chandler convinces Joey that

Janine wants to take over his apartment. In the "C" story, the setup is Phoebe making out with the copy guy. In the payoff, Rachel spreads rumors about Phoebe, but her boss thinks that Rachel slept with Ralph Lauren.

"SEX AND THE CITY"

"A" story: Charlotte forces herself into a romance after all of her friends end up single at the same time.

In the "A" story, the setup and driving force is Charlotte discovering that all of her friends are single again. In the payoff, she forces herself into a romance.

"A" story: A friend's funeral prompts Carrie to resurrect her romance with Big. "B" story: Miranda fears she might die after buying an apartment that induces panic attacks in her. "C" story: Sam is ostracized for going after a socialite's hubby, and Charlotte picks up a man at a cemetery.

In the "A" story, the setup and driving force for Carrie is the death of her friend. It forces her to rethink and resurrect an old romance. In the "B" story, the setup is Miranda's anxiety attacks about her apartment, which convince her she might die. In the "C" story, the setup is Sam's going after a socialite husband. The payoff is her being ostracized. And Charlotte picks up a man at a cemetery.

"COACH"

"A" story: Hayden attempts to recruit the country's top high school player.

The driving force is set up when Hayden finds out about the availability of a top high school player. The Coach is motivated to do anything he can to succeed. That's the nature of his character as created by Barry Kemp. It is the Coach's fatal flaw—and his susceptibility. The payoff is his actions to accomplish that goal. He will inevitably result in relationship clashes with his wife Christine and daughter Kelly.

"THE SIMPSONS"

"A" story: With Lisa's help, Homer becomes the food critic for the local newspaper, but fellow critics criticize his always-positive reviews, prompting a radical change—and revenge by the restaurant owners.

In the "A" story, the setup is Lisa helping Homer become a food critic for the paper. She is always positive, and so are the reviews. Fellow critics criticize him for being so kind. The payoff occurs when Homer changes the reviews, and the restaurant owners want revenge.

"A" story: Homer and Marge win a Harley in a dance contest. Bart teaches Homer how to ride.

In the "A" story, the setup is Homer and Marge winning the bike at a dance contest. Bart must teach Homer how to ride. But Homer takes it everywhere, becoming a nuisance. He forms a motorcycle gang called "Hell's Satans," with Moe, Carl, Lenny, and Ned Flanders. In the payoff, the "Hell's Satans" motorcycle gang arrives to claim back their name. They take Marge when they leave. Homer takes off to find her.

Drama Series

"LAW & ORDER"

"A" story: An entire police precinct comes under fire when Briscoe and Logan investigate the death of a homosexual police officer who was killed in a drug bust.

The universe of the show is New York realism, as creative-executive producer Dick Wolf conceived of the series, playing effectively off the gritty headlines. The premise here is story-driven. The driving force of the story is set in motion when a police car dispatcher relays a call for emergency backup: a police officer has been shot. But that backup never arrives. The cop dies waiting for it. The twist occurs when Briscoe and Logan uncover the fact that the cop was homosexual and that the motivation was hatred toward gays in uniform. The DA (District Attorney) forcefully uncovers evidence that the cops on the force harassed homosexual police officers. When the cops are investigated, tension builds in the city.

The defense lawyer is a strong antagonist. He plays on underlying social fears of gays in uniform, and the cops are eventually acquitted. At the tag, Briscoe and Logan try desperately to undo the damage, but the emotions of the jury overshadow the evidence. Richard D. Lindheim and I are planning to co-author a new book, *Law and Order: The Inside Story*, revealing how the Emmy award-winning series was developed. (Our previous book, *Inside Television Producing* for Focal Press is out of print.)

"A" story: Briscoe and Logan's investigation of insulin overdose deaths at a diabetes treatment center reveals a bizarre suspect— the hospital's computer system.

This is another story-driven episode, consistent with the series' intention to have stories as current as news headlines. It deals with a complex case of human glitches in a high-tech computer system.

"THE PRACTICE"

"A" story: Berluti is given his first case—a year-old dog-biting incident. "B" story: Lindsay and Ellenor are caught in a legal quandary when a juror flirts with Lindsay on an elevator and reveals a possible verdict.

In the "A" story, the setup and driving force for Berluti is to handle his very first case, the year-old dog-biting incident, as best he can. In the "B" story, the setup is the juror who flirts with Lindsay on an elevator. The payoff is how it may impact their legal actions.

"A" story: Tensions rise when Lindsay requests a partnership.
"B" story: Eugene defends a gang member on murder charges.
"C" story: Rebecca receives an animal-rights activism award.

In the "A" story, the setup is Lindsay requesting a partnership. It sets off a furor over her request. In the "B" story, the setup is Eugene having to defend a gang member on murder charges and how he handles it. In the "C" story, Rebecca's set up to win an animal-rights activism award.

"STAR TREK: VOYAGER"

"A" story: The Doctor learns that Lewis Zimmerman, a father of modern holographic technology, who invented the matrix that made his program possible, is acutely ill.

The Doctor's driving force is quickly set up in Act One to save the man who created him, at all costs. But there are problems getting there, and Zimmerman is too self-centered to get help from the Doctor. The payoff is how the Doctor handles this most difficult patient to try to save him.

That logline is from a shooting script entitled "Life Line," story by John Bruno and Robert Picardo, teleplay by Robert Doherty and Raf Green. The "Star Trek: Voyager" script excerpts are reprinted in Chapter 15.

"CHICAGO HOPE"

"A" story: Shutt and Simon try to help a patient who's mute and paralyzed to communicate by putting a computer chip in his brain. "B" story: McNeil gets into hot water for performing an operation before getting financial authorization.

In the "A" story, Shutt and Simon are set up to help a mute and paralyzed patient communicate with a computer chip in the brain. Their driving force is to succeed at all costs. In the "B" story, McNeil is driven to perform an operation before getting the authorization. The payoff is how the hospital administration will handle it.

"WEST WING"

The staff faces the following problems: "A" story: a memo criticizing the President that Mandy wrote while working for the opposition; "B" story: meetings about gays in the military; and "C" story: meetings about campaign funding.

There are three interwoven stories in this logline. In the "A" story, President Bartlet and his staff must deal with the impact of Mandy's critical memo written while she was working for the opposition. The "B" story sets up the controversial meeting about gays in the military, and the divergent viewpoints of the staff. The "C" story sets up the staff conflict about campaign funding, which must be resolved.

"X-FILES"

"A" story: Digging for an X-file, Mulder finds one, in a photograph of an odd trio: a Negro baseball great, former agent Arthur Dales, and the alien bounty hunter—taken in 1947 Roswell, New Mexico.

The setup and driving force for Mulder is digging into the X-file. He finds a photograph of the odd trio taken in Roswell and is driven to investigate. He finds evidence that some of America's greatest athletes might have been aliens.

Television Films and Movies of the Week

In network long-form, television films and movies of the week, exploitation reigns supreme. At ABC, CBS, NBC, and Fox, exploitive premises and adaptations are at the heart of the television films and movies of the week they develop. Some quality character-driven projects with big stars can occasionally surface, but that's rare. HBO and the other pay cable companies compete vigorously and should be considered for your original and creative long-form projects.

In the early days of primetime programming, television movies and miniseries were high-prestige items. Based on books or original scripts, they featured top writers, producers, actors, and directors. But as costs have escalated, and as audiences have fled from the network landscape, much has changed. Television movies and miniseries are extremely expensive to develop and produce, and have little opportunity to win back their costs. The typical cost for a long-form script in 1994 was $25,000 to $100,000. The scale for writing television films is much higher today (see Chapter 18 and Appendix B, available on website at www.focalpress.com/companions). In 1994, production budgets could exceed $3.6 million, and the costs are higher today. The networks provide only a small portion of the production costs. A license fee is negotiated, but it is much less than the production budget. Consequently, producers must find other resources for "deficit financing."

As a result, development executives find themselves in a frantic race to outbid each other for high-visibility, exploitive projects based on fact. During "sweeps" weeks, their appeal to sordid interests is unflappable. The topic has to be relevant, sexy, and exploitive for marketing appeal.

Think about the headlines surrounding Amy Fisher, the "Long Island Lolita," who tried to kill the wife of her alleged lover, Joey Buttafuoco. Three of the major networks put together deals to produce films from slightly different angles. And they got high ratings. *Variety* correctly identified the fiasco as a "form of cultural humiliation."[25]

Yet despite the promise of restraint, the acquisition chase became unshackled. The networks battled for the rights to two different long-form films about the Menendez brothers, who were accused of murdering their wealthy parents. Then they brawled over acquisition rights for television films based on the attack on Nancy Kerrigan, the Olympic ice skating medalist winner, by her rival, Tonya Harding. As reported in *Variety*, ABC's leading bid for a story on Nancy Kerrigan came from Steve Tisch, in association with Disney.[26]

Deals revolving around this scandal included an ABC movie, a prime-time special, an association for Nancy Kerrigan with Disney theme parks, and a Disney book deal. The movie fee, negotiated by William Morris, exceeded $1 million. In the meantime, Fox developed the story from the perspective of the plot to injure Nancy Kerrigan. The producers, Citadel Productions (partly owned by HBO), used court documents as their public domain resource.

Michael Weisbarth, co-executive producer of the Emmy-winning miniseries "Lonesome Dove," told me that his project had a difficult birth at the network. Based on a Larry McMurtry novel, the script promised quality, atmosphere, and complex characters; however, no Western had been on the air in some time, and the network did not think it would get an audience. The script, like every script in Hollywood, was put through multiple revisions. Weisbarth is a creative producer with integrity and vision, and the final shooting script closely matched the atmosphere in the book, focusing on complex character development. As a result, the script was eminently castable and made a uniquely literate miniseries that found an audience.

Think about what this kind of assignment means for writers. They need to find the right story angle for the characters featured, undertake extensive research from public records, tie the story elements together, and deal with ethical issues. They also face unrealistic deadlines imposed by the networks on producers.

"In the Line of Duty: Ambush in Waco" was produced by Kenneth Kaufman, who specializes in television movies about law enforcement officers. The film was about David Koresh and four agents from the Bureau of Alcohol, Tobacco, and Firearms (ATF) who were shot by members of the Branch Davidian cult. The producer conceded facing enormous pressure to get the film completed in time. He was also overwhelmed by the extensive amount of research that was required. The writers investigated public records, hired consultants from law enforcement, and interviewed people from the cult.[27]

John McMahon, producer of "Without Warning: Terror in the Towers" specializes in psychological mystery films for the USA cable network. His project dealt with people trapped in the building during the World Trade Center bombing. The producer was determined to develop the premise as an heroic story, rather than focusing on the disaster: "We put together enough to dramatize the story in quite an uplifting way. That was the whole point. We weren't planning to do a story about a disaster and dead and injured people. . . . The core of the movie was heroic acts in one of the worst terrorist attacks on U.S. soil ever."[28] One of the most challenging problems he faced was meeting the accelerated timeframe mandated by the networks.

Another long-form producer, Brian Pike, producer of "Triumph Over Disaster," relates the same problems. The premise for his movie centered on a TV weatherman who calmed Miami during the storm that ravaged Florida: "This is microwave moviemaking. I've never done anything this fast in my life."[29] Pike received the assignment from Warren Littlefield, NBC Entertainment president. At first, he refused, saying he did not want to exploit someone else's tragedy. Then he decided to handle the story in a way that would focus on heroes—people who calmed Miami in the face of disaster.

Brian Pike is a respected veteran of television drama who spent almost a decade developing dramatic programs for NBC. He has a particularly relevant perspective about ethics and creativity for writers and producers of long-form drama: "Real life events have always been a mainstay of television. . . . What is new is this frenetic rush to the screen. . . . To me, drama is about the introspection of character, and when you are rushing to the screen, there is no time for that. You are limited to recreating the events. A writer and a producer do not have the time to wrestle with ethics and morality. My fear is that we are going to breed a generation of writers who are efficient regurgitaters. There is something very creative in this process, but that's not drama—that's a new form."[30]

As a direct result of violence depicted in sweeps weeks shows, industry executives from networks and cable companies met with Senator Paul Simon (D-IL) at a hearing of the Judiciary Subcommittee on the Constitution. At that session, Warren Littlefield, NBC Entertainment president, apologized for the network's response to competition for viewers and advertising. He said he regretted airing "Murder in the Heartland," based on the killing spree of Charles Starkweather. That TV film inspired a copycat killing in Canada. "We thought it was a good idea at the time, but it got poor ratings and was an economic disaster."[31] George Vradenburg, executive vice president of Fox Broadcasting, argued that his network put violence in the proper social perspective. Shows like "America's Most Wanted" and "Cops" are dedicated to the prevention of violent crimes. He pointed out that "America's Most Wanted" has directly led to the apprehension of hundreds of felons.

In an effort to solve the problem of gratuitous violence, an unprecedented meeting of executives from broadcasting, cable, and motion pictures was held in Los Angeles. For a full discussion of "Writing Violence in Films," see Chapter 18.

Animation

If you're interested in writing animation, be sure to contact the WGAw, Department of Industry Alliances, 7000 West Third Street, Los Angeles, CA 90048-4329. Their Website is www.wga.org; phone is 323/782-4511; fax is 323/782-4511; and e-mail is industryalliances@wga.org/. The department furthers the cause of writers who work in fields other than traditional movies and television shows, with particular emphasis in four areas: interactive, nonfiction entertainment, animation, and informational films.

Also contact the WGA Animation Writers Caucus, WGAw, 7000 West Third Street, Los Angeles, CA 90048-4329. You can also get information on animation writers at this website: www.awn.com; phone: 213/782-4511; fax: 213/782-4807.

For information on writing for animation series, formats, and the WGA Animation Writers Caucus and Animation Contract, see Chapter 13.

Interactive and New Media

If you're developing projects for interactive, animation, or new media, then get in contact with the WGAw, Department of Industry Alliances, 7000 West Third Street, Los Angeles, CA 90048-4329. Their Website is www.wga.org/ialliances; phone is 323/782-4511; fax is 323/782-4511; and e-mail is industryalliances@wga.org. The department furthers the cause of writers who work in interactive, nonfiction entertainment, animation, and informational films.

For details on writing for interactive and new media format, and a sample interactive program contract, see Chapter 13.

Nonfiction Entertainment

Nonfiction entertainment includes documentaries, news, nondramatic programming and programs, minimal writing, and reality shows. Included within these categories are reality shows, magazine shows, "making of" shows, travelogues, "how-to" shows, certain talk shows, certain children's shows, and infomercials. For a sample informational program contract, see Chapter 13.

ENDNOTES

1. Michael Gill, "Robert Kosberg, The Pitch King," *Hollywood Scriptwriter: The Trade Paper for Screenwriters,* May 2000, 5.
2. Ibid., 4.
3. "American Beauty: An Interview with Alan Ball," *Creative Screenwriting,* January/February 2000, 26–27.
4. Ibid., 30.
5. Daniel Argent, "An Interview with M. Night Shyamalan," *Creative Screenwriting,* September/October 1999, 41.
6. Ibid., 41.
7. Ibid., 45.
8. Ibid.
9. Robert Feld, "On the Edge with David O. Russell," *Written By,* December/January 2000, 26–27.
10. Ibid., 27.
11. Daniel S. Duvall, "A Witch's Broomscript: Or How to Make a Screenplay without Really Writing, An Interview with Dan Myrick and Eduardo Sanchez," *Written By,* September 1999, 40–41.
12. Ibid., 40.
13. "Crying All the Way to the Bank," *Variety,* March 22, 1993, 68.
14. "Art House Heavyweights," *Variety,* March 22, 1993, 68.
15. Peter Bart, "Mythic Megapix," *Variety,* June 21, 1993, 6.
16. Jeffrey Ressner, "Gonzo Screenwriter," *Time,* May 31, 1993, 64.
17. Gregg Kilday, "Taking Liberties," *Variety,* January 10–16, 2000, 58.
18. "Novel Roots," *Variety,* January 10–16, 2000, 66.
19. Gregg Kilday, "Taking Liberties," *Variety,* January 10–16, 2000, 58.
20. Ibid., 61.
21. Ibid., 63.
22. Ibid., 58, 66.
23. Jamie Painter, "Writing His Own Rules," by *Written By,* February 2000, 25.
24. Ibid., 31.
25. "Skategate Puts Webs on a Slippery Slope," *Variety,* February 7–13, 1994, 1.
26. Ibid., 65.
27. Patricia Brennan, "TV Drama Recipe," *Washington Post* TV Week, May 23–29, 1993, 7.
28. Ibid.
29. Ibid.
30. Ibid., 45.
31. "TV Networks Promise Lawmakers a Harder Line Against Violence," *The Washington Post,* May 23, 1993, A-5.

PART TWO

STORY DEVELOPMENT

3

How to Develop a Marketable Story

Genres and Themes

The following are the main genres in feature films: comedy, drama, thriller, romantic comedy, action-adventure, black comedy, science fiction, romance, horror, war, children's, Western, animated, fantasy, and musical.

In all film premises, try to keep the genre consistent. Comedies are comic, dramas are dramatic, thrillers keep you in suspense, and animation provides fantasy worlds. An early analysis can help you keep a better handle on the focus of the story. If a story was meant to be dramatic but comic elements come into play, then the plot might be enriched by that interweaving of genres; however, if comedy dominates, or a subplot becomes a main plot, then a different story is in the making.

When you're developing an idea, it's helpful to keep the genre consistent in the story. Some writers mix genres to add to the richness if they are writing a screenplay for the independent film market. Think of genre-mixing films such as AMERICAN BEAUTY written by Alan Ball, THE SIXTH SENSE, written by M. Night Shyamalan, and THREE KINGS, written by David O. Russell. But these are the exceptions to the rule.

You can identify the plot according to genre, theme, and plot patterns. Theme is important to set the protagonists and antagonists in recognizable conflicts and to establish action for audiences, such as redemption of a character. But if the situation and dialogue are too heavy, then it becomes melodrama, which will stick out like a sore thumb. If a writer deliberately pushes a political message, then the entertainment value is lost and the ideological statement overshadows it. Theme material is most effective when it springs naturally from the integration of plot, character, and action.

Plot Patterns

In the process of writing the story, certain plot patterns become identifiable. One generally is dominant, whereas others serve as background or subplots in the evolution of the script. It's helpful to keep track of your main plot and subplots this way, but remember this is just a general conceptual tool meant to be explored. Your script may involve several overlapping patterns, or none of them.

Decades ago, a critic named George Polti identified 36 dramatic plot situations that seemed to be at the heart of all dramatic stories. Lewis Herman reduced that number to nine in his book, *A Practical Manual of Screenplay Writing.* More recently, I modified those patterns in an earlier version of this book, and in *Primetime: Network Television Programming,* where Richard Lindheim and I added plot patterns to identify generic television stories.

In this edition, I've modified that list further, to encompass the following plot patterns for both motion pictures and television: love and romance, jeopardy and survival, vengeance, success and achievement, search and quest, group and family ties, fantasy, and return. The list is not exhaustive, but it does outline the potential for dramatic conflicts faced by lead characters in features and television.

Love and Romance

This kind of story deals primarily with romantic conflicts faced by lead characters and how they overcome those obstacles. In a traditional love pattern, boy and girl meet, lose each other, and must win each other back. The story usually centers on a character's desire to maintain a relationship in the face of serious threats. The story may draw on elements of the classic love triangle, in which an outsider enters into the romantic competition.

The love pattern is a predominant one that helps sustain audience involvement in the lives of the lead characters and conflicts. In YOU'VE GOT MAIL, comic obstacles get in the way of the leads meeting. They finally meet, conflicts ensue, and they fall in love. The same is true of THERE'S SOMETHING ABOUT MARY. THE STORY OF US is a comedy about the ups and downs of a 16-year marriage. MICKEY BLUE EYES focuses on a man who falls for a mobster's daughter. THE BEST MAN is about a writer who is best man at the wedding of two old college friends. His steamy new novel, which is based on their lives, is about to become public. RUNAWAY BRIDE is about a woman who left three grooms at the altar and the cynical reporter who decides to do a story on her. Similarly, SLEEPLESS IN SEATTLE focuses on how two lovers destined for each other will eventually meet and fall in love, from opposite sides of the country, and wind up loving each other.

In the television comedy "Friends," the leads are always in romantic conflicts. "Ally McBeal" deals with the susceptible lead characters in a law firm, who fall in and out of love. The HBO comedy "Sex and the City" centers on a female writer in New York who tries to understand the contemporary sexual antics of men and women.

Jeopardy and Survival

The jeopardy pattern is usually centered on a life-and-death situation, testing the survival instincts and prowess of the leading characters. In this story pattern, characters confront extremely difficult odds (e.g., earthquake, avalanche, hijacking, terrorists, obsessed antagonists). They use every mental and physical trick to overcome extraordinary obstacles. In some situations, those obstacles are compounded by a "timebomb" situation (i.e., something must be done before time runs out and disaster occurs).

Motion pictures have had smash successes with high-concept jeopardy films. Think of the incredible survival skills needed by lead characters in action films such as END OF DAYS, ARMAGEDDON, ENEMY OF THE STATE, TWISTER, THE THOMAS CROWN AFFAIR, James Bond films, RAIDERS OF THE LOST ARK and the two Indiana Jones sequels, and JURASSIC PARK.

Television movies rely heavily on survival story patterns for television films, as well as reality-based shows like "Survivor."

Vengeance

Stories in the vengeance mode deal with lead characters who personally seek revenge for some wrongdoing. Characters in this type of story want to solve crimes that are unsolved, get an eye for an eye, or simply "right" some earlier injustice.

In features, the plot pattern is one of the most successful at the box office. Think of the powerful revenge and vengeance motives for lead characters in films such as LETHAL WEAPON and its three sequels, THE FUGITIVE,

RUSH HOUR, BATMAN, TERMINATOR, and ROBOCOP. In THE HURRI-CANE, the search is set up to save a man wrongly accused of murder.

This type of story pattern is prominent in virtually every mystery, suspense, or action-adventure television series. Think of the premises of shows such as "Law & Order: Special Victims Unit," "NYPD Blue," and "X-Files."

Success and Achievement

Success is another story pattern that stands on its own but also fits comfortably into the fabric of other story types. In the success pattern, the lead character needs to achieve something *at all costs*. The goal may be self-serving (e.g., money, romance, promotion), but the character is consumed by the drive to succeed.

In features, the need to succeed is the force behind manic leading characters. In AMERICAN BEAUTY, a magazine professional takes a self-improvement course to extremes when he quits his job, starts to pump iron, buys a hot car, and gets a job in a fast-food joint. In BOWFINGER, Steve Martin plays a down-and-out producer who will do anything to get a star to commit to his next movie. In JERRY MAGUIRE, a sports agent is driven to succeed at all costs. In FOR LOVE OF THE GAME, Kevin Costner plays a baseball pitcher nearing the end of his career. He battles his personal weakness, a sore arm, to win the game. Other films in this plot pattern include QUIZ SHOW and WALL STREET.

Search and Quest

The search or quest pattern is centered on the notion of a person trying to find something of great importance. The quest might be external or internal. In an *external* quest, the character can be searching for a missing witness, clues to buried treasure, or missing information. The search stands on its own as a story but can also be tied to larger story patterns, such as vengeance or romance.

The external search provides a more action-packed framework for stories, whereas the *inner* quest is more difficult to convey on screen. In an inner quest, the search might encompass a character's drive to "find" himself or herself or deal with traumatic personal crises.

An external search is at the heart of the premise for THREE KINGS, in which the Special Forces soldiers hunt for a cache of hidden gold bullion in post–Gulf War Iraq. In SAVING PRIVATE RYAN, the search is for a missing soldier in World War II.

An inner search is at work in films like THE TALENTED MR. RIPLEY, QUIZ SHOW, and BULLETS OVER BROADWAY. In HUSBANDS AND WIVES, a relationship that breaks up has an enormous impact on the couple's closest friends.

Group and Family Ties

This pattern involves a group of characters who normally would have nothing to do with each other, but because of circumstances, are tied together in the story. Because of the arena/setting, they are forced into interrelationships that become the thrust of the story.

This pattern can work anywhere in features; think of dramatic stories about characters bound together by their shared environment, such as in THE GREEN MILE and THE SHAWSHANK REDEMPTION, both of which are set in prison. The film ENCHANTED APRIL is about four British women who rent an Italian villa. They are incompatible strangers at the beginning, who develop deep friendships by the resolution.

This story pattern is a classic setup for sitcom character conflicts in television series. The setup is perfect for lead characters in their home ("Malcolm in the Middle," "Friends," "Everybody Loves Raymond," and "3rd Rock from the Sun"); a law firm ("Ally McBeal" and "The Practice"); a hospital ("ER" and "Chicago Hope"); a police station ("Law & Order: SVU" and "NYPD Blue"); a radio talk show ("Frasier"); work ("Becker," "Coach," "The Drew Carey Show," and "Veronica's Closet"); an apartment complex ("90210," and "Melrose Place"); and even outer space ("Star Trek: Voyager"). Some classic sitcoms were set up in a Boston bar ("Cheers"); a taxi dispatch center ("Taxi"); and even an army camp ("M*A*S*H").

Fantasy

In variations of the Cinderella tale, lead characters become more "whole" as a result of their fantasy experience, and the audience is permitted to act out their own fantasies on some level.

In BICENTENNIAL MAN, an android learns over the course of two centuries what it is like to experience emotion and be human. In BEING JOHN MALKOVICH, an unemployed puppeteer/filing clerk finds a mysterious portal into actor John Malkovich's brain. He and his girlfriend charge fees for the privilege of entering John Malkovich's brain. At the end of the foray, the lead character's life has changed, and so have all those he's touched, including the girl he pines after, his wife, and actor John Malkovich.

In TOY STORY 2, Buzz Lightyear and his toy friends are on their own when their owner goes to summer camp. The animated film PRINCESS MONONOKE is a mythic story about the balance between civilization and nature. THE IRON GIANT is an animated feature about a boy and his robot friend. Other examples of the fantasy pattern are PLEASANTVILLE, THE TRUMAN SHOW, and THE LION KING. In ROOKIE OF THE YEAR, a 12-year-old pitcher has a 100-mph fast ball. An earlier film, FIELD OF DREAMS, deals with the same kind of baseball fantasy from an adult perspective.

Some of the television shows in this genre provide viewers with an outlet for their own lighter fantasies, including "Touched by an Angel" and game shows like "Who Wants to Be a Millionaire." The characters in "Ally McBeal" deal with quirky personal and sexual fantasies. So do the quirky lead characters in the comedy "Sex and the City." Earlier forerunners of fantasy include "Heaven Can Wait" and "Love Boat."

Return

Within one of the larger story patterns, a character may have to confront the sudden reappearance of someone or something from the past. This story element forces the character to readjust the comfortable status quo. For example, the lead character may suddenly be faced with the return of an ex-husband, high school sweetheart, wandering father, missing child, long-lost lover, or long-forgotten criminal record. This pattern may serve nicely as the driving force for individual characters in a series, but it is not generally the overriding motif for a series.

The feature THE STRAIGHT STORY is the tale of a 73-year-old man who rode across the Midwest on a lawn mower to visit his ailing brother. In the feature PASSION FISH, a paralyzed star of daytime TV is reclusive and returns to her home in Louisiana. At home, she strikes up an unexpected friendship with her nurse. They share poignant stories, and each has an impact on the other's life.

Plot patterns are not mutually exclusive, and any number of subplots can emerge within a given story; however, this type of plot identification provides you with a clearer overview of the dominant story elements and the concurrent identification of background material. Once the dominant pattern is identified, there's a smaller chance of being sidetracked by intriguing subplots or minor characters.

4

How to Write the Story

Where to Begin: Choosing the Story Area and Lead Characters

A story idea can be derived from any personal experience, relationship, observation, music, film, or article that intrigues you—any source that sparked your imagination. But the *story area* must be capable of standing on its own as the spine of the story, vital to the motivations of your lead characters.

The story area needs a *hook*—a unique premise that will set it apart and grip the audience. If the hook is strong, then the story will have marketing appeal and a much better chance of eventually reaching the screen. Here are a few workable story areas:

- "FIERY METEOR NEARLY HITS U.S."
- "ASTRONAUTS MUST BE RESCUED BY MILITARY FORCES IN A HURRICANE"
- "U.S. WORRIED ABOUT TERRORIST SECURITY RISKS IN SECRET NUCLEAR MISSILE SITES OF FORMER SOVIET UNION"
- "WOMAN HAS FATAL ATTRACTION FOR JUSTICE DEPARTMENT OFFICIAL WHO IS TRYING HER FATHER FOR WAR CRIMES"
- "CAMPERS LOST IN UNSEASONABLE BLIZZARD"

Each idea offers intriguing potential for functioning as the story's spine; however, the story areas are much too broad in their present form. They need to have lead characters and a point of view. The pivotal step is to choose a susceptible lead character and identify the conflict that he or she has to overcome. That process ensures a clear point of view for the story.

For example, the first story area deals with a near catastrophe—a meteor slamming into the United States. That story could be told from any number of vantage points. This might be one approach: "An aging scientist discovers that a fiery meteor is about to hit the U.S.—but no one believes him."

Now the story has a lead character who is vulnerable. It's told from the perspective of an aging scientist. It also has a built-in dramatic conflict with a "timebomb" situation. The scientist must find a way to convince others, and to act, before the meteor strikes. As the story develops, other characters and subplots might be incorporated, but the basic premise is fairly well-defined at the outset, and the hook can be told in a logline.

Let's look at the next story area: "ASTRONAUTS MUST BE RESCUED BY MILITARY FORCES IN A HURRICANE." This is based on the book *Mode VIII*, written by Dr. Gregory A. Rogers. I optioned the novel and adapted the screenplay. This is the action logline:

MODE VIII

Logline: When a Kennedy Space Center shuttle develops problems during its ascent, the only option for the astronauts is a bailout into the Atlantic Ocean—with a hurricane raging. Military rescue forces must enter the storm to find and rescue the astronauts.

Screenplay by Rick Blum

Based on the Novel by Gregory A. Rogers

Producer: Rick Blum

Technical Adviser: Dr. Gregory Rogers is an insider who has worked in space shuttle support operations at Kennedy Space Center for 31 missions. He wrote the Department of Defense flight surgeon manual for Mode VIII rescue procedures at Kennedy Space Center and performed Mode VIII rescue exercises. He had assistance from many of their crewmembers flying these missions, as well as working with the astronauts themselves. These experts provided him with their authoritative viewpoints in helping to write this story. He has also authored two other shuttle-related novels.

©1999, these and other scripts excerpts reprinted with permission from Gregory A. Rogers.

In the MODE VIII logline, I had to set up the fact that there was a credible reason for a shuttle problem and the necessity of rescue forces to be on alert. This is a high-budget action film, so I also wanted to incorporate the expertise of the book's author, Dr. Gregory Rogers, as technical adviser. In script development, I relied heavily on his feedback. He knew every aspect of the shuttle and rescue forces, as well as the characters and storyline.

Because this is an action film, I needed to set up the first pages with a strong opening hook. In the novel, the crisis was unraveled over time in several official mission meetings. In the screenplay, I wanted to set up a quick, visual opening action teaser. In the first scene, we see the shuttle ready for takeoff, then something goes terribly wrong. The rescue forces are called into action. Then we discover it is all an exercise. We get to meet the lead key characters, see how professional they are. They must get up the shuttle with a particular multimillion-dollar mission payload—and within a selected window of opportunity.

For the next story area, "U.S. WORRIED ABOUT TERRORIST SECURITY RISKS IN SECRET NUCLEAR MISSILE SITES OF FORMER SOVIET UNION," Frank Tavares and I played on that fear in the action-comedy screenplay THE ELTON PROJECT. This is the logline for that film:

THE ELTON PROJECT

Logline: A secret military project in Nevada is accidentally uncovered by a low-level government employee and his reporter friend. Learning that a paranoiac military colonel has aimed a nuclear missile at a friendly country, the two interlopers attempt to abort the mission.

©1999, story and script excerpts reprinted with permission of Frank Tavares.

In the screenplay, the spine of the story is centered on two middle-aged friends, one a newly divorced bureaucrat from the Department of Energy, the other a journalist doing research on hazardous waste. They head to Las Vegas and encounter a secret Department of Energy missile defense plant in Elton, Nevada. The paranoid military Colonel assumes they are on terrorist payroll. They are the driving forces for the project to be activated. The missiles have hidden codes connecting them to bases in the former Soviet Union. The missile is aimed at Israel. Our leads hook up with a woman CIA agent to halt the flying missiles with virtual-reality weapons.

The next story area is this: "WOMAN HAS FATAL ATTRACTION FOR JUSTICE DEPARTMENT OFFICIAL WHO IS TRYING HER FATHER FOR WAR CRIMES." This is based on a screenplay I wrote with Allan Gerson, SONJA'S MEN, which was based on a true story, with dramatic license. Finding the spine of the story, though, posed some creative challenges. In the feature script, Allan Gerson and I struggled to find the right perspective. Gerson was the first Jewish prosecutor for the Justice Department's Office of Special Investigation, which was set up to investigate and deport Nazi war criminals in the United States. He is also the son of Holocaust survivors. In this story, a woman who is the daughter of a Nazi collaborator falls in love with the prosecutor. For dramatic purposes, we needed to set their passion against his drive to prosecute Nazi collaborators and her drive to save her father at all costs. That became the film's driving force for the lead characters. The step outline for SONJA'S MEN appears later in this chapter.

Finally, look at the last story area: "CAMPERS LOST IN UNSEASON-ABLE BLIZZARD," and try to define the best dramatic angle. You might choose the point of view of one camper or a number of them. Or you might want to tell the story from the point of view of the rescuers. The basic conflict and plot pattern centers on a survival situation, but who is in jeopardy? And how great is the sense of urgency for escape and survival? Those decisions dictate the direction and visual approach of the story. Later in this chapter, we'll see how they were developed for a TV film, "The Wind Chill Factor," which Dan Wilcox and I wrote.

How to Advance the Story Effectively

In order to move from the narrative treatment into script, there is an ongoing need to set proper story sequences in order. I've found that the use of *dramatic action points* is an effective way to select and arrange key incidents in the story so that the dramatic drive of the story is clear. I call them "dramatic action points" in deference to Irwin Blacker's analysis of how to strengthen stories with Aristotelian playwriting theory. There are roughly 26 to 35 major action points in a 120-minute film, which translates to four or five pages for each sequence in the script. Those are, of course, very general figures, but they do provide some guidance in assessing the time count for an eventual script.

Dramatic action points are referred to by some writers as *dramatic beats.* They are the basic dramatic units and events that advance the story. Once these beats are identified, they can be placed in different contexts—much like the restructuring of a puzzle—to strengthen the plot structure. They can be used to orchestrate the pacing and balance in the story.

How do you know which sequence begins the story? It helps to identify an *inciting incident* or a point of attack for your lead character. Why is this day, this moment, this situation critical to his or her life? Then you can build the most effective combination of scenes to unravel the story. But which scenes go where? Which characters are needed at what points? Which scenes build the conflict? Which scenes are extraneous?

Aristotle talked about the importance of the proper arrangement of incidents in a plot to have the greatest impact on the audience. Twentieth-century writers agree. Eric Bentley (*The Playwright as Thinker*) contended that a carefully arranged sequence of actions is essential to achieve maximum effect. He called it a "rearrangement" of incidents as opposed to a simple chronological arrangement. In short, *dramatic action* rather than literal action.[1]

The use of *dramatic action points*—or *dramatic beats*—is an ongoing process in the story development phase. As an example of how it might work, let's look at one of the premises mentioned earlier: "CAMPERS LOST IN UNSEASONABLE BLIZZARD." We might try to outline these points for the opening sequences:

1. A family is en route to the Berkshires for a camping weekend.
2. They arrive and find the campgrounds in disarray, but decide to stay.
3. They get snowed in.

Even in this sketchy form, it becomes apparent that the inciting incident, or point of attack, is not strong. There is no suggestion of conflict or character. The action points can be revised accordingly:

1. A couple's marriage is shaky. The husband works too hard and they need a vacation.
2. They head up to the Berkshires for a camping weekend. He brought along work anyway, and they argue.
3. They arrive at the campground, which is in disarray. It's late at night, and they decide to stay.
4. It snows.

But even here there are some problems. The points are too choppy and are not really composed of individual dramatic sequences. The action needs to be clarified, and the characters need more definition. It might be possible to merge the first two action points for the sake of pacing and add other people to the story—their children, other campers, perhaps even a pet that is lost in the storm. This is what the revised outline might look like:

1. BARRY, SHARON, and KIDS ride to the campsite. We learn they have marriage problems.
2. They arrive at the campgrounds and find it in disarray. It's late, they're tired, they decide to stay.
3. Setting up camp, we meet other campers, and follow up the marriage conflict.
4. It snows as they sleep.
5. An expensive trailer reaches camp, finds no power. The irate owner blames Barry.
6. In morning, Barry's kids play in the snow. Their dog gets swept away in the river.

And so on. Dramatic action points provide a very bare but specific blueprint for the structure of the story.

The Treatment and Step Outline

The story must be written in a form called the *treatment,* which is the narrative version, or the *step outline,* which is a detailed outline of proposed action sequences for the script. Both forms are acceptable. They make it easier to move directly into script form. Examples of each format are provided on following pages.

The purpose of the treatment is to work out story problems and to get feedback from people you trust to strengthen plot and character development. It has to have a beginning, middle, and end, character conflicts, act builds, story twists, comedy moments, high points of crisis, and the story's resolution.

In features, the treatment is about 10 to 30 pages. You can depict the genre, dramatic setup, character development, crisis, and story progression. In episodic television, treatments are about 5 to 10 pages in length—the shorter, the better. Give an accurate picture of the setup, characters, conflicts, universe of the story, tone of the show, act breaks, and plenty of laughs if you're doing comedy. You can sprinkle in dialogue to show where the jokes play.

Sample Narrative Treatment

This is an excerpt from a longer narrative treatment for "The Wind Chill Factor." It is an example of the tone and atmosphere in a treatment for a feature or TV film. Here is the opening act. It demonstrates how the action points translate into the treatment. The following act is derived from those action points.

THE WIND CHILL FACTOR

April. A bright spring day.

> This derives from Action Point #1

We follow BARRY STERN, mid-30s, SHARON, early 30s, and their SON, 10, and DAUGHTER, 7, riding in a new but small camper from New York City to the Berkshire Mountains. Throughout the trip, we hear innocuous commentary from the radio about a cold front moving in from Canada. But the noise is lost in the sounds of the children at play and the dog barking.

The marriage is rocky. Barry is a lawyer who works too hard and is constantly afraid he won't be advanced. This family weekend was arranged to save the marriage, but Barry has brought along a legal brief anyway.

> Action Point #2

They reach the Berkshires just at dusk, and follow the signs to the campground. They drive down a steep dirt road into a valley nestled among the mountains. But when they arrive, they find the campgrounds in disarray. A sign that reads "OFFICE" points to some prefabricated walls lying unassembled on the ground.

Another camper is parked nearby—a Toyota. The couple inside, CARLOS, mid-30s, and JENNIFER, late 20s, commiserate with the Sterns. They too, made reservations, but the campground obviously went bankrupt before it could open.

> Action Point #3

They're all undecided about what to do. They should find another campground, but it's getting dark and there's a storm brewing. Besides, this place can shelter them—the campsites are cleared, there are picnic tables, fireplaces, there's a centrally located water pipe, and there are two outhouses, one male, one female. The two couples decide to stay until morning, when the storm will be over.

Barry struggles through the unfamiliar tasks of setting up a campsite, and he is forced to finish in the rain. Thunder and lightning follow him as he returns to the camper, drenched to the bone. The kids think it's outrageously funny.

Another car arrives, drawn by the light from the lanterns. It's a group of YOUNG FRIENDS, two boys, and a girl, in their early 20s, who set up a rudimentary tent in a nearby campsite.

Action Point #4

Inside the Sterns's camper, after dinner, the family goes to bed, accompanied by the sound of rain on the roof. Sharon bickers with Barry, who refuses to go to bed without reading over his brief. Angry, Sharon gets into bed. Barry reads. The sound of the rain peters out. Barry offers his wife some minimal consolation—at least it's stopped raining. But outside in the campground, we see that it's begun snowing.

Action Point #5

During the night, a sleek, flashy, expensive-looking silver trailer arrives in the snow, driven by CHARLES EVANS, late 40s, who is camping with his wife, MAGGIE, 30s, and their teenage daughter, BETH. The family is dismayed to see the condition of the campground, and an irate Charles follows the only visible light—Barry's— to register his complaint. Barry is surprised to see it snowing, but he suggests that Charles do what everyone else has done: camp here for the night. After all, how long can a snowstorm last in April?

Charles tries to connect his electrical system to the power outlet at the campsite but finds that the power has not been turned on. He's furious; now he has no heat. And, like everyone else, he has no cold-weather clothing. Disgruntled, he bundles his family into the silver trailer for the night. Gradually, the campground lights go out, first in the Evans's camper, then in Barry's.

In the morning, it is still snowing heavily. The Stern kids, eager to build a springtime snowman, find makeshift winter clothing— dishrags for their ears, pinned-up blankets for sweaters, plastic bags for galoshes. And they rush out into the snow, with their dog, to play.

Action Point #6

When Sharon calls them to breakfast, the dog—a city dog, who is used to a leash—bolts and races along the edge of a small river. The pup loses its footing in the snow, falls into the water, and is swept downstream.

The kids race along the riverbank, following their pet, plodding through the snow, calling to him. Stephen spots them, races over, and restrains them from following the dog. He tries to explain that they can't save their pet. It couldn't see the footing in the snow; neither can they. But the children are unheeding; they scream and cry as they watch their pet sweep out of sight . . .

Sample Step Outline

This is a step outline from SONJA'S MEN, which I wrote with Allan Gerson about his experiences as a prosecutor with the Justice Department's Office of Special Investigations. The screenplay is based on fact and deals with many different issues, so we had to be sure that the script didn't become too broad. It is a screenplay dealing with the prosecution of Nazi collaborators for war crimes. The research involved reading emotionally compelling depositions and trial transcripts. Yet, we couldn't have the script deal exclusively with the issue of responsibilities for war crimes, or it would seem thematic, rather than dramatic.

After much deliberation, we decided that the focus of the story is about how characters deal with personal betrayals. Deception takes many different forms. Aaron deceives Sonja, she deceives him. Sonja's father deceives her, and he is deceived by the government. Aaron feels betrayed by the government, and the government feels he betrayed them.

Because it was a character-driven screenplay, we built the film around a three-act structure. We placed a story twist at the end of Act I (beat # 16), where Aaron discovers that his lover's name is the same as that of the Nazi collaborator he's investigating: Tyrowicz. The second story twist occurs at the end of Act II (beat #23), when Aaron discovers that his supervisor was the one who leaked information about Aaron's parents lying on their visas. In a later twist, we learn it was Sonja who leaked the information to save her own father.

In the step outline, we uncovered a problem in the perception of Aaron's character at the setup (beat #2). He appears unsure about why he wants to join the Justice Department. It was suggested by a producer that Aaron's character would be more susceptible if he was driven and passionate about the reason for the change. So, in the script we made that change. Aaron is driven to right the wrongs inflicted on his parents and family during the Holocaust. That drive conflicts with his supervisor's intention, which is to get as many political wins as possible. And it conflicts dramatically with Sonja's intentions—to save her father. That change made Aaron a more likable and identifiable character.

We had another problem at the resolution (beat #34), where Aaron returns to his old job. Given the change in his character arc, it wasn't likely that he'd go back. He needed more at stake, so we set it up in the script that he couldn't return, and instead had to deal with more intense dramatic consequences.

<u>SONJA'S MEN</u>
<u>BY ALLAN GERSON AND RICHARD BLUM</u>

STEP OUTLINE

1. Tidal basin. Jogging early morning, we meet Aaron, running toward his office. The atmosphere of Washington, D.C. is vivid.

2. Law office. His current boss, Jim, congratulates him. Aaron's still not sure why he's decided to take the new position with Justice. Something is compelling him, maybe just the need for a change of pace.

3. Georgetown restaurant. His friend Charlie toasts him. He notices a lovely woman nearby, arranging photos in a portfolio. This is Sonja. Aaron initiates small talk, asks for her card. She's prepping for a show, has a studio in Dupont Circle.

4. Dupont Circle studio. Aaron is taken by the sophisticated photos in her exhibit, all on the Ukraine. He notes another portfolio, and she, embarrassed, explains that those are boudoir photos. That's how she can make a living. Her father would wring her neck if he found out what she was doing. The photos in the Ukraine were enough. He kisses her. What was that about, she asks? He's not sure. His parents would kill him for kissing a shiksa. He sees a self-portrait, a small photo of her. He can have it if he wants.

5. His parents' house. This is strained. They don't know why he's moving to another job. Why he is so restless. He thought they'd be proud of him. We're always proud of you, mom answers vaguely.

6. Director's office—OSI. Parker is a no-nonsense superior who wants wins. He briefs his new staff on the status of two cases, Osidatch, who was chief of police, and Tyrowicz, who was the S.S. liaison. Charlie will set up two depositions in California.

7. From his office, Aaron calls Sonja, tells her he'll be out in L.A. for a deposition, will call when he gets back. She tells him she's on her way to California. She has a show in L.A. County and will be seeing her dad. She'd love to see Aaron when he's free. She gives him her number in La Jolla.

8. Flight to L.A. Aaron reads the files, absorbed by the photos of young men from another era. Then looks at his photo of Sonja. On the back, she's jotted something we can't see.

9. LAX. Charlie meets Aaron in a rented red thunderbird. They've got interviews that night and in the morning.

10. Ida Kempner, an older woman, identifies both Osidatch and Tyrowicz. She feels comfortable with Aaron, who speaks Yiddish. She recounts how she was forced to save herself by jumping from a train heading to a "work" camp.

11. Tyrowicz is interviewed in his home, overlooking a rose garden. He is a Nazi collaborator who is a greasy bastard. He admits knowing Osidatch, but refuses to answer straightforward questions about his own work with S.S. headquarters.

12. Marriott Hotel—night. Aaron is asleep, fitfully, reliving the nightmare-flashback of Ida being thrown from the train. He wakes up, very disturbed. Sees Sonja's picture and calls her. They'll meet tomorrow.

13. La Jolla. Beautiful settings. They discuss how much she missed her dad. She used to live in D.C. when her husband used to work with NASA, but since he died, there's nothing holding her to D.C. Now she considers California home, much closer to her family and friends. They wine, dine, and make love.

14. Parker's office. The debriefing. Parker tells Aaron they have enough to go after Osidatch and Tyrowicz, but warns him not to get moral in the prosecution's brief. This is immigration fraud, not historical justice. To see how it will be handled, go to the Supreme Court hearing next week. Another Nazi collaborator, Federenko, is appealing his extradition. Aaron is uneasy about this.

15. U.S. Supreme Court . . . marble steps . . . full nine judges' trial of Federenko. He's been sentenced to be extradited, but appealed on grounds that what he did was involuntary. Justice Stephens demands to know whether the prosecution's argument is about historic justice or about illegal aliens? Parker's comeback: "aliens." Aaron has a major disagreement with Parker—he didn't say one word about Jews or Nazis in his argument. Parker warns Aaron to stick with the legal strategy in dealing with Osidatch and Tyrowicz or he's gone.

16. New Orleans, Mississippi river boat. Aaron's feeling tense from the animosity with Parker. Sonja asks him what's wrong, he can trust her. He talks evasively, but emotionally, about people's responsibility for the past. Sonja's taking photos and reveals how worried she is about her father. Some people from the Immigration and Naturalization Service started asking him what he did during the war. They've accused him of being a Nazi. My dad's no angel, but he could never have done those things. Aaron tries to be noncommittal—advises that he should get a good attorney. Then he asks her last name. She's just known as Sonja T. "Tyrowicz," she announces proudly.

17. Parker's assistant finds the bills for the L.A. trip. On the car rental extension, Sonja's charge card was marked on the bill. Parker also found an open letter sent to Aaron's old law firm; it was forwarded here, marked "S. Tyrowicz" on the return. She's the only daughter of Tyrowicz. Parker orders a complete FBI and INS investigation of Aaron.

18. Parker's office. A bombshell is about to drop. Parker knows Aaron's been screwing the daughter of a Nazi collaborator. He also hits Aaron with a new charge—Aaron's parents lied on their immigration visas. Background checks revealed they used false names on an application—just like Osidatch and Tyrowicz. If the Ukrainians find out, it could prejudice the case against Tyrowicz. Parker doesn't know if Aaron can stay on the job.

19. He talks to Sonja, to share some of the burden of lies uncovered. She asks why he didn't tell her about being with the OSI. He tells her he was afraid it would push her away. Now he needs to put things in perspective. He doesn't believe his parents could have lied all these years about their name. He's got to visit and take care

of them. Sonja defends her own father, guilty of the same thing—lying on an immigration form in the past. This is a rough moment for her, deeply concerned about her father. They both realize they're prisoners of their parents' past, and intricately bound up in their survival and way of life today.

20. Aaron's parents. They're frail and worried. Painfully, they recount the truth. They used another family's visa to escape the brutality of Ukrainian forces. They were close enough in physical features to get away with it, but their names were different. They adopted that family's name in the United States. Aaron is astounded that they never told him about it. He sees how upset they are and promises to protect them. Everything will be okay.

21. A Ukrainian reporter calls Aaron. He got the information from a "well-placed" source. Tomorrow's headlines will demand that Aaron's parents go on trial, just like Tyrowicz. Both lied on their visas, both should go on trial. They want the same treatment for the Jews and Ukrainians.

22. Parker's office. Parker informs Aaron that he's got to place him on leave. He's been besieged with calls to take him off the case. He'll put him on leave until this blows over. Aaron is outraged; he needs to clear his parents' name.

23. Aaron tries to track down the source of the news leak with Charlie's help. Aaron knows the leak could have been implemented by Sonja in a desperate bid to save her father. Charlie comes up with evidence that it was Parker himself who leaked the information because he wanted to bring proceedings against Aaron's parents. It would mean a promotion in his home district.

24. Preparing for the Tyrowicz trial, it's apparent that they need depositions from Moscow, Israel, and other sensitive sources. Aaron is the only one who speaks Russian and Yiddish, and he can get difficult witnesses to testify. Charlie convinces his boss to bring Aaron back as the prosecutor. The witnesses feel comfortable with him.

25. A deal is struck. Parker will see that the charges against his parents are dropped, if Aaron strictly adheres to the immigration strategy as prosecutor. Get Tyrowicz extradited to the Soviet Union

because he lied on his visa. He'll be executed in Russia. Needless to say, Aaron must also stay away from Sonja.

26. He lets his parents know that the charges will be dropped. They're happy, but this has taken its toll emotionally and physically on them.

27. He meets Sonja discreetly in L.A., lets her know he's going to prosecute her father. She tells him she'll be staying with her father throughout the deportation process. She asks why he ever wanted to be with the OSI. He tries to explain: to bring a semblance of responsibility for what happened in the past. And they can't be in communication after this.

28. Sonja and her father in Del Mar Beach. They talk about the lies of the past. He claims there was no choice. If he didn't carry out his responsibilities, he would have been killed. It was a different time and place.

29. In California Superior Court, the trial begins. Aaron introduces Soviet and Israeli depositions. We hear revelations from witness after witness that Tyrowicz was guilty of war crimes. He was chief S.S. liaison, working closely with Osidatch. The Ukrainians are outraged, claim the Russians are sending wrong information about him. Judge bangs the gavel. Sonja watches the proceedings solemnly.

30. Trial wraps up. Aaron proves that Tyrowicz was guilty of lying on his immigration visa. He would not have been allowed to become a citizen if the material facts were known. Judge's decision: deport Tyrowicz to the Soviet Union. Parker's team has been effective.

31. Kennedy Airport. Sonja is with her father as INS agents escort him toward a waiting Soviet Aeroflot.

32. Aaron hands in his resignation.

33. He calls Sonja; there is no answer.

34. Washington, D.C. Aaron takes early morning jog before returning to his old job.

Roll Credits:

CHARGES AGAINST AARON'S PARENTS WERE DROPPED.

SONJA'S FATHER WAS EXTRADITED TO THE SOVIET UNION WHERE HE WAS EXECUTED.

Storylines for Television

If you are writing the half-hour comedy episode for television, then you need to write an outline called a *two-pager*. The two-pager is a condensed narrative of your story, which defines the spine at the story.

A very helpful story tool for comedy writing is called a "Beat Sheet," which is a one-page blueprint of the story. It is a list of all the beats that define your story episode. It lets you see how each of the points works, and what doesn't.

The storyline, itself, is four to six pages. It conveys all the comic feats for the characters in the show.

Know that there is a different industry jargon for story outlines for drama. If you're writing a story for a one-hour dramatic episode, television film, or miniseries, then you'll write a treatment or "Step Outline," using "dramatic beats," which are discussed previously.

ENDNOTES

1. Eric Bentley, *The Playwright as Thinker: A Study of Drama in Modern Times*, San Diego, Harcourt Brace, 1987.

5

Dramatic Elements and Act Structure

Dramatic Elements in a Story

A useful artistic resource for film writers is the inclusion of dramatic elements established by Greek playwrights to heighten the effectiveness of a script: inciting action, complication, crisis, climax, reversal, and denouement.

- *Inciting Action:* event at the beginning of the story that forces your lead characters to move into action. It's the point of attack.
- *Complication:* occurs when your character tries to deal with a conflict and faces unforeseen obstacles.
- *Crisis:* a dramatic conflict that builds story momentum as your character faces enormous odds against achieving his or her goal.
- *Climax:* peaks the story as your character confronts the most fateful consequences of the rising action.
- *Reversal:* a turning point twists the story in a new direction at the end of the act. It usually occurs at the ends of Act One and Act Two.
- *Denouement:* resolution to the story. It happens at the end of Act Three.

Classical Three-Act Structure

Both screenwriters and television writers can use a dramatic structure that parallels effective playwriting strategy. Classical playwrights used three acts to build actions and complications for the characters.

- *Act One* sets up the inciting action, characters, and conflict. At the end of the act, a turning point twists the story in a new direction.
- *Act Two* develops the complication and builds the dramatic crisis. At the end of the act, a turning point twists the story in a new direction.
- *Act Three* builds the story's crisis to a climax. At the end of the act, the crisis is resolved in the denouement.

Act Structure in Motion Pictures

A theatrical motion picture screenplay is constructed as if it followed a classical three-act structure, but there is no act designation in the written script. This is the generally accepted act structure.

- *Act One* sets up the action in about 1 to 15 pages. It starts with an inciting action, builds the conflict, and unravels the first plot point or story point that turns the story in a new direction.
- *Act Two* can be about 45 to 60 pages. It develops the story with rising action to heighten the conflicts. It unravels the second plot point or story point, which twists the story in a new direction.
- *Act Three* is about 25 to 30 pages. This act is paced quicker. The conflict builds to a climax. Then the story is resolved in the denouement.

The development of an act rests on the established principles of story plotting and scene construction—hook the audience early, and build the action and conflict at a steady pace. The entire story has to be told within the parameters of a given number of acts and about 120 pages.

Act Structure in Television

In television, act structure is defined by the story length, so it can be confusing for writers to think about the right act structure to build the story. The act breaks in television are set up to accommodate commercial breaks, and each act should have enough story twists to keep an audience interested in seeing how the story unfolds. It might be helpful to think about a three-act structure as the building blocks to reach the beginning, middle, and end.

Half-Hour Sitcom Act Structure

In a half-hour television comedy series, the scripts can have a *teaser* of 30 to 60 seconds. Act One is about 10 to 12 minutes; Act Two is about

10 to 12 minutes. A *tag* or *wraparound* closes out the action in less than one minute. A half-hour show can be written in two acts or three acts, with each act about the same length (see Chapter 11).

One-Hour Dramatic TV

Many dramatic 60-minute television scripts are broken down into four acts. All are approximately equal length, totaling up to 60 pages (see Chapter 14).

Long-Form Television

Television movies of the week or TV films are broken down into seven acts. All are about equal length, totaling 90 pages for one-and-a-half hours, or 110 to 120 pages for a two-hour film.

Plotting Audience Interest in Your Story

As a former studio executive and producer, I know how studios depend on audience testing techniques to measure the appeal of story and character elements in features and television. Most films and television programs go through the process of audience testing to provide studios and networks with some idea of the script's effectiveness. By means of electronic testing, a graph is generated and instantaneous viewer response is recorded. Producers can literally see how every joke, line, car chase, action sequence, or romantic intrigue holds audience interest.

Conceptual devices for story development can help sharpen a script's impact and appeal. An audience's interest curve is especially helpful in conceptualizing the story needs for each act. You can block out the major crisis point in each act and build the story conflict accordingly. With the interest curve in mind, you can examine the function of each act and determine its effectiveness in the total plot structure. You can see whether an act sustains or builds audience interest, and whether it makes effective use of dramatic beats or action points throughout the show.

Sample Audience Interest Curves

For motion pictures, the screenwriter has more time to develop characters and can build a slower pace that increases throughout the film. The result is a classic three-act structure and a skewed bell-shaped curve, as shown in Figure 5-1.

As mentioned previously, motion pictures are not formally written with act breaks, but the classical three-act structure underpins the screenplay. In this case, Act One sets up the film's story, characters, and conflicts. Act Two develops the complications and builds to the dramatic crisis. Act Three builds the conflict and action to a climax. At the end, the crisis is resolved in the denouement.

A sample audience interest curve from a 60-minute dramatic television production is shown in Figure 5-2. It has four acts.

As with many shows, it begins with a short teaser, which hooks audience interest in one minute or so. The script builds the rising action and complications throughout each act, peaks to a climax at the end of Act Three, and resolves the intensity of conflicts in Act Four, where the denouement falls. The end of an act usually peaks audience interest—to hold viewers throughout the commercial—and reflects a natural break in the storyline. You can apply that same principle to the plotting of any film story, creatively guiding audience interest levels.

A sample of a two-hour TV film audience interest curve is shown in Figure 5–3. It has seven acts.

If you read from left to right, you can see that the short teaser was very effective as a hook, and that each act break was designed to maximize audience interest up until the commercial breaks. Interest picks up, with a snowballing effect throughout the entire show, and sustains until the end of Act Seven.

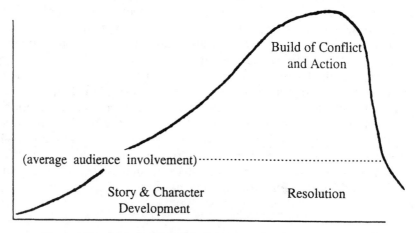

(No Act Breaks in Feature Films)

Figure 5-1
Sample Audience Interest Curve for Motion Pictures

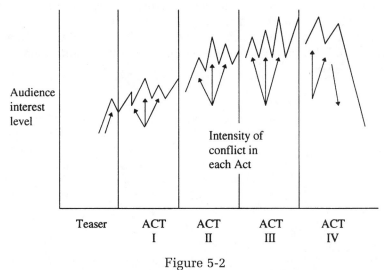

Figure 5-2
Sample Audience Interest Curve for 60-Minute Dramatic TV Show

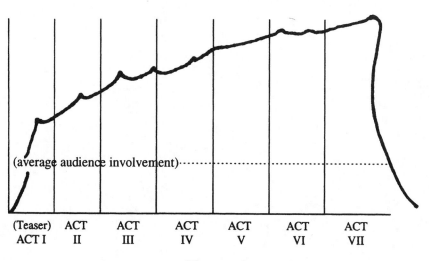

Figure 5-3
Sample Audience Interest Curve for a Two-Hour TV Film

The plot interest curve, or audience interest curve, is just one more conceptual device to visualize the story in development. It helps to consider the pacing of the story as it unfolds, and it suggests the intensity of action sequences and dramatic interrelationships that can sustain—and build—audience interest.

PART THREE

CHARACTERS AND DIALOGUE

6

How to Develop Credible and Castable Characters

How to Create Credible and Castable Characters

As emphasized throughout this book, *characters are the driving forces of your story.* Your hero must be someone the audience cares about—identifiable, susceptible, and vulnerable. That makes him or her appealing and castable.

To push the edges of conflict as far as possible, it helps if a protagonist faces powerfully motivated antagonists. Think of leads who face extraordinary opponents, in films such as THE THOMAS CROWN AFFAIR, all of the James Bond films, RAIDERS OF THE LOST ARK and the two Indiana Jones sequels, ENEMY OF THE STATE, LETHAL WEAPON and its three sequels, END OF DAYS, THE FUGITIVE, RUSH HOUR, BATMAN, THE HURRICANE, THREE KINGS, and UNFORGIVEN.

If you create lead characters who are *proactive,* then they are even more appealing to actors and audiences. In other words, they take positive action to get themselves out of a crisis, rather than sitting back passively.

Characters must resonate like real people, with a consistent pattern of behavior and dialogue and a complete, holistic, psycho/socio/physical being. The development of unique characters is indispensable to a compelling story and script. In the heat of sexual liaisons, or during encounters with aliens, car chases, or preparation for a trial, characters must be consistent in things they do, say, and think.

Creating Credible Characters

Knowing the character's inner life is a crucial part of story development and scripting. You might not be able to define inner realities at the conceptual stage, but in the process of development, the character's personality emerges. It helps to know who the character is, how the character thinks, reacts, interrelates, and behaves in any given situation. When characters are first created, detailed biographies can serve as springboards for story development. But the script must unveil that development through astute dramatic exposition.

One technique that helps identify realistic characterization is tied to the way actors interpret and analyze their roles. This approach is called "the Method" and is taught by proponents of Stanislavski's acting system. Constantin Stanislavksi was artistic director of the Moscow Art Theatre in Russia, and his techniques provided actors with tools for realistic character development. He brought his techniques to America in the early twentieth century.

Those techniques were modified, criticized, attacked, and misunderstood over the years, but they played a prominent role in the way actors, directors, and writers approached a script. In the United States, the system was adapted by Lee Strasberg, Stella Adler, and others at the Group Theatre in New York in the 1930s. Later, at the Actors' Studio, Lee Strasberg put his emphasis on exploring inner techniques and psychoanalytic realism, which became the cornerstone for Method training. It was also at the heart of artistic controversy in the 1950s and 1960s.

Stella Adler, who studied with Stanislavski, came to a different conclusion. Like Stanislavski, she had the greatest respect for playwrights and scripts. She taught that actors must derive their understanding of characters from analyzing given circumstances in the script.[1]

Using Method Acting Techniques: "The Method Writer"

I've found that television and screenwriters can benefit from the tools used by Method actors. Just a word of caution: Don't tell anybody you're using "the Method," or you'll get funny looks like you escaped through a time warp from Greenwich Village in the 1960s. But the fact is, no technique has more relevance for screenwriters because every word you write is meant to be cast and performed in larger-than-life closeups. In addition, variations of the Method remain the staple for acting training in television, film, and theatre today.

An actor trained in the Method approaches his or her character with a disciplined sense of creativity and spontaneity. In this sense, "disciplined" means using tools to create a sense of inner life for the characters in every scene of the script, from beginning to end.

As a "Method writer," you can flesh out the text and subtext in every scene. You can explore the motivations of characters, the consistency of attitudes, the justifiable actions and reactions in the plot structure. As the writer, you get to play every part, and if a behavioral problem is discovered, there's still time to fix it in a rewrite.

Here are some of the tools you can use to sharpen the realism and credibility of your characters: super objective, throughline of action, intentions, motivations, sense of urgency, state of being, moment-to-moment realities, and the "what if—?" technique. Ask yourself the following questions as you write your screenplay and create your characters:

1. What is the Super Objective?

The *super objective* is the main reason the character has been created. Each character, no matter how briefly he or she appears on screen, has a major objective to accomplish. This differentiates each character from the next.

2. What is the Throughline of Action for Each Character?

The *throughline of action* is a conceptual thread that shows how each character fits into your main objective. Each character serves a very specific function in relation to the plot development and the realization of the super objective. Each scene should bring you closer to those goals.

3. What is the Character's Intention?

The *intention* is the character's physical action in each scene. Intentions can change from scene to scene, and even within a scene—*if properly motivated.* Intentions are usually expressed as physical objectives. The character wants to do something (e.g., find a killer, experience a new theme park, fight a conspiracy, clear a cousin of murder, trip up burglars at home).

4. What is the Character's Motivation?

The *motivation* explains *why* a character needs to achieve a specific intention. The analytical edge provides a more dimensional understanding of the character and imprints a uniqueness on everything he or she does and says. It helps to convey the emotional subtext of each character.

If a character wants out of her marriage, there might be any number of emotional factors contributing to that decision. She may be frustrated, unfulfilled, afraid, or attracted to someone else. The motivation imprints a uniqueness on her character and provides a psychological framework for action and reaction throughout the treatment and script.

In BASIC INSTINCT, Nick, a homicide detective, knows the ins and outs of criminal minds, and is eager to close this case. But he's motivated by a steamy attraction he feels for Catherine. He knows she could be the murderer, but he places himself in jeopardy because he's sexually enmeshed by her. Catherine is motivated by the complex psychological cat-and-mouse game she plays, her power over men (and women), and her need to hide her secrets.

In JURASSIC PARK, John Hammond, billionaire developer, is motivated by egotism when he invites a select group to tour the park before it's ready to open. Dennis, a computer hack, is motivated by greed when he knocks out the security system to steal valuable vials. And when the dinosaurs run amok, all of the characters, including the kids, are motivated by another basic instinct—survival.

In UNFORGIVEN, Munny, the bounty hunter, is motivated by the need to earn money to support himself and his kids. He's a widower who barely ekes out a living as a pig farmer.

5. What is the Character's Sense of Urgency?

The sense of urgency is tied into the concept of intentions and motivations. It tells viewers how badly the character needs to achieve some goal or fulfill an intention. A rule of thumb: the greater the sense of urgency, the greater the dramatic conflict. If a character desperately wants to achieve a goal, and some obstacle is thrown in the way, then the dramatic tension heightens in direct proportion to that emotional intensity.

In BASIC INSTINCT, Nick needs to find out who's responsible for the ice pick murders before she strikes again. It may be the woman he's sleeping with.

In JURASSIC PARK, the characters are fighting for survival at all costs—using their wits against predatory dinosaurs.

In MY COUSIN VINNY, an attorney who just passed the bar needs to save his cousin and friend wrongly accused of murder. If he fails, they'll go to prison for life.

Something important always needs to be at stake.

6. What is the Character's State of Being?

The *state of being* is a character's total psychological and physical frame of reference in a scene. A writer creates more realistic dimensions by incorporating given circumstances into the character's thoughts, behavior, and attitudes.

Let's create a scene with these given circumstances as an example. Joel is frantic to see Maggie. He runs over to her place and finds it empty. It's been raining; it's late at night. What behavioral reality needs to be conveyed? Joel is wet, cold, out of breath, concerned, anguished. We can convey it all without a line of dialogue. The stage directions might suggest this: "Joel slams open the door, glances anxiously around the room, sees no one. Breathing hard, he wipes the rain from his face." And so the stage directions can paint reality through description, keeping alive all of the elements in the circumstances of the scene.

7. Are the Moment-to-Moment Realities Established in the Scene?

These are the character's reactions to everything she or he experiences in the scene. These realities take into account all of the circumstances of the scene, including the imprint of other characters, the imposition of the physical environment, and the psychological realities of each moment in the scene.

The *moment-to-moment reality* is a character's reaction to each and every dramatic unit, giving time to build attitudes and make internal adjustments. Let's set Tony up as a supervisor in a defense plant that's scheduled to close because of the recession. His orders are to reduce his staff, including Mona, his executive vice president. When she learns about it, she may argue and storm out in anger. But Tony remains resolute. Only after the conflict is over does he take a beat (a *beat* is a dramatic moment in which the character makes internal transitions in thought or attitude). He picks up the phone and tells the president he'll quit if he has to do anything like that again. That action, in the privacy of his office, makes him a more sympathetic character in the eyes of the audience.

Such private moments are important for establishing the true inner nature of characters. The audience can see how genuinely concerned they are, how brutal, how comic, how gentle, how disturbed. It helps to build in a sense of vulnerability or susceptibility for each character. That makes them more identifiable and provides a more interesting dimension to their behavior.

Let's suppose "Seinfeld" were still on the air and that a particular episode deals with a power failure hitting New York. When the lights go out, Jerry would never think that the whole city is powerless. He would have to build logically to that moment of discovery. First, he might try the light switch or test the bulbs. Then he might discover that the light is out in Kramer's apartment. They both search for a flashlight and check the circuit breaker. And that's where they discover that the whole apartment building has gone dark. Jerry still has no idea of the scope of the blackout. He and Kramer go out into the street and find that the whole block is out. Then, through a neighbor, he learns the momentous reality—the whole city is dark.

Meanwhile, what are his moment-to-moment attitudes? This depends on Jerry's state of being, intention in the scene when it opened, motivations, and sense of urgency. If he was getting ready for an appearance on the "Tonight Show with Jay Leno," then the power loss is frustrating. And he would go through each moment credibly to build that frustration. At first, he would simply be annoyed. That motivates him to correct the situation by finding a lightbulb; however, the power is out in the other room. His reaction? Greater annoyance. He can't complete his intention. Now he learns that the whole apartment building is dark. His attitude? Frustration! He'll never have time to get ready for the "Tonight Show" appearance. When he learns that the whole city is dark, his attitude is coupled with anxiety and curiosity.

Each moment can be played out credibly, and each reaction conveyed effectively to the viewer. With the proper builds and reactions, we can avoid inconsistent or manipulated action that forces an incident or telegraphs the story. A viewer may know that the lights went out in New York, but there is no way for the character to know it until the actual moment of discovery.

That same technique can be used for building tensions in a scene. Suppose we create an all-obsessed escaped convict in the house of police siren Lynn. The viewers may know the danger, but she doesn't. That orchestrates the pacing of the drama. Once the audience knows the danger, we can take our time bringing Lynn to that confrontation scene—and heighten the suspense. The obsessed convict takes a weapon and glides silently into a closet. Lynn may come into the room, take off her police uniform, and head to the closet—then spot a newspaper on the table. She tosses her uniform on the chair, glances anxiously at the paper's headlines about the escaped convict. Instinctively, she locks her front door. Now Lynn picks up her uniform, moves to the closet—and the phone rings. She answers. It's Molly, a partner who wants to know if she's all right. She reassures her partner, then hangs up. Now she heads to the closet. This time she opens it, and—nothing. She gets a hanger for her uniform and turns to go. Then, suddenly, a hand reaches out and grabs her!

We can play all of those realities in the plot to heighten the eventual confrontation. Hold the audience, surprise them, and play out all the moment-to-moment tensions. But now the story needs a twist to help Lynn escape. Perhaps she breaks away through some ingenious action or special skill as a police siren. If she has some special skill, then it's important to plant it earlier in the story, so it won't appear to be contrived. A *story plant* provides a logical and proper buildup for action on the screen.

8. *"What if—?" Techniques.*

A good suspense story is usually brimming with unusual turning points for characters—twists and turns in the plot, "red herrings," the unexpected. If a character gets into a hopeless situation, and the audience is totally caught up in the action, then it is anticlimactic for the police to burst in and save him or her. The audience has seen it a hundred times before. The action becomes predictable and clichéd.

One of the most useful devices for finding innovative twists is the *"What if—?"* technique. As the story develops, ask a steady stream of "What if—" questions, until you find several different possibilities. "What if this happens? What would my character do?" Try to go beyond the first, immediate response. Give yourself several alternatives. Try any combination of thoughts that are consistent with the credibility of the piece.

Think of the visual and dramatic turning points faced by lead characters in films such as RAIDERS OF THE LOST ARK and the two Indiana Jones sequels, James Bond films, THE THOMAS CROWN AFFAIR, ARMAGEDDON, ENEMY OF THE STATE, LETHAL WEAPON and its three sequels, END OF DAYS, THE FUGITIVE, RUSH HOUR, BATMAN, THE HURRICANE, THREE KINGS, and ROMANCING THE STONE.

The more you ask "What if—?" the greater the possibility of keeping the characters alive, appealing, and castable. The flip side was aptly illustrated by a cartoon I remember seeing. A frustrated writer sits by a computer, pages strewn all over the room. The caption went something like this: "Oh, to hell with it! 'Suddenly a lot of shots rang out, and everyone fell dead. The End.'"

Character Arcs

And that brings us to the subject of a *character arc*. Over a span of time, *motivated changes* occur in your characters, forcing them to act and react in ways that are driven by dramatic events. As a result, your character changes by the end of the film, but in a way that is consistent with who he or she was at the beginning.

In motion pictures, a character arc should seem natural and self-fulfilling. For example, in AMERICAN BEAUTY, the middle-aged character of Lester has the biggest character arc or transformation. As screenwriter Alan Ball reveals, the character parallels his own midlife crisis experiences: "I think you do reach a major point where you realize you have more of your life behind you than you do ahead of you. You start to reassess. All of a sudden things that seemed incredibly important don't seem quite so important anymore. I think men especially yearn for the passion that they felt about life when they were younger. . . . I think there's a wakeup call in everybody's life, but it's an incredibly painful journey. Most world mythologies have some myths in which the hero goes into the underworld, and I think those myths are based on that psychological truth that people undergo this sort of transformation at some point in their lives. . . . Lester's choice not to follow through with it redeems him, because she is not really the goal, she's the knock on the door. And I didn't even know that myself when I read the first draft of the script." In the first draft of the screenplay, Lester had sex with her. The screenwriter Alan Ball realized it was a "completely horrible, disgusting thing. And I'm really glad that I saw the error of my ways. . . . But I very quickly realized that was not the way it should be."[2] He realized that the character arc of Lester would not give in to the sexual temptations.[3]

In HOME ALONE, we meet Kevin, an eight-year-old, who is susceptible to the barbs and mishaps of his chaotic family. When he's left alone, he enjoys the new freedom, successfully overcomes his fear of furnaces, and then is ready to deal with two burglars. He is proactive—initiating booby traps. At the climax, he has more confidence and an understanding of himself and his family. The character arc is fully motivated by the events that transformed him.

At the beginning of THE CRYING GAME, Fergus befriends a British hostage whom he's been ordered to execute, which sets him up as a sensitive character. The driving force occurs when his hostage is accidentally killed. Fergus is proactive—he flees to London and initiates a search to find his hostage's girlfriend. Fergus finds Dil and becomes romantically and sexually entangled with her, only to discover that she is a he. It forces him to change his political alliances and his life choices. In the climax, he sacrifices himself in jail for the sake of Dil. That character arc is credible because Fergus is initially shown to us as a sensitive character.

In television, character arcs refer to something different. They are the planned evolution of the characters and relationships in a series. That evolution is usually determined by a *show runner* (writer-producer) after a series has been on the air and the relationships are still changing. Some characters may be targeted for romance, breakup, promotion, or unemployment.

Sexual tension that bubbles between two leads is a wonderful way to maintain audience interest in a series. Think of the romantic undercurrents between leads in sitcoms like "Friends," "Ally McBeal," and "Sex and the City."

If the romantic tension is successful, then that's one of the reasons audiences tune in. It is a daunting leap to have the character arcs resolved with an affair, marriage, breakup, or living together. But those elements do add freshness to series characters and have appeal for big audiences (especially during sweeps weeks). Nonetheless, the audience expects characters to have the same kind of tensions after the big event. Character arcs allow actors to grow in ways that are credible for the character and conflicts already established.

Setups and Payoffs

In all well-constructed screenplays, especially comedy, be sure to set up your characters individually for everything they encounter. Make sure it's all relevant to the characters' scene, action, reactions, and dialogue. Something is there for a reason. And then you have to deliver a credible and appropriate payoff in the script.

ENDNOTES

1. For more on the Method, see Richard A. Blum, *Working Actors: The Craft of Television, Film, and Stage Acting,* Focal Press, 1989; R. Blum, *American Film Acting: The Stanislavski Heritage,* UMI Research Press, Ann Arbor, MI, 1984; Stella Adler, *The Technique of Acting,* Bantam Books, 1988; David Garfield, *A Player's Place: The Story of the Actors' Studio,* New York, Macmillan, 1980.
2. Peter Chumo II, "American Beauty: An Interview with Alan Ball," *Creative Screenwriting,* January/February 2000, 26–27.
3. Ibid., 30.

7

How to Write Realistic Dialogue

Dialogue is an integral part of scripting and is intricately bound up with character development. Inner values and motivations are communicated by the uniqueness of dialogue. What a character says—or *doesn't* say—tells us about that character's state of being.

Ideally, dialogue should be motivated by the circumstances in the scene and should be consistent with the character development already established. Just as the writer has an "inner eye" for visualization, you've also got to have an "inner ear" for dialogue that makes the character come to life, adding a dimension of spontaneity and realism to the roles.

Problems and Solutions in Writing Dialogue

Often, the first run at dialogue presents some problems. Lines may be choppy, staccato, unrealistic, or perhaps melodramatic. The script might be peopled with film characters transposed from an English drawing room comedy ("quite grammatically correct, but evuh so bor-ing, dahling"), or with characters misplaced from an unedited version of reality-based TV ("Well . . . um . . . uh . . . y'know what I mean . . .").

To help identify and overcome those problems, with some deference to David Letterman, here is a list of the top-ten worst dialogue problems and solutions. It deals with dialogue that is too head-on or too on the nose, too choppy, too repetitious, too long, too similar, too stilted, too preachy, too inconsistent, or too unbelievable.

The Top-Ten Worst Dialogue Problems and Solutions

1. Too Head-On or Too On The Nose

This dialogue is much too literal and embarrassingly obvious. It sounds contrived. For example:

JENNIFER comes in the door and CARLOS smiles.

CARLOS

Jennifer, I'm so glad to see you. I love you so much.
I've been waiting to see you for so long.

That kind of dialogue is pretty embarrassing. No subtlety at all. It would be more effective if he were too overcome to speak. Or he might grab her close and say nothing. Then, after a beat, he might say:

CARLOS

Y'know, I can't stand to see you.

And they hug.

Well, of course, actions speak louder than words, and you've built a nice counterpoint to the action. Jennifer knows what he means, and so does the audience. Subtlety can be achieved through understatement, "playing against" the expected material, and playing out the characters' subtexts and inner attitudes.

2. Too Choppy

This dialogue is staccato. Filled with one-liners. A word or two. When you thumb through the script, it looks like an early Pinter stage play rather than a cinematic project. This is an example of dialogue that's too choppy:

DREW

I'm hungry.

KATE

Me too.

                                    DREW
Let's go out to eat.

                                    KATE
Okay.

                                    DREW
Is the deli okay?

                                    KATE
Yes, it's okay.

One solution to this problem is providing credible motivation for dialogue. The characters need a motivation and intention for speaking. They need a preestablished pattern of thought and behavior. Drew, for example, might be checking out the refrigerator through an earlier piece of action, then:

                                    DREW
Hey, there's nothing in here. Wanna go out?

                                    KATE
Mmm. I'm famished.

                                    DREW
How does the deli sound?

                                    KATE
Like chicken soup heaven.

And they race each other out the door.

In essence, the dialogue is the building block for moment-to-moment realities in the scene. It should spark behavioral action and reaction to be most effective.

3. Too Repetitious

Dialogue becomes repetitious when a character repeats himself or herself in a number of different ways. The character offers redundant information or repetitive phrases.

ILENE
I had such a good time on the trip. It was one of the
best trips I ever had.

ARTIE
I'm glad you enjoyed the trip.

ILENE
It was so good to be away. It was a terrific trip.

It seems as if the writer doesn't know what the character should say next,
and so relies on earlier dialogue—or is afraid the audience won't "get" a
specific point unless a character emphasizes it. One solution is to go back
into the script and clearly motivate each speech—or delete the speech alto-
gether. This is how the previous dialogue might be handled in revision:

ARTIE
You must have had some time. I never saw you so
relaxed.

ILENE
It was wonderful. I'm sorry it's over.

The simple character interchange affects the whole point of the dialogue
exchange. One character reacts to the other's emotional and physical state
of being in the scene. As for points the viewer should "get," put some preliminary plants in the script. Then a casual line of dialogue by a character
is sufficient to trigger the "Aha!" syndrome for the audience.

4. Too Long

Dialogue that is too long reads like an editorial speech or a philosophical
diatribe. It creates static action in the script and often includes related problems of redundancy and preachiness. Let's examine this speech:

JESSICA
(to Anne)
You didn't get the position because you're a woman,
not for any other reason. If you were a man, you
would have been hired on the spot. Don't let them do
that to you. Go back and fight for what you believe
in. They wouldn't get away with that on me. I can

assure you of that. I remember when I was growing
up, my mother always told me to look out for sexists. You've got to stand up and let them know you're
not going to take that kind of treatment.

The speech tends to dominate visual action and incorporates too many different thoughts, without essential breaks for transitions or reactions. It would
be helpful to intersperse reactions and stage directions at the end of each
major unit of thought. That makes the speech seem less formidable and its
impact more immediate. Here's what it might look like.

JESSICA
(to Anne)
If you were a man you would have gotten it.

Anne tries not to pay attention. She's in no mood for Jessica's
tirade.

JESSICA (CONT'D)
Don't let them treat you that way. Go back and fight
for what you believe in.

Anne says nothing. Jessica sees she's getting nowhere, crosses
over to her friend, and speaks softly but urgently.

JESSICA (CONT'D)
I was always warned about sexists like that. Let them
know you're not going to take it.

A BEAT, then Anne turns to look at her friend. The conviction is
sinking in.

The idea is to integrate emotional reactions into a long speech and trim the
excesses. Long speeches are not always a problem, especially in court dramas. But emotional reactions add much to the context. It might be possible for Jessica, for example, to blurt out the dialogue in anger and frustration.
That emotional reaction might be germane to her state of being. If so, the
speech can stand on its own merits.

5. Too Similar

Sometimes characters sound the same. Their dialogue patterns are indistinguishable from each other. Once that happens, the character's individuality has been lost. Can you distinguish between these two?

> BEN
> Hey, did you bet on the car race?

> ALEX
> Yeah, I did. Did you?

> BEN
> Yeah. Did ya win?

> ALEX
> Nah, not when I needed it.

The characters sound precisely the same, and they're redundant on top of it. One way to counter the problem is to provide some psychological richness to the scene. The characters need to be reexamined in terms of motivations, intentions, and sense of urgency.

Because Ben and Alex are two different human beings, their inner thoughts and attitudes might be expressed in totally different dialogue structure. Here's how the scene might play.

> BEN
> (tentatively)
> You bet on the race?

ALEX shrugs off the question.

> ALEX
> Sure.

> BEN
> Did you win? Alex?

No response. Then:

ALEX

Not this time. Not when I needed it.

Ben crosses to him and touches his arm, reassuringly.

The conflicts are implied. When creating dialogue, remember that your characters are unique human beings, with the ability to interact at the highest levels of subtlety and complexity.

One producer told me he covers the names of characters during the first pass at a script, to see if they're drawn dimensionally. If he can't distinguish between the blocks of dialogue, then he discards the script as "characterless."

6. Too Stilted

This dialogue sounds as if it came from a history book, a poem, a newspaper, a grammar text, but not from a person. This is an example of stilted dialogue:

JEFF

It is my responsibility to provide you with my interpretation of the event. You are the only person that might accept that perspective. You must hear me out.

Unless Jeff has a particularly pedantic problem, it would be more appropriate for him to colloquialize and get to the bottom line quickly.

JEFF

You gotta listen to me!

And that says it all. Don't be afraid to use contractions in dialogue. That's the way real people speak.

It helps to read dialogue aloud to hear the character in action. If the speech pattern is stilted, then you can improvise to find a more spontaneous feel to the character's actions. At your desk, with no one else around, put the same characters into different conflicts. You'll be surprised how much you learn about them.

7. Too Preachy

This problem is related to being "head on," "redundant," "too long," and "too stilted." The character tends to sound very formal and espouses thematic ideas or philosophical notions. He or she becomes an ideological mouthpiece for the writer, rather than a dimensional being. This speech, for example, borders on the preachy:

> MIKE
>
> Do you see what happens when convicts run free? They belong in jail, or they threaten the very fiber of society. This sort of thing would never happen if we had stronger lawmakers and laws.

If a character must speak with strong convictions, it doesn't have to sound like an editorial. Mike can get the same point across by growling:

> MIKE
> The bastard oughta be locked away.

The exact nature of the dialogue, of course, depends on the unfolding action in the scene, and the consistency of the motivations and behavior of the character throughout the story and script.

8. Too Introspective

This problem deals specifically with the character who is alone and speaks out loud. This cliché is typical:

> MICHELLE
> (to herself)
> Oh, how I long to be with him now.

That's enough to make any writer cringe. How often does a person actually talk to herself or himself? Not very. And when we do, it's *not* in complete, logical sentences. Logic is antithetical to the emotion of the moment. The dramatic conventions of a Shakespearean soliloquy are very different from the cinematic expectations of television and film.

It makes more sense for the character to build a private moment on screen. She might glance at a picture, close her eyes, and try to regain her composure. Once again, actions speak louder than words.

9. Too Inconsistent

This means that a character is saying something that doesn't fit the personality already created. The dialogue is incongruous with character. In some cases, that inconsistency results from a lack of proper transitions in the scene. This is an example of erratic dialogue or attitudes that change too quickly to be believed.

                        JASON
        I wish you would both listen to me.

                        JENNIFER
        No! Carlos and I have better things to do.

                        JASON
        I'm telling you this for your own good.

                        JENNIFER
        Okay, we'll do it.

The thought transitions are simply too quick to be credible. It might work better if the proper actions and reactions are built into the scene through suggested transitions. This is one way of handling that problem.

                        JASON
        I wish you would both listen to me.

                        JENNIFER
        No!

She glances up at her brother, and sees the hurt in his eyes.
Then she tries to explain.

                        JENNIFER (CONT'D)
        Carlos and I have important things to do.

That obviously has no impact. He tries to control the urgency in his voice.

JASON

I'm telling you this for your own good.

A long BEAT, then Jennifer turns away, heading toward the couch. She mulls it over. Finally:

JENNIFER

Okay, we'll do it.

Jason breathes a sigh of relief.

Sometimes the problem of inconsistent dialogue can be helped by analyzing the character's inner drives and attitudes on a moment-to-moment basis in the scene. The solution might simply be to build more transition time, or to build more character development into the script.

10. Too Unbelievable

This is a catch-all category that implies that a character doesn't sound real for any number of reasons. You can test the credibility of dialogue by speaking it aloud to judge whether or not it rings true. It should sound like a real person responding to the immediate circumstances we've just seen.

If there is a problem, then try this exercise: *improvise.* Out loud, or on your computer, put the same characters into a different conflict. It should be a direct conflict of wills, each with totally opposing intentions. The two characters might thrash out the conflict in two or three pages. One may give in, one may walk out, or both may compromise. The outcome is not important; however, the dialogue, motivations, and behavior must be logical and consistent. Once you know how the individual characters interact, then the integrity of the characters is assured. The original dialogue can be tested against your heightened insight into motivations, intentions, and attitudes.

PART FOUR

MOTION PICTURE SCREENPLAY FORMAT

8

Spec Screenplay Format

Spec Screenplay Format

When you write a spec screenplay, it has to look like a professional screenplay. Professional screenwriters write a screenplay that can be called a "master scene" script. A master scene script offers a vivid description of action within each scene, but it does not break down specific camera angles or shots. You identify each new scene and set up all of the characters, dialogue, and action, but you won't write camera or technical directions. Save all that for the director.

Only when a script has been purchased and is ready for production is it ready to be put into shooting script form. The shooting script sets up all of the scene numbers and directorial requirements. With feedback on each scene, you can rewrite as necessary for production. The shooting script is the director's final blueprint for production and has every shot numbered in the margins.

Master Scene Screenplay

On the following pages, you'll find a master screenplay script sample, which is appropriate for motion picture screenplays, long-form television films, and television film episodes. Film scripts run about one minute of screen time per page.

A full-length screenplay is about 120 pages, with no act breaks—the slimmer the better. A two-hour television film is around 110 to 120 pages and has seven acts. A 90-minute film is about 90 pages, with seven acts. A one-hour dramatic episode is approximately 60 pages long, broken into four acts.

> The title goes here capitalized and underlined

SAMPLE FILM SCRIPT FORMAT TITLE ←

Written By

Your Name ← Writer's name

Your Name, Agent, or Lawyer ←

> This can be your address, agent, or entertainment attorney

Address

Phone

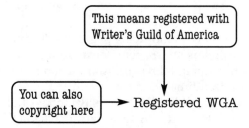

> This means registered with Writer's Guild of America

> You can also copyright here

Registered WGA

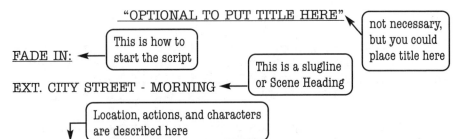

Every scene in the script begins with a SCENE HEADING, which is called a <u>slugline</u>. This is the location of the scene. It identifies the location as EXT. (exterior) or INT. (interior). Then the specific location (e.g. PARKING LOT, RESTAURANT, DAVID'S BEDROOM, APARTMENT - BEDROOM, THE HOTEL BAR). Then the time of day (e.g., DAY, NIGHT, MORNING, AFTERNOON, EVENING, DUSK, SAME, LATER, MOMENTS LATER, CONTINUOUS, THE NEXT DAY). That information is necessary for the director and production manager to determine the set, location, and lighting requirements of your script.

Next, you put the action, describing the characters and locale in the scene. It is basically a place to describe the ESTABLISHING SHOT. You can specify what the street looks like and any characters or cars we may see. Don't worry about typing in CREDITS because that is the director's prerogative.

> Double space implies new angle

You can simply skip a paragraph to describe another angle in the scene, without actually having to label it. This is particularly true if you are thinking of a related piece of stage action in a master shot or wide shot. This saves you from overdirecting your script and permits ease of reading.

The suggested angle does not have to include any other scene heading because it is still part of the same scene. You are merely calling for a different angle within that scene. This helps move your plot forward in a linear fashion.

EXT. JEN'S CAR - MORNING ◄— This indicates a different scene and location

Describe Jen's car and whatever and whoever we see outside the car, using clear and concise visualization.

INT. JEN'S CAR - DAY ← [New Scene]

If you change the physical locale of the scene, you must provide a new scene heading. When you describe your CHARACTERS or any information pertaining to CAMERA ANGLES, VISUAL EFFECTS, or SOUND EFFECTS, be sure to cap that information.

Try to be as visual as you can in your description of the CHARACTERS. Set up their ages, who they are, what they look like, and what they're doing at the moment we see them. Don't forget the setting in the scene. You'll have to describe it in vivid detail, to give a rich and clear picture of the mood, atmosphere, and dramatic action. [This is how to set up characters]

JEN, late 20s, short and brunette, puts the key in the ignition. FRANK, 35, slim and balding, is sitting next to her, reading a map.

[This is how to set up dialogue]
                    JEN
    Let's move on to something else, okay? How about
    numbering shots in a script?

                    FRANK
        (mock disgust)
    That's just for a shooting script.

[This is how to indicate reactions]
Jen shrugs, starts the car, and pulls away.

EXT. STREET - DAY [New scene heading]

We see the car pulling away from the curb and disappearing down the street in light traffic.

Notice that it is necessary to provide a new scene heading because we are now shooting outside again.

I/E. JEN'S CAR - TURNPIKE - DAY ← [One way to indicate interior and exterior car scenes]

If we cut between the interior and exterior of Jen's car, this is one way to indicate it. Another is to write INT/EXT. - JEN'S CAR.

We can use another technique to keep the dialogue alive and the visuals wide open. That's the use of OS (OFFSCREEN) and VO (VOICEOVER).

                          JEN (OS)
          So, you can still hear me talking while Frank is on
          screen.

Jen reaches for a CD and puts it in the player. We HEAR a light rock song play.

This is how to indicate a "Voice Over"

                          FRANK (VO)
          Right. And there is a technical difference between the
          voiceover and the offscreen voice. The VO is gener-
          ally used like this over some other visual action. Or
          sometimes by a narrator.

This is how to indicate "Off-Screen" dialogue

                          JEN (OS)
          Sounds confusing. But the OS is used when one of the
          characters isn't seen in the shot but we know he or
          she is in the scene, perhaps on the other side of the
          room.

We see the car blend into the light maze of traffic on the city streets.

Here is the end of a scene description

                                                        CUT TO:

EXT. BEACH - DUSK   New scene heading

We're in a totally different location now, so there is a transition CUT TO. Use this command as little as possible since it is implied for editing.

In the action line, describe who and what we see. If we see Frank and Jen, where are they? Try to set the right visual and emo-tional atmosphere with your description. Do they look tired after

driving all day? Are they wearing different clothes? Are they
tense? bored? anxious? happy? Be sure to set up character reactions. Perhaps Frank has a look of concern.

In the distance, he sees the light of a bonfire. Three MASKED
FIGURES are huddled nearby. ⟵ (Here is how to suggest a point-of-view shot)

Note that we don't have to say a point-of-view shot because it is
implied.

                                   JEN (OS)
                 Frank? What's the matter?

                                   FRANK
                 (tense) ⟵ (Parenthetical directions for characters
                 Nothing's the matter.   should be short)

The parenthetical information should be used if the attitude of
the character is not clear by dialogue alone. It wouldn't be necessary for you to say "Frank speaks angrily" if he shouts "Get out
of here!"

You might also include some relevant action for the character, if
this can be done succinctly. For the most part, however, try to let
the dialogue speak for itself. For example:

Jen glances down the beach, squints to see the figures, and looks
back at Frank. A BEAT, then she packs their belongings hurriedly.

                                   JEN   (A "Beat" is described here)
                 Let's go.

The BEAT is a film version of the dramatic pause, or the
Chekovian pause. It implies a second or two for the character to
digest the information before he or she acts on it.

(How to describe background and foreground)

Note, too, that if some background action is occurring, you identify it as b.g. (not spelled out); similarly, if the camera is focused
on foreground action, you would say f.g.

EXT. JEN'S CAR - BEACH - DUSK

Jen and Frank race through the beach to their car and hastily climb in. She starts it up, but the engine won't start. In the b.g., we can make out the figures by the bonfire, moving toward them.

                        FRANK
        Hurry!

INT. JEN'S CAR - BEACH - DUSK

A BEAT before the ignition catches and starts up.

Note that the character doesn't have to repeat any visual information (i.e., he wouldn't say, "Hurry, the figures are coming toward us!"). We can assume that Jen sees the same thing that he does.

EXT. BEACH ROADS - DUSK

We see the car skid through dusty beach roads.

> This is how visual and sound effects are written

When you have special sound effects (e.g., the WAVES CRASHING, the FIRE CRACKLING), place those directly in the scene description to add atmosphere and mood to the piece.

Keep the action moving from scene to scene, and be sure your characters act and react like real people. Each one is unique and must sound and behave like a credible, identifiable person.

Once the script is finished, you can type FADE OUT or THE END.

> The last transition in the script is FADE OUT or THE END ⟶ FADE OUT.

How to Prepare Your Screenplay Professionally

A full-length screenplay should be no more than 120 pages. Read as many screenplays as possible in the genre you are writing for to see how the professional screenplay is set up. Remember that you will be reading scripts that are shooting scripts, which means they will have shot numbers and camera shots. You will be writing a master scene screenplay for submission, with no camera shots and little or no technical directions. Save all that for the director.

You can order from thousands of motion picture or television scripts at sources like *Script City* (Website: www.scriptcity.net; address: 8033 Sunset Blvd., Box 1500, Los Angeles, CA 90046; phone: 818/760-8292), or *Larry Edmunds Books* (address: 6658 Hollywood Boulevard, Hollywood, CA 90028; phone: 323/463-3273). Or get a catalogue from *Hollywood Collectables* (120 San Fernando Blvd., Suite 446, Burbank, CA 91502; phone: 818/845-5450). You can also order shooting scripts of current films from *Newmarket Press* movie books at 18 East 48th Street, New York, NY 10017; phone: 212/832-3575.

All script pages should be three-hole punched. Put roundhead script fasteners (or brads) and washers through the first and third holes of the script. Keep the center hole empty. Script fasteners come in two sizes: 1.5 inches for scripts over 100 pages, and 1.25 inches for scripts under 100 pages. Ask your local office supply store for the right supplies. If they don't carry them, you can also purchase them from the Writers Store (Website: www. writersstore.com; address: 2040 Westwood Blvd., Los Angeles, CA 90025; phone: 800/272-8927). You can also order professional card stock and brads from the *NY Screenwriter* (Website: www.nyscreenwriter.com; address: *The New York Screenwriter Monthly*, 655 Fulton Street, Suite #276, Brooklyn, NY 11217).

Other Format Distinctions

Your script covers should be card stock cover of at least 80-pound weight. Keep your colors neutral, and the cover page blank.

Title Page

The first page of the script is your title page. It has the script's title by you, the screenwriter. Be sure to print a contact address and phone number, so someone can know how to reach you, if interested. The name and address can be your agent, your entertainment attorney, your company, or your personal address. On the title page, you can also indicate that your screenplay is "Registered, WGAw" or "Registered, WGAE" and/or copyrighted (for information on the script registration and copyright, see Chapter 18). Don't put the date on your script, and don't type any draft on it.

Development strategies and feedback decisions take a long time. Projects will look old if you date them.

The industry-standard font is Courier or Pica 12 point, looking as if it's typed on a typewriter.

According to *The Screenwriters Bible* by John Truby, a film script usually abides by the following margin and tab guidelines.[1]

Margins

Text should be 1.5 inches from the left margin and .5 inches from the right margin, which should be ragged.

Tabs

Left margin at 15 spaces (1.5 inches) from the left edge of the page

Dialogue at 25 spaces (2.5 inches) from the left; 10 spaces from the left margin. (Make sure your dialogue does not extend beyond 60 spaces, or 6.0 inches.)

Actors' instructions at 31 spaces (3.1 inches); that's 16 spaces from the left margin

Characters' names at 37 spaces (3.7 inches); that's 22 spaces from left margin

Top margin: One inch from the top of the page

Bottom margin: One inch from the bottom of the page

As for page numbers, they should be one inch from the right and one-half inch from the top. Your first page does not carry a page number. If you revise a page, you can simply type the page number, then 6-A or 6-B.

Here are some other distinctions in a film script:

1. Words are generally capitalized to identify NEW SCENE HEADINGS, NEW CAMERA ANGLES, SOUND EFFECTS, SPECIAL EFFECTS, and scene transitions such as CUT TO or DISSOLVE TO.

2. Use CUT TO or DISSOLVE TO sparingly. Most scenes that are written in the script are implied cuts that will be edited in postproduction. Use CUT TO only if you think that the scene location and time sequence are

substantially different from the earlier scene. As for DISSOLVE TO, use this only to set up a long transition in time, or to set up a dream or fantasy sequence.

3. If a scene is continued on a new page, it may be indicated by a "(CONTINUED)" at the bottom right-hand page of the script, and "CONTINUED" at the top left of the following page.

4. If dialogue is broken at the end of a page, it should end with a full sentence. Then "(MORE)" is added under the broken dialogue, and "(CONT'D)" is typed on the following page, after the character's name.

5. The names of CHARACTERS are capitalized to indicate who is performing in the scene and who is speaking at the moment. If a character is simply mentioned by another, there is no need for capitalizing. There is latitude about capitalizing a character's name throughout the script. Most writers prefer to capitalize it just the first time the character appears in the script. Others will capitalize the name throughout each scene in the script.

How to Set Up Camera Angles

Most film scripts are written without complicated, extensive camera directions. You can simply skip a paragraph to describe the action in a new angle.

There is no need to clutter scripts with over-the-shoulder shots, reverse angles, medium shots, two shots, or crane shots. The director will make all of those decisions in preproduction planning. The writer's responsibility is merely to *suggest* the potential for camera coverage without complicating or overdirecting the script. But if you need to suggest angles on characters or locations in the scene, this is how to do it.

- STABLER or ANGLE ON STABLER: This focuses our attention on a specific person in the scene; in this case, a character named Stabler. The first direction is leaner looking in the script. Be sure to set up the actions and reactions of Stabler right away.
- CLOSE ON STABLER or CU STABLER: This describes the magnified coverage of Stabler's face on screen. "CU" means closeup. You might also see "ECU," which means extreme closeup. Try to keep the closeup coverage minimal by describing it creatively in the script, since it is a director's call.
- SOLID ROCKET BOOSTER: This is a different view of a shuttle, with an angle on a solid rocket booster.
- BATHROOM: Describe the bathroom and characters we see in it.

- HALLWAY: This is an angle featuring the hallway, with the description of characters we see near the hallway.
- BACK TO SCENE: This is a way of suggesting a director can use a previous angle. It can be used after a montage or insert.

How to Structure Scenes

A scene is one link in a dramatic sequence of events. It consists of action and dialogue that occur in a single place and time. Once the location changes, so does the scene. The dictates of the story determine how long each scene will be, but many writers try to economize. Some scenes may run for a few sentences, whereas others are as long as a few pages.

Here is a dramatic sequence that takes place at the airport. It actually consists of three separate scenes:

1. outside the airport
2. inside the terminal
3. inside the baggage compartment

Within each scene, several different camera angles and shots may be required to put the sequence together. But the general location remains the same, and the production crew will not have to move elsewhere.

<u>"AIRPORT SEQUENCE" SCRIPT SAMPLE</u>

EXT. AIRPORT - DAY

We're at L.A. Airport, clogged with traffic, the lines of cars backed up as far as we can see. A large 707 sits waiting for takeoff at one of the terminals.

INT. TERMINAL - DAY

As busy inside as it was outside. Lots of people milling around, waiting for the crowd to board the plane to Washington. A small coterie of FIRST CLASS PASSENGERS make their way into the plane, obviously important. They're government VIPs.

In another section of the terminal, watching the action, are THREE MEN near a food stand. One wears a suit and tie, the others wear baggage handling outfits. The MAN IN THE SUIT slips open his attaché and manages to pass a small packet to the BAGGAGE HANDLER.

A quick glance around. No one has seen them. We HEAR a muffled call over the P.A. system for all passengers to board the flight. The MAN IN THE SUIT, attaché firmly in hand, waits on line for the security check. He passes through the gates without a problem.

INT. PLANE'S BAGGAGE COMPARTMENT - DAY

The two BAGGAGE HANDLERS work furiously to attach electronic wiring to the wall of the compartment. One HANDLER opens a plaid piece of luggage, exposing some kind of crude bombing device. Time is pressing, but they complete their mission. One of them reaches down into the luggage and hits a switch. The countdown has begun. They scramble out of the compartment and slam the door shut, leaving us in darkness.

The first scene—outside the airport—is an establishing shot, which provides a visual orientation to the viewer. When the scene is shot, the director may use several different angles (a high angle of the airport, various angles of the traffic, a closeup of the large 707, etc.), but the actual scene location (EXT. AIRPORT - DAY) does not change.

The second scene takes place inside the terminal. It identifies and focuses the action on some key characters. The director may use several different setups (camera angles and lighting changes) to achieve the total effect of passengers waiting, men interacting, passengers boarding, and so on.

The third scene takes place in the baggage compartment and completes the dramatic action in the chain of events. The scene's action is specifically related to the previous scenes in the sequence.

Scenes can be viewed as links in the dramatic action chain, holding story sequences together with a clear purpose. They move the story forward with skill and maintain a tempo and rhythm for the entire script.

Let's look at some special problems you may encounter in writing certain types of sequences in your screenplay, and how to handle them.

Special Techniques

Montages and Series of Shots

A MONTAGE is a succession of different shots that condense time, emotions, and action into just a few short scenes. The story may call for a quickly established romance or an historical progression of images leading to the present time. This is one way to set up the MONTAGE SEQUENCE:

MONTAGE - ILENE AND RICK HAVE ROMANTIC FUN TOGETHER

—Ilene and Rick have pizza in a small Italian restaurant.

—They go to a Sarasota Beach together.

—They go to a hotel room, he opens some wine, and it spills all over.

END MONTAGE or

BACK TO SCENE

Sometimes, the montage sequences are numbered. Very similar is the SERIES OF SHOTS that defines quick scenes that push the story forward. The individual scenes are sometimes listed by number. If a writer needs to show a character undertaking different activities in a progression of time, then this technique is ideal. It gives the viewer a sense of completed action and pacing.

Let's look at the screenplay format in the following sample, which is reprinted with permission of the software program Final Draft, Inc. At the beginning of the sample, you'll notice how different series of shots are set up with a dash (–) to identify the different scenes. Also note the scene transitions DISSOLVE TO 5 MINUTES LATER and then DISSOLVES TO MINUTES LATER. That is a valid way to set up a montage without specifying it.

—Bryan turns on the shower and tests the water temperature. He grabs his toothbrush, squirts some toothpaste on it, and climbs into the shower, brushing his teeth.

—Back in his bedroom, a towel wrapped around his waist. He slides open the closet and pulls out some clothes: black slacks, white and gray buttondown shirt, black leather shoes.

—He is fully dressed with the exception of his tie, which hangs around his neck, unknotted. He bends down to scan one of the open road maps, takes a pen from his inner pocket, and circles the town of Sayerville, New Jersey.

—He grabs a large sample case containing mirror samples and hurries out the door.

EXT. STREET OUTSIDE BRYAN'S APARTMENT - DAY

—He crosses the street and gets into his big, beat-up green 1979 Cutlass Supreme. He sits down, puts on his seatbelt, and unbuttons the top button of his pants. He grabs a piece of chewing gum off the dash and throws the foil in the back seat, which is full of newspapers and takeout bags from McDonald's and Burger King.

I/E. BRYAN'S CAR - PHILADELPHIA STREETS - DAY

—He drives through the streets of Philadelphia, passing various recognizable landmarks: City Hall, Independence Hall, the Liberty Bell.

—The car heads across the Walt Whitman Bridge, out of Philadelphia and takes an exit marked "NEW JERSEY TURNPIKE NORTH."

—The car sits stopped in traffic, which isn't moving.

I/E. BRYAN'S CAR - TURNPIKE - DAY

Bryan grabs a watch, which is sitting on the dashboard. He glances at it, sees that he is late.

> BRYAN
> No!

He turns the wheel to the left and pulls onto the shoulder, driving past all of the stopped cars.

I/E. BRYAN'S CAR - SUBURBAN STREET - DUSK

Bryan is stopped at an intersection, staring at a street map in his hands. He looks at the map, glances up at the street sign, down at the written directions in his appointment book, and finally back to the map.

> BRYAN
> (muttering)
> Stupid broad doesn't even know where she lives.

EXT. HOUSE IN SAYERVILLE - DRIVEWAY - DUSK

Bryan's car pulls into the driveway of an upper-middle-class
home. He parks behind a new Mazda Miata, gets out, and buttons
his pants. He notices a satellite dish on the roof and smiles. His
face reads: "I can sell these folks." He grabs his sample case and
walks to the front door, avoiding a barking dog chained to the
basketball hoop. He rings the doorbell. It is opened by BOB
WILLIAMS, white, 31-year-old yuppie-type. In his arms is a one-
year-old baby girl, crying loudly.

> BRYAN
> (loudly)
> Mr. Williams? Bryan Lerner, Contemporary Mirrors.
> I'm not too late, am I?

> BOB
> No, perfect timing. We're just getting done feeding the
> baby. Come on in.

Bryan enters the house, wipes his feet, and closes the door
behind him. As he follows Bob down the hall, he gestures upward
with his hands and eyes as if saying "why me?".

> BOB (CONT'D)
> (continuing)
> Any trouble finding the place?

> BRYAN
> No . . . no problem at all. Your wife's directions were
> perfect. Gorgeous home you have here, Mr. Williams.
> Did you decorate yourself? . . . Silly question, I'm sure
> you did . . . wonderful taste.

INT. HOUSE IN SAYERVILLE - KITCHEN - DUSK

Seated on one side of the kitchen table is Bryan, his sample case
on the floor next to him. Across from him sit Bob and his wife,
BETTY WILLIAMS. In Betty's arms is the baby, still crying.

While he talks, Bryan reaches into his sample case and pulls out
a large, fancy mirror sample with gold, leafy trim. It looks great.
Making sure it remains in full view, he sets it aside and reaches
back into his sample case, pulling out a small, plain, obviously
junky mirror. It has no trim or edging and looks more like
something a girl might pull out of her purse to check her
makeup. He holds it in his hand and speaks of it as if it were the
greatest thing since sliced bread.

> BRYAN
>
> As you know, we're Contemporary Wall Mirrors. What
> makes us different from the competition is we make
> all the components ourselves. That means we can sell
> directly to the consumer, eliminating the middle man,
> which in turn saves you money. The bottom line is
> that I can cover your entire foyer with the best qual-
> ity at the lowest price, and that's really the most
> important thing, isn't it Bob?

Bob nods his head in agreement.

DISSOLVE TO:

FIVE MINUTES LATER. Bryan is still pitching to them about the
wonders of the junky mirror with such intensity and emotion
that the Williams are at his complete attention. Even the baby
has stopped crying and seems to be listening.

> BRYAN (CONT'D)
>
> . . . Now, not everyone can pick this up, but if you
> look closely at the surface of the mirror, you'll notice
> that it's coated with our patented anti-fog inhibitor,
> Phenoprophine. It keeps dust and steam from build-
> ing up on the mirror's surface. It always looks clear
> as day.

Bob and Betty lean closer to the mirror, trying to see the
chemical for themselves.

> BRYAN (CONT'D)
> (continuing)
> As a matter of fact, it's the same stuff NASA uses on
> the windows of the space shuttle to keep the space
> dust off.

                                        DISSOLVE TO:

TEN MINUTES LATER. Bryan is standing behind Bob and Betty, pointing to some papers that are sitting on the table in front of Bob.

Point of View (POV)

When you indicate a characters' POINT OF VIEW, you can just imply what the character sees and describe that.
For example:

JENNIFER stops as she sees her brother, JASON, across the room, and smiles.

That avoids camera direction, and the point of view is implied. It is also acceptable to type the following:

JENNIFER'S POV

She sees her brother Jason, across the room.

BACK TO SCENE

This suggests another angle without specifically identifying it.

Intercuts

INTERCUTTING is cutting between two or more scenes consecutively. For example, a script may call for parallel action and dialogue during a phone conversation. If you play the scene in one location, it could result in static dramatic action. If the script cuts back and forth between characters, it might result in awkward repetition of scene descriptions.

The most common solution to this kind of problem is to identify the ongoing scenes in an INTERCUT SEQUENCE. The appropriate scenes are defined, and action and dialogue are written as usual. That provides the director with more latitude. This is how it can be written:

INTERCUT - JEN'S DEN/CARLOS' OFFICE - DAY

Jen is on the cordless phone in the den, pictures scattered all over the floor.

                    JEN
                (on phone)
        You okay?

In his office, Carlos is on the phone, near the company computers.

                    CARLOS
                (on phone)
        Fine, but I miss you somethin' awful. When will you
        come back?

She takes a deep breath.

                    JEN
                (on phone)
        Not for a long time.

Carlos's eyes widen. He didn't want to hear that. He hangs up.

END INTERCUT

If you CUT TO another scene heading, you don't need to indicate END INTERCUT. The need for an intercut sequence is dictated by the length of the required scene and the importance of seeing consecutive dramatic action on the screen. The sequence allows the director to edit as he or she sees fit.

Dreams and Fantasies

In scriptwriting, dreams and fantasies are used interchangeably. They permit the viewer to enter the character's mind, to literally see imagination, daydreams, fantasies, and nightmares. A "dream sequence" can be distinguished from "reality" to keep the production realities clear. Here is one way it can be done:

INT. BEDROOM - NIGHT- CAROL'S DREAM

She's fast asleep; a look of anxiety twists her face. A poisonous spider moves toward her at an inscrutably slow pace . . .

INT. BEDROOM - NIGHT - REALITY

She snaps her eyes open and looks around. There's nothing there.

In this case, the dream sequence is almost a flashcut. It is a very fast insert into the "real" world of Carol sleeping. Once the sequence is over, the "real-time" sequence picks up the pace and helps sustain the mood.

A longer sequence is generally identified in advance, and the first "real" scene is distinguished. Here's what a longer dream sequence looks like. It is from the screenplay I wrote with Allan Gerson, SONJA'S MEN. To set the scene, Aaron has just taken a deposition from Ida, an elderly victim of the Holocaust. She revealed how she escaped from a death train by jumping from a bridge. It had a tremendous impact on him. The characters of Tyrowicz and Osidatch are under investigation by his office as Nazi collaborators.

INT. AARON'S HOTEL ROOM - NIGHT

Aaron is asleep. A fitful, deeply troubled sleep.

DREAM SEQUENCE:

EXT. UKRAINE TRAIN STATION - DAY - AARON'S DREAM

We see TYROWYCZ and OSIDATCH, barely in their 30s, in uniform, officiously directing the UKRAINIAN POLICE as they forcefully push JEWISH CITIZENS into the waiting train. We see men, women, children, not sure what's happening. Once the doors are locked, the train moves off.

INT. TRAIN - NIGHT - AARON'S DREAM

The train is crowded, dusty, noisy. We see a YOUNG IDA KEMPNER, late teens, blonde, energetic, concerned. She reaches for the window, desperately trying to open it.

> IDA
> (in Yiddish)
> We've got to get out. They're going to kill us!

The OTHERS look at her as if she's crazy.

> OLD LADY
> They're work camps. That's all.

IDA struggles to open the window, with bars above. No one helps. She pries the window open and tries to push herself through the bars. Finally, one or two PASSENGERS help her. She scrapes her way through the window as the train passes over a river.

AARON'S PARENTS

They, too, are passengers. They grab their son, AARON, 10, and try to get him through the window to safety.

EXT. TRAIN - NIGHT - AARON'S DREAM

The train crosses the bridge from Ukraine to Poland. From the train window, we see IDA push her way out of the open window and silently fall twenty feet below. We hear GUNSHOTS.

The boy Aaron is FALLING from the train, down into the water. We're falling, spiraling, down into the water. Water is rushing up toward us. We hear the sounds of RUSHING WATER and the sounds of GUNSHOTS.

<u>END DREAM SEQUENCE</u>

CUT TO:

INT. AARON'S HOTEL ROOM - NIGHT - PRESENT

Aaron sits bolt upright, grabs his chest, gasps for breath. He wakes with a start, catches himself in a silent scream. He tries to orient himself. The room is dark; there is no sound other than his own heart pounding. The clock reads 12:00 midnight. The dream was too real for him. He turns on the table lamp.

Flashbacks

A flashback distinguishes "time remembered" from real time and is set up just like the montage sequence. If a memory is very brief, then the writer can identify the flashback in the master scene heading. For example:

FLASHBLACK - ALEX IN ATTIC

It's a dingy place, no air, no light. In the corner, something moves . . . We can't make it out, but it's alive.

Alex is on his knees, a flashlight in hand. He tries to switch it on, but the batteries are dead. He throws it toward the moving object and races toward the attic steps.

BACK TO PRESENT DAY

Jarred by the memory.

If a flashback sequence is much longer, it would be written just like a montage sequence or dream sequence. Always be sure to end it with a designation of BACK TO PRESENT DAY.

This might be the time to caution against the unnecessary use of flashbacks. The technique is helpful to provide some exposition about characters or to establish a "backstory" to the plot; however, if it's used too often, the effect can be detrimental to the story. The more a writer relies on flashbacks, the more he or she intrudes on the forward thrust of the plot. If a story begins in the present tense, then slips back in time, the viewer already knows the outcome. The audience is waiting to see the characters work their way out of the current situation. That action is forestalled with the intrusion of flashbacks. If you must use flashbacks, do so sparingly.

Insert

If your character reads a book, letter, or newspaper, then you can let us know the content by calling for an INSERT. Here's how it's done:

Jennifer tears open the manila envelope, and reads it:

INSERT - THE LETTER

"Congratulations! You've just won $2 million."

BACK TO SCENE

Jennifer breaks into a huge grin.

Shooting Script Format

When you receive a deal from a producer, then you can type the shooting script for production. The shooting script has all of the shots numbered and directorial input noted. You can "lock in" the script pages and submit it. Invariably, you will receive notes and feedback from the director on scenes and dialogue.

You can easily revise the pages with any revision system, such as revising dialogue on page 12 as 12-A. Some production companies print revised script pages on different color pages. Any of the screenwriting software programs will easily guide you through the process.

Screenwriting Format Software

Fortunately, there are some exceptional screenwriting software programs on the market that can make your life as a writer much easier, from first draft to final draft. You can concentrate on the creative aspects of scripting and let the script formatting programs do the complicated work.

Before purchasing software, however, you should investigate. Make sure the software works for you, and with your computer. You'll find informative computer software reviews on Websites such as the Writers Guild of America (WGA) Website at www.wga.org. It links to detailed and objective script software reviews, at www.wga.org/tools/scriptsoftware/index.html. You can also find rankings and evaluations of standalone software programs, as well as script programs that work with your computer software in magazines such as *Written By, Creative Screenwriting, Script,* and *Hollywood Scriptwriter.*

You can test-drive some of the top screenwriting software on their Websites. You can also select professional screenwriting software from The Writers Store (www.writersstore.com/, or phone: 800/272-8927), which has the most current information on computers and screenwriting software.

As of the date of this publication, these are some of the most respected professional software standalone programs.

- *Final Draft, Inc.*—Version 5.0 is an exceptional professional screenwriting program that can be used on either a PC or a Mac. It's the top-of-the-line, with enormously helpful professional tools for television and screenwriters, as well as playwrights. There are too many useful, powerful tools to mention here. It includes samples from 50 current television scripts, with character names. The professional software has it all, and technical support is excellent. Company information: www.finaldraft.com; address: C & M Software, LLC, Final Draft, Inc., 16000 Ventura Boulevard, Suite 800, Encino, CA 91436; phone: 800/231-4055 or 818/995-4422.
- *ScriptThing*™—A professionally powerful and easy-to-use scriptwriting software program. It includes two TV sitcom formats and a multimedia script format. Company information: ScriptPerfection Enterprises, Inc. merged ScriptThing with MovieMagic Screenwriter to form Movie Magic Screenwriter 2000; www.ScriptPerfection.com or www.Screenplay.com; address: ScriptPerfection Enterprises, Inc., 4901 Morena Boulevard, Suite 108, San Diego, CA 92117; phone: 800/450-9450.

- *Movie Magic Screenwriter 2000*™—This is the new name for the merger of Script Perfection's ScriptThing and Screenplay System's Movie Magic Screenwriter. It is the penultimate tool for screenwriters, television writers, playwrights, and interactive and multimedia writers. The software is powerful and intuitive. Included are seven script formats, an outstanding index card system, unique real-time Internet collaboration with writing partners, notes commander, text to speech, a scene pilot, fifty television templates, and excellent Multimedia writing software. It has enhanced powerful production features and includes standard numbering and revision tools, as well as extras for animation writers. Screenplay Systems also offers a stripped down version called *Hollywood Screenwriter* that is inexpensive but lacks many of the program capabilities. Tech support is also superb. Company information: www.screenplay.com; address: Screenplay Systems, Inc., 150 East Olive Avenue, Suite 203, Burbank, CA 91502-1849; phone: 800/84-STORY.
- *Scriptware*™—Another professional, powerful, and easy-to-use screenwriting program for film, television, audio-video scripts. You can order it for Mac or Windows. Company information: www.Scriptware.com; phone: 800/788-7090. Download a free demo from their site.

Software for Script Development

When computer software was first developed to help construct stories and characters, fierce debates raged about the potential to propagate formulaic plots and characters. The arguments peaked when *Dramatica*, which was developed by Screenplay Systems, Inc., predicted what could happen in a story, based on nine or ten questions.

Today, there are some sophisticated developments in software programs to help focus stories and characters. Some have changed little, whereas others require a long learning curve. A comparative review is offered at the Writers Guild of America Website (www.wga.org/tools/scriptsoftware/index.html). You can look at story development software as tools to help you flesh out character and plot problems. Here are some examples of current script development software packages:

- *Dramatica Pro*™—The new version is 4.0. It is sophisticated and powerful story development software. It permits you to examine all aspects of the story and character development. Among other things, it offers step-by-step tools for creating powerful stories, and it includes creative tools, such as characters, story engine, reports, brainstorming, and theory. It can take a very long time to learn the new theory and manage the concepts. Company information: www.screenplay.com; address: Screenplay Systems, Inc., 150 East Olive Avenue, Suite 203, Burbank, CA 91502-1849; phone: 808/84-STORY. A

- *Writers Blocks*—Version 2.0 is for Windows. It's subtitled: "The easiest way to organize your story ideas." And it is. It's a very visual and creative way of developing stories and treatments. They are like electronic three-by-five-inch story outline cards that you can detail and change. Company information: www.writersblock.com; Ashley Software, 27758 Santa Margarita Parkway, Suite #302, Mission Viejo, CA 92691; phone: 949/713-9222, or 800/229-6737.
- *COLLABORATOR III*™—Based on Aristotle's six elements of drama and Lajos Egris' dramatic theories. It poses hundreds of questions about story and character development, but it does not construct a story. It is for PC only and is good, but getting technical help is difficult.
- *PLOTS UNLIMITED*™—Has a database of more than thirteen thousand plots. Writers mix and match, deriving story elements from columns a, b, and c. It has thousands of potential story ideas, which can be cumbersome and confusing. The software hasn't changed significantly since it was developed, but its creators indicated that by the time this book is published it will be updated and revised.

Using script development software is a personal thing. It may help organize your work, cut time on story and character choices, and build creative juices. On the other hand, it might seem more like a diversion from a video game, or be frustrating to use and stop you cold.

ENDNOTES

1. John Truby, *The Screenwriters Bible,* Revised Edition, Los Angeles, Silman-James Press, 1995, 68.

9

How to Write Effective Scenes in Screenplays

In motion pictures, scene descriptions can be long enough to establish the full flavor of the place and action, but short enough to keep the pacing alive and the reader interested in the story flow and dialogue.

Problems and Solutions in Writing Scenes

Just as there are problems in dialogue, so there are predictable pitfalls in scene descriptions. Here are eight of the more common stylistic problems and solutions: Too choppy, too confusing, too redundant, too long, too expository, too technical, too expensive, and too potentially litigious.

Eight Pitfalls in Scene Descriptions, and How to Solve Them

1. Too Choppy
Some scene descriptions are written too choppily, presumably to account for each piece of stage business. Here's an example of that problem:

Joan picks up the garbage. She stops to feed the dog. She goes to the back door.

The writing style can be smoothed out by avoiding separate sentence units and excessive use of pronouns. The action can be described more comprehensively:

Joan picks up the garbage, stops to feed the dog, then continues on her way out the back door.

2. Too Confusing

A similar problem occurs when several different characters are in a scene, and the writer wants to keep them alive. The tendency for pronoun confusion increases with the number of characters interacting in the sequence. For example:

The dog barks. Arty enters. Ilene sees him and tries to calm him. She gets him coffee from the kitchen and he barks louder.

Confusing to say the least. The problems can be corrected by addressing the specific characters and compressing the action:

As Arty enters, Ilene tries to calm the barking dog. Unsuccessful, she heads toward the kitchen and gets Arty some coffee. The dog barks louder.

3. Too Redundant

A related problem is redundancy in visual description. Several key words might be repeated needlessly. It helps to "flag" those words. You can literally circle them to see if they intrude on the reading flow:

Jennifer smiles and Carlos smiles back. Carlos crosses to the fireplace and he starts the fire and lights the wood. He pokes the fire with brass tongs and the fire begins to crackle.

The stage directions need to be smoothed out. The phrasing can be modified and polished:

They exchange smiles as Carlos crosses to the fireplace. He lights the wood, pokes the brass tongs into the flames. The fire begins to crackle.

Limiting the amount of repetition—in both words and phrases—cleans up the description and makes the script more readable. Clean and well-written scene descriptions help keep the tempo of the script alive and the rhythm flowing naturally from scene to scene.

4. Too Long

Descriptions become too long when you put in too much narrative detail. There is sometimes a fine line between having a creative, literary quality to a script, and having so much detail that it confuses the reader. Remember, this is a cinematic vehicle, meant to be produced. A book can take its time unraveling atmosphere, but you have only a prescribed number of pages to write a script.

5. Too Expository

Be careful of scene descriptions that tell us things we can't possibly know, like the fact that Frank and Jennifer met in Washington, D.C., grew up in the same town, or married and divorced twice. The only way we can know it is if one of your characters reveals it in dialogue.

6. Too Technical

This happens when you try to direct the film, rather than write it. As a general rule, stay away from camera angles, over-the-shoulder shots, medium shots, or any other directorial call. You'll only get in the way of the director.

7. Too Expensive

This happens if you call for unnecessary locales and production require-ments, including aerial shots (require expensive helicopters and cameras), snow or rain, hundreds of people who have talking parts (extras must be paid extra if they speak), scenes requiring travel to many different cities, or many different locales.

8. Too Potentially Litigious

A different kind of problem arises if you want to incorporate recognizable names of real people, or stories from real life that you don't own. In our litigious society, be cautious, and obtain the necessary rights and clearances.

The same is true for the use of songs or lyrics. Unless a particular song is critical to the needs of a script, you can simply suggest a song style rather than provide someone else's lyrics. For example:

In the b.g., we hear the strains of a blues song, and the husky voice of a nightclub vocalist. Over the song, we hear the din of the supper club crowd, ignoring the music behind them.

This scene description sets atmosphere, without defining the song or the lyrics. On the other hand, some screenwriters deliberately choose a song to establish the period atmosphere of a piece. The appropriateness is determined by the needs of a specific project and your artistic style.

How to Write Effective Opening Scenes in Screenplays

The first pages of a screenplay have to grab the reader, setting up the characters, their driving force, and pacing of the film. The first page is critical in setting up a "hook" for readers, and the first ten pages have to build even stronger momentum to stay with the script. That momentum has to build throughout every scene in the script.

As an example, I have included the opening sequence of two screenplays. The first sample is from an action screenplay I wrote, MODE VIII, based on the novel by Dr. Gregory A. Rogers. I optioned the book from the author and adapted it for the screen. At the time, studios developed and produced many big-budget action films. Given the author's credibility and expertise, I wanted to make this screenplay the most credible in the genre and as tight as possible. When the screenplay was completed, it was a potential multimillion-dollar film, with a lot of characters to cast, expensive hurricane weather effects, and shooting in the ocean. The studios "passed" because of those reasons, as well as because it was too similar to other projects.

The following script pages are the opening scenes of MODE VIII, reprinted with permission of Dr. Gregory A. Rogers. See how quickly it sets up the lead characters in a test crisis, and the importance of getting the shuttle up into space quickly and safely. I thought the dialogue might seem too technical and confusing. It can be revised and tightened up.

FADE IN:

SUPER TITLE:

THIS FILM IS DEDICATED TO THE RESCUE FORCES OF THE UNITED STATES ARMY, NAVY, MARINES, AIR FORCE, AND COAST GUARD.

EXT. LAUNCH COMPLEX 39A - KENNEDY SPACE CENTER - DAY

SUPER: KENNEDY SPACE CENTER, FLORIDA.

It's a beautiful summer day. The space shuttle Enterprise is on the launch pad, elegant. It sits like a sparkling diamond, bathed in brilliant light.

It HISSES and GROANS from the mechanical preparations for launch.

INT. FIRING ROOM - DAY

The Firing Room is Launch Control, with rows of computer screens on the ground floor.

We see the TEST DIRECTOR, 43, African American, slightly overweight, checking with the OTC (Orbiter-Test Communicator), 35, Hispanic, balding. Both talk to shuttle crew and floor TECHNICIANS.

EXT. LAUNCH COMPLEX 39A - DAY

Air Force helicopters pass by the shuttle pad.

White and blue Huey helicopters of NASA pass the busy Press Site as REPORTERS stand talking. The countdown clock rolls on. The CHATTER between the various workers and astronauts can barely be heard.

OTC (V.O.)
We're coming out of the T-minus nine-minute hold and
are proceeding toward launch.

INT. FLIGHT DECK OF THE SHUTTLE - DAY

Mission Commander, Col. TOM STABLER, 51, cultivated, grey-haired gentleman, glances at his pilot LEE HARGIS, 38, nice appearance, modest physique.

> OTC (V.O.)
> Enterprise, this is Launch Control. Event timer is started. Over.

> STABLER
> Roger that, Control. Event timer is rolling. Enterprise, out.

Commander Stabler smiles at Hargis, then over intercom tells the crew.

> STABLER (CONT'D)
> We're getting close to launch time, crew. Get ready to rock and roll.

INT. MIDDECK - SAME TIME

CREW MEMBERS

TIFFANY CHURCHILL, mid-30s, small, British payload specialist, smiles at YOSHIKI TAKAHASHI, early 40s, tall, Japanese payload specialist. He smiles back.

Takahashi gives a "thumbs up" to the American specialists.

TED SLAJESKI, early 50s, Polish, medium build, NICHOLE JOR-GENSEN, early 30s, brunette, tall, and JENNIFER ADLER early 30s, African American, all exchange "thumbs up."

> STABLER (V.O.)
> Alternating current sensor to monitor.

INT. FLIGHT DECK OF THE SHUTTLE - SAME TIME

Hargis reaches over to panel to his right and flips three switches down for one full second, then to the monitor position. He reports.

> HARGIS
> Three AC BUS sensors to monitor.

CUT TO:

EXT. SHUTTLE LANDING FACILITY - DAY

Air Force helicopters have landed. Rotors stop. The crews climb out.

JOLLY ONE

From the first helicopter, JOLLY ONE, we see flight surgeon STEVE COBB, late 30s, athletic-looking, climb out.

Cobb grabs his medical gear, then greets a second flight surgeon, EVANS, late 20s, from the second helo. They're laughing as they head into Operations Building.

INT. FIRING ROOM - SAME TIME

In the Firing Room, CHATTER and light activity at the computer consoles. The Public Affairs Officer [PA] announces.

> PA
> All systems aboard Enterprise are functioning well.

EXT. ENTERPRISE - DAY

We have a compelling view of the shuttle, as the catwalk moves away from the orbiter. The astronauts used it to climb into the orbiter, but it is now being RETRACTED.

> OTC (V.O.)
> We are at T-minus seven minutes and counting. This
> is the voice of launch control.

SOLID ROCKET BOOSTER

Now we are on the aft skirt of the Left Solid Rocket Booster [SRB], and an area of the metal skin of the SRB.

INT. FIRING ROOM - SAME TIME

On a computer screen, a small YELLOW WARNING box appears, accompanied by one SMALL BEEP.

A TECHNICIAN, 31, leans forward in surprise, then hits his transmit button to report.

                    TECHNICIAN
          Test, we've got a pressure fluctuation in the Number
          One SRB HPU fuel supply module.

Test Director stands next to him.

                    OTC
          Say again?

                    TECHNICIAN
          We have a pressure spike in the Number One SRB HPU
          fuel supply module.

                    TEST DIRECTOR
          How large a spike?

                    TECHNICIAN
          It's not critical yet, but it's elevated to 4-38 psi. Above
          standard launch parameters.

INT. FLIGHT DECK OF THE SHUTTLE - SAME TIME

On the orbiter flight deck, Stabler and Hargis are chatting, when a single YELLOW LIGHT on the Master Caution Board illuminates. The chatter immediately stops.

> STABLER
> OTC, Enterprise.

> OTC (V.O.)
> Go, Enterprise.

> STABLER
> Control, we've got a caution light illuminated in the Number One SRB APU controller. What's the deal?

> OTC (V.O.)
> We're working it, Enterprise.

> STABLER
> Enterprise copies, OTC. Enterprise, out.

The pilots glance at each other, concern on their faces.

INT. FIRING ROOM - DAY

Technician is scanning the monitor. A SECOND YELLOW WARNING box appears.

> TECHNICIAN
> Test, high-pressure relief valve has just been activated on Number One HPU!

Test Director and OTC exchange worried glances.

> TEST DIRECTOR
> What is the fuel flow pressure?

Technician hits a couple of buttons, stares at screen, reports.

> TECHNICIAN
> Five-Ten, Test.

> TEST DIRECTOR
> Electrical, what's going on down there?

We see an ELECTRICAL TECHNICIAN, early 30s, scanning computer pages. He replies.

> ELECTRICAL TECH
> We're looking, Test. We're looking.

Test Director is upset.

> TEST DIRECTOR
> We've got a potentially explosive problem at the base
> of an SRB with one point three million pounds of
> rocket fuel. Don't tell me you're looking. Find the
> damn problem!

INT. FLIGHT DECK OF THE SHUTTLE - SAME TIME

On the flight deck, Stabler is staring at the Event Timer, which is counting down from 6:13.

> STABLER
> Thirty seconds to APU Pre-start. We're nearly there.

We watch as the seconds count down, but no call comes across. At 5:55, Stabler calls in:

>   STABLER (CONT'D)
> Enterprise is ready for APU Pre-start.

No response. This concerns both pilots.

>   STABLER (CONT'D)
>   (more forcefully)
> Kennedy, we are standing by for APU Pre-start.

Before any response, the Event Timer STOPS. OTC answers.

>   OTC (V.O.)
> We're going into a hold at this time, Enterprise.

Stabler stares at the single illuminated YELLOW CAUTION LIGHT, then asks.

>   STABLER
> What's the problem, OTC?

INT. FIRING ROOM - SAME TIME

Test director and OTC are staring at each other. The director finally gestures and says.

>   TEST DIRECTOR
> Tell them.

OTC nods solemnly, then states.

>   OTC
> We have a pressurization problem with the HPU fuel
> supply module on Number One SRB. The high-pres-
> sure relief valve has been activated.

INT. FLIGHT DECK OF THE SHUTTLE - SAME TIME

Stabler slams his hand against the side wall of the orbiter. Hargis lets out a short, worried grunt. The commander looks over at Hargis and shakes his head with obvious worry.

                    STABLER
        I hope you're doing something about that!

                    OTC (V.O.)
                    (flatly)
        We're working on the problem.

Now Hargis makes a fist, hits the intercom switch, tells his crew.

                    HARGIS
        You heard the report, crew. Be ready to book it if that
        thing acts up. If that HPU blows, it could set off the
        SRB whether we like it or not.

In middeck, all Crew are concerned. Tiffany Churchill reaches for her seat belt.

                    CHURCHILL
        Should we unbuckle ourselves, just in case?

STABLER AND HARGIS

Stabler glances at his co-pilot.

                    STABLER
        Not yet. Not until I give the Egress, Egress, Egress
        command. Stay buckled in for now. They won't leave
        us in here if they think that SRB is gonna blow. They
        just wouldn't do that.

He glances over to Hargis with a look that says, "I sure hope they won't, anyway."

INT. FIRING ROOM - SAME TIME

Technician observes the first caution box FLASHES RED. He anxiously reports.

                    TECHNICIAN
          Large pressure spike in Number One HPU!

Test Director turns to OTC.

                    TEST DIRECTOR
          Get that crew out of there!

                                        CUT TO:

INT. FLIGHT DECK OF THE SHUTTLE - DAY

Stabler spots the yellow caution light turn RED, then, before he can act, two more RED LIGHTS appear and a WARNING KLAXON SOUNDS.

He simultaneously begins flipping switches and orders.

                    STABLER
          Egress! Egress! Egress!

CREW

The crewmembers begin scurrying, as they unbuckle themselves from their seats.

                      OTC (V.O.)
Enterprise, begin immediate egress procedures . . .
Begin emergency shutdown procedures . . .

STABLER

Stabler, still flipping switches.

                      STABLER
Already underway, Kennedy. Just get the damn crew
access arm back to the side hatch!

EXT. ENTERPRISE - DAY

The middeck crew OPENS the side hatch, as the White Room SWINGS
into place. The astronauts climb out of the hatch and scurry across
the platform toward a set of escape buckets.

EXT. SHUTTLE LANDING FACILITY - DAY

The rotors of the Air Force helicopters are turning as their crews
pile in. They shut the doors as the helicopters are already moving
forward.

The Jolly One pilot, Taylor, calls in tensely.

                    TAYLOR (V.O.)
Jolly One flight is on the move, NASA Tower.

                    NASA TOWER (V.O.)
You're cleared for takeoff from the towway-taxiway
intersection at your discretion. Good luck, Jolly One
flight.

HELICOPTERS

The helicopters ROLL OUT in sequence to the concrete taxiway and immediately lurch up into the air.

EXT. LAUNCH COMPLEX 39A - CREW - DAY

The astronauts climb into the escape buckets two at a time, slam their hands down on the release levers, and begin the LONG SLIDE DOWN to the capture nets at the end.

Five are down.

INT. FLIGHT DECK OF THE SHUTTLE - DAY

Stabler is directing his pilot.

> STABLER
> Get out of here, Lee! I'll get the last switches.

Hargis takes a beat, Stabler says.

> STABLER (CONT'D)
> We can't both climb out of these seats at the same time, so get going!

Hargis climbs out of his seat, as Stabler hits last switch.

> STABLER (CONT'D)
> Kennedy, Enterprise crew is out of here! Get those Jollies down to Helipad seven.

Without waiting for a reply, he disconnects his comm-line, hits his quick-release lever for the restraint straps, then follows Hargis out toward the exit.

EXT. SHUTTLE LANDING FACILITY - DAY

We see the helicopters flying low and fast across the front of the Vehicle Assembly Building, toward the launch complex.

EXT. ENTERPRISE - DAY

The first five astronauts climb into the white Armored Personnel Carrier (M-113) and the engine STARTS UP.

Another slide bucket SLIDES DOWN the escape wires. Stabler and Hargis joins them.

The M-113 lurches forward as they head for the rendezvous point with the helos.

EXT. LAUNCH COMPLEX 39A - DAY

ARMORED PERSONNEL CARRIER

The M-113 carrier arrives just as the first helicopters HOVER into position to pick them up. Four of the astronauts head for the helo as the cargo door slides open.

HELICOPTERS

The helo crew grabs the astronauts, HAUL them in, and the helicopter takes off, before they can close the door.

The second helo lands, the last three astronauts climb aboard, then it takes off.

From behind the launch complex, we see the helos heading off for the Shuttle Landing Facility.

                                                        CUT TO:

EXT. SHUTTLE LANDING FACILITY - DAY

As the helicopters land and open the doors, we see the crew climb out.

COBB AND STABLER

Climbing out of Jolly One helicopter, we see the flight surgeon, Cobb, and Stabler. Cobb has a big smile on his face. He slaps Stabler on the back.

                    COBB
          What a great Mode Four Simulation that was!

Stabler smiles back at the Air Doc.

                    STABLER
          Want to join me for coffee?

Cobb glances at his watch.

                    COBB
          Can't. I'm running late for a briefing.

He waves and heads back to his helicopter.

                                        CUT TO:

EXT. BUILDING 401 - PATRICK AFB - DAY

We see Cobb, running to find the right building. Finally, he spots "Building 401," and a nondescript sign "shuttle mission briefing."

He hits a magnetic device, the door slides open, and he rushes inside.

INT. CONFERENCE ROOM - BUILDING 401 - DAY

SUPER: 13 AUGUST, THURSDAY, 12:56 HOURS - U.S. SPACE SHUTTLE MISSION BRIEFING - PATRICK AFB.

At the head of the conference table we see Col. WILLIAM SHERI-
DAN, 49, once attractive, with gray hair.

The senior staff members of the space mission sit patiently, includ-
ing his assistant MITCH WALLER, 30s, crewcut, plump, and Lt.
Commander VAN RODEN, late 40s, a body-building vet of the Coast
Guard.

Sheridan watches as Lt. Col. ART BELL, mid-50s, trim, black hair
with grey stripes on the sides, saunters in with an exaggerated air
of self-confidence.

                    SHERIDAN
        How's it going, Art?

Bell nods.

                    VAN RODEN
        How you doing, Air Boss?

                    BELL
        Fine.

Bell pulls out a chair on the side of the table, sitting next to
Sheridan.

Cobb comes through the door, very rushed and tired. Trying to be
inconspicuous, he secures a seat next to the other Flight
Surgeons.

Sheridan looks around the table.

                    SHERIDAN
        Lets get started. I want to brief you on the mission's
        payload . . .

Mission Staff take out their briefcases and notepads.

> SHERIDAN (CONT'D)
> The payload is the Werner Von Braun Deep Space
> Explorer, designed to fly past Jupiter and Uranus,
> then send information back to earth from beyond the
> edge of the solar system.

Van Roden glances at Bell, who is making a note to himself.

> SHERIDAN (CONT'D)
> The astronauts will have only twenty-two minutes
> each day to launch, and if they don't launch within
> the next five weeks, the mission will be delayed for
> six years.

Bell is circling notes to himself.

It's very important to sustain the pacing and scene momentum with the scene descriptions. The astronauts learn they have no choice but to eject in the Atlantic Ocean, with a hurricane heading toward central Florida. After a series of shots, the shuttle crew ejects into the Atlantic Ocean, in ferocious waters. The action is unrelenting toward the single goal of rescuing everyone possible.

Now, let's look at the opening of another screenplay, THE ELTON PROJECT, an action comedy that I wrote with Frank Tavares, reprinted with permission of Frank Tavares.

At the open, we see the mysterious research facility in the Nevada Desert, then we meet our heroes, Mark and Tony. In Tony's apartment, we quickly learn that Mark's newly divorced, works for the Department of Energy, and that Tony is a writer doing a series on unusual salvage sites. He knows Mark's vulnerabilities and plays on them to set up a driving force for a trip to Nevada.

THE ELTON PROJECT

<u>FADE IN:</u>

EXT. ELTON RESEARCH FACILITY - NEVADA DESERT - SUNSET

SUPER: "ELTON RESEARCH FACILITY, NEVADA"

It's sunset, and the desert colors are fading. Cactus plants throw long shadows. Everything is still.

TWO COYOTES survey the landscape. Their ears move like antennae, listening for the approaching night. Their eyes dart. Noses twitch. Senses are sharp.

The coyotes cautiously approach a high chainlink fence. Razor wire lines its top, a sign is posted below: "PRIVATE PROPERTY! ABSOLUTELY NO TRESPASSING!"

Far beyond the fence, blurred in the distance, we can just make out what appear to be a string of large satellite dishes.

One animal sniffs at the base of the sign. Something curious has passed this way. Its head jerks up . . . nose straining . . . ears searching.

A RIFLE SHOT CRACKS the stillness. Almost instantly, the animal is thrown against the fence. Before its partner can react, ANOTHER SHOT splits the dusk, and this animal, too, is violently wrenched from the hunt.

DIRT BIKES

In the distance, we see two dirt bikes buzzing toward us.

Each RIDER wears a sand-colored jumpsuit and an ominous helmet with a sun visor that covers the face.

The bikes are noisy as they race across the terrain kicking up clouds of dust. We hear the FILTERED VOICE of one of the riders. He's yelling into his helmet radio above the noise, amply impressed by his companion's shooting.

                    RIDER
                 (filtered)
Damn, Lieutenant, that had to be half a mile! Even
with the scanners, that's good!

The bikes lead the dust, closing in on the dead targets.

We get a better view of the riders now. Both carry sidearms. One
of them, the LIEUTENANT, also has a scoped hunting rifle slung
across his back.

He stops and dismounts the bike, walks over to the remains of the
desert critters, and lifts his visor. Behind a small helmet microphone
we see the face of a tough, 40-year-old, no-nonsense hunter. His
expression is angry. With his boot, he shoves one of the carcasses
toward the sign.

                    LIEUTENANT
        Too bad you can't read.

The other rider lifts his visor and laughs. He's in his 20s, slim,
well-built.

                    RIDER
        Lieutenant, I've never seen a G-2 quite like you before.

The Lieutenant says nothing. He climbs back on the bike and
kick-starts the engine. He lowers his visor and we hear his
emotionless voice over the radio.

                    LIEUTENANT
                 (filtered)
        Let's move it.

The Lieutenant REVS the engine, lifting the front wheel off the
ground as he races away. The second bike follows.

Beyond them, a convoy of unmarked trucks moves slowly across the horizon as the riders leave us in a pocket of dust.

                                                            CUT TO:

INT. KARATE STUDIO - DAY

SUPER: "WASHINGTON, D.C."

We're in a Washington, D.C. Karate dojo, smack in the middle of a practice. TONY MILLER, mid-40s, athletic, tall, and sturdy, parries blows and kicks from his friend MARK COLE, 40s, short and stocky. Mark is moving like a man possessed. He's spastic but determined. He's drenched with perspiration.

Tony moves deftly as his friend tries to catch him off guard. With a practiced move, Tony sidesteps a kick and easily throws Mark to the floor. We hear a loud gasp as Mark hits the mat.

                    TONY
         You okay?

Mark is breathing heavily. He wipes perspiration from his eyes, looks up and nods. Tony needles him.

                    TONY (CONT'D)
         You're a goofball. No control.

Mark ignores the comment. Tony pokes a little harder, trying to get a reaction.

                    TONY (CONT'D)
         No wonder Judy threw you out. She probably couldn't
         figure what floor you'd bounce off next.

It works.

> MARK
> She didn't "throw" me out.

Mark gets up from the mat.

> MARK (CONT'D)
> You want control? I'll give you control.

Mark's ready for the next move, just a little bleary.

Tony smiles at his friend's bravado, and slowly circles around him.

> TONY
> We'll see.

The move is quick and Mark almost doesn't see it. But this time he manages to deflect Tony's arm, and with a combination of luck and resolve, throws his friend to the ground.

A surprised Tony looks up from the mat. Mark smiles over him.

> MARK
> You were saying?

INT. TONY'S APARTMENT - NIGHT

It's a bachelor one-bedroom apartment. In the living room, two suitcases are open in a corner, their disheveled contents visible. Several shirts and a suit are hung on a chairback. It's obvious someone has spent more than a couple of nights on the sofabed.

Across the room is the desk of a writer. Books, stacks of paper, and magazines cover its surface. A phone with a tangled cord shows lots of use.

On the desk is a computer. Mark is sitting in front of it, joystick in hand, racing at Indie. We hear the sounds of his AUTO RACING computer game.

At the counter that separates the little kitchen from the living room, Tony cleans up the remnants of a takeout pizza.

> TONY
> I think you've got that defense move down.

> MARK
> So there's hope for a black belt?

> TONY
> Maybe before you retire.

Tony wraps the pizza in tinfoil.

> TONY (CONT'D)
> Want to save this for your lunch tomorrow?

Mark nods in appreciation.

> MARK
> Yeah, sure.

At the computer game, Mark fights the curves of the computer track. His body language shows he's really into it. He tries a gutsy inside move. His on-screen car careens out of control. We hear the sound of the fiery CRASH.

> MARK (CONT'D)
> Damn! That's the third time.

He puts down the joystick and leans back in the chair.

> TONY
>
> So your fine motor skills are a little short.

Mark looks up, mock indignation.

> MARK
>
> And now the famous reporter's gonna make short
> jokes? Payback for having his ego bruised?

Tony laughs.

> TONY
>
> Better me than your wife's attorney.

He puts the leftover pizza in the refrigerator.

> MARK
>
> Speaking of which, the lawyer lady called personnel
> this morning.

> TONY
>
> Sniffing out your retirement bennies, no doubt.

Mark shakes his head. He looks exhausted.

> MARK
>
> Jeez. I'll never get through it.

Tony reaches back into the refrigerator and pulls out two beers.

> TONY
>
> Yes you will.

He tosses one to his friend. Mark makes a lucky catch.

                    TONY (CONT'D)
    The same way I did.

                    MARK
    One alimony check at a time?

They laugh. Mark struggles with the beer tab. It pops open and
spills over his lap.

                    MARK (CONT'D)
    Damn.

He grabs a pillowcase from the sofabed to wipe it up.

                    TONY
    Maybe you need a little time off. Come with me to
    Nevada next week.

Mark tosses the pillowcase into a growing pile of dirty clothes by
his suitcase.

                    MARK
    Yeah, like Ebert-the-troll is gonna give me time off to
    watch you write stories on salvage operations in a
    desert.

Tony opens his beer with one hand.

                    TONY
    You're a senior project advisor for the Department
    of Energy, for chrissake. Tell him one of your research
    sites needs a visit. You got something in Nevada?

    The opening sequence sets up the right atmosphere for this action-
comedy. It also sets up the driving force for Mark and Tony to get to Nevada

as quickly as possible. The audience knows something mysterious is happening in Nevada, but our leads do not.

The action helps to build the pacing throughout the screenplay.

10

Script Revisions

Revising Your Script

Screenwriting and television writing mean rewriting, as any writer who gets notes from producers, directors, agents, and friends can attest. Once you've completed the draft, you enter the bottomless abyss of revising.

Before sending out your spec script, make sure it's in the best shape it can be. With stoic objectivity, read every scene, dialogue, character reaction, visualization, and pacing. It is a time-consuming process, but it will help make your script more professional, competitive, and producible. Build and refine the story's pacing, the visual imagery, and the credibility of the characters and dialogue. Here is how.

A Checklist for Script Revision

You can use this checklist of critical questions to help you analyze the first draft of your work.

1. Is the Script Visual?

A script should be cinematic. As you read the draft, can you actually visualize the scenes unfolding? Are the descriptions clear? If not, camera angles can be suggested, character actions amplified, locations sharply defined. As you spot problems in the draft, note them in the margins.

2. Is the Script Producible?

No matter how good the script, it won't be produced if it calls for $535 million worth of sets, period costumes, worldwide locations, hundreds of stars, thousands of extras, and impossible camera shots. The script should be realistically conceived in terms of production requirements, locations, and casting needs.

3. Is the Script Format Professional and the Content Readable?

Even the most powerful script can end up by the wayside if the format looks amateurish to a reader. If you have questions about script form, check the sample formats in this book. In addition, look at the clarity of writing in the script. Sometimes scene descriptions are too choppy, cluttered with information, or too repetitious. Smooth out the writing style for the greatest impact on the reader.

4. Is the Story Focused and Well Developed?

Here you must examine the structure of the dramatic action points. Some scenes may lag, whereas others may be redundant. As you read the script, assess the effectiveness of the plot sequences. If the story is unclear or erratic, then it's time to cut and paste. One sequence might work better at the beginning or end, which means reorganizing the entire storyline, dropping scenes, adding new ones, and polishing others.

5. Is the Dramatic Conflict Strong and the Pacing Effective?

The script should hold and build audience interest throughout each act. If the conflict is cleverly set up, and the stakes are high—the sense of urgency is great—then audience involvement with the characters and conflicts increases. The pacing is most effective when scenes build on each other in a careful, logical sequence of dramatic action.

6. Is the Mood Accurately Conveyed?

Each scene should help create the atmosphere of the project. If the descriptions are not vivid enough, then take time to rewrite them. Don't settle for less than the most illustrative images of the place, action, and characters.

7. Are the Characters Likable, Identifiable, and Consistently Developed?

Be sure the characters are fully and credibly motivated. Are the interrelationships clearly drawn? If not, see if you can strengthen them through

Method writer constructs, using superobjectives, throughline of action, intentions, motivations, sense of urgency, and moment-to-moment realities.

8. Is the Dialogue Realistic and Sharply Defined?

If the dialogue appears to be awkward in some places, check all the pertinent problems. Characters are unique individuals, and their dialogue should reflect that individuality. If a word seems off, write "b.w." (find a "better word") in the margin, or write "b.l." (find a "better line") to point out the problem for later revising. It may seem like nitpicking, but don't let those little problems slip away. If your characters make it onto the screen, those lines will make you, and probably others, cringe.

The Final Polish

Once all of the points are addressed, and the major revisions are incorporated into the script, there's one more stop-check point. It's called the polish. Once more, go over the script with a fine-toothed comb. Be sure the story is focused, the characters are three-dimensional, the dialogue is refined, the action is visual, the mood is conveyed, and the pacing is effective. After all, this is the script that may eventually wind up in the archives of the Academy of Motion Picture Arts and Sciences—or at least in the hands of a reputable agent.

PART FIVE

TELEVISION SCRIPTS

11

Television Sitcom Script Format

Writing Spec Sitcom Scripts

If you're writing a spec script for comedy, choose a current, successful series that is *not* the same show you are writing for. Legal and creative issues discourage producers of shows from accepting spec scripts based on their own series. Producers agree that submissions from other current sitcoms are the best way for new writers to submit scripts. Series producers know dialogue and character arcs of their shows intricately, as well as nuances about the history, present, and future problems of the program that you can't possibly know.

So, write a spec script for a similar genre show. Watch the series, tape the episodes, and analyze the characters and structure intimately. That's how you will find the right act breaks and comic tone of the series.

Try to create your spec script as a perfect professional sample of the series. Be sure to get sample episodic scripts from the show you're interested in. You can find numerous televisions scripts in sources like *Script City*, or *Larry Edmunds Books*, as mentioned in Chapter 8. Remember that these scripts will likely be in shooting script form, with shot numbers throughout. But they will give you insight into the actual series format, structure, and production pragmatics of each show.

Keep the spec script focused around the lead characters, and pepper the right comic pacing in your pages appropriately. Use the right comic tone, with the right edges for the characters, dialogue, and pacing.

The idea is to submit the spec script to the producer of a different sitcom series. If your script is professionally written, with respect for the comic tone, characters, dialogue, and production, then the producer may invite you to "pitch" an idea for their series. At that pitch, you come in with several story ideas specifically created for their series. For a full discussion of "pitching" for television, see The Art of Pitching Ideas section in Chapter 17 and Pitching in Chapter 19.

Comedy Theory

In his superb new book, *Laughing Out Loud*, award-winning screenwriter and author Andrew Horton blends history, theory, and analysis of comedy with invaluable advice.[1] In this outstanding book, he uses examples from Chaplin to Seinfeld, Aristophanes to Woody Allen. He describes comedy as a perspective rather than merely as a genre and then goes on to identify the essential elements of comedy. His overview of comedy's history traces two main branches—anarchistic comedy and romantic comedy—from ancient Greece through contemporary Hollywood, by way of commedia dell'arte, vaudeville, and silent movies. Television and international cinema are included in Horton's analysis, which leads into an up-close review of the comedy chemistry in several specific films and television shows. (Horton is also the author of *Writing the Character-Centered Screenplay,* a classic book on the character-based screenplay).[2]

Evan Smith, in *Writing Television Sitcoms*, offers an interesting overview of complex comedy theory. He provides a list of "Characteristics of Comedy," including these elements: incongruity, surprise, truth, aggression, and brevity.[3] Smith also discusses the importance of establishing, building, and releasing tension in comedy.[4] He also provides sample stories and scripts, with advice from top sitcom producers.

Another excellent resource on TV comedy writing is *Successful Sitcom Writing: How to Write a and Sell for TV's Hottest Format*, by Jurgen Wolff.[5] It includes many relevant examples and samples from sitcom story and television script samples. For additional information on comedy writing, see *Funny Business: The Craft of Comedy Writing*, by Sol Saks.[6] It includes an anatomy of the "Bewitched" pilot script, which he created. I worked on that series as a program executive.

In all of your sitcom stories and scripts, be sure that the setup is strong and the payoff or punchline is clever and worth it. Also, make sure the action, reaction, and punchlines are right for the characters.

TV Sitcom Format

Sitcoms are usually written in one of two formats: tape or film format. Specific shows may vary slightly. A half-hour sitcom script can have a *teaser* of 30 to 60 seconds. Act One is about 10 to 12 minutes; Act Two is about 10 to 12 minutes. A *tag* or *wraparound* closes out the action in less than one minute. A half-hour show can be written in two or three acts, with each act about the same length.

Title Page

Whether you write a spec script for tape, film, or animation, the Title Page must look like the following:

> This is how to set up the
> page for TV film, tape and
> animation

TITLE OF THE SERIES

"Your Episode Title"

Written By

Your Name

Copyright/ WGA Reg.   CONTACT:

Your Agent, or Lawyer

Address

Phone

At the bottom, put your contact address for your agent, yourself, or your entertainment attorney. You can also indicate if it is Copyright, "Registered, WGAw," or "Registered, WGAE." For information on how to copyright and register your script, see Chapters 18 and 19. Don't put the date on your script, and don't type any draft number on it.

To help format TV scripts, screenwriting software makes it easier. Final Draft, Inc. software includes 50 television series formats as free templates in their screenwriting program. Movie Magic 2000 offers templates for 50 television series. Scriptware also provides many television samples. See Chapter 8 for more discussion on screenwriting software.

Tape and Film Formats for Current Comedy Series

If a program is to be produced on tape, with multiple cameras, then a spacious format is used, which is derived from the early days of live television. The margins are wide enough for directors and talent to jot down their needs. The script uses less camera coverage and fewer angles than feature film scripts. Consequently, the page count is much longer. In tape, a 30-minute script can run anywhere from 40 to 50 pages.

This tape format has several distinct features:

1. New acts and scenes are centered at the top of the page.
2. The margins are wide, so directors can mark them up.
3. Business and action are flush left, single-spaced, and capped. In multicamera tape, actions are set in parentheses.
4. Dialogue is double-spaced and not capped.
5. Characters appearing in the scene are identified before the scene begins.
6. Page numbers are consecutive throughout the script.
7. There are no "Continueds" on pages to indicate continuing scenes. In this case, scenes are identified as part of the same sequence at the top right-hand of the page.

In episodic comedy scripts, stage directions are single-spaced, but descriptions are still kept to a minimum. The scene sets up the basic information concerning place, characters, and action, and the director takes over from that point. Compared to film, there is not much latitude for embellishing mood and atmosphere.

Format Samples for Current Sitcom Series

Here are sample TV formats from current successful, sitcom series. These TV script format samples are reprinted with permission of the software program Final Draft, Inc. The script notes for the shows are reprinted as text before the format sample.

"Frasier"

"Frasier" is split into two acts; scenes run roughly from A to H. The script is roughly 50 pages. The show is ended by simply calling it, "End of Act Two" rather than "End of Show." The "Frasier" script format sample follows, reprinted with permission of the software program Final Draft, Inc. All dialogue should appear double spaced.

FRASIER

"Title goes here"

#episode number goes here

ACT ONE
A

FADE IN:

INT. FRASIER'S LIVING ROOM - DAY - DAY/1
(Frasier, Niles, Daphne, Roz, Eddie, Martin)

DAPHNE IS SETTING THE TABLE, AS NILES AND FRASIER FOLLOW HER.

DAPHNE

Says some smart dialogue.

CONTINUED:

2.

(A)

> NILES
>
> Witty reply.

> FRASIER
>
> Even wittier retort.

MARTIN ENTERS.

> MARTIN
>
> Says some smart dialogue.

FRASIER FALLS OVER EDDIE WHO ENTERS RUNNING.

FADE OUT.

2.

(B)

B

INT. RADIO STATION - DAY

(Niles, Roz, Frasier)

FRASIER BROWSES THROUGH THE PAPER.

> NILES
>
> Witty, nutty observation.

(CONTINUED)

CONTINUED:

3.

(B)

> ROZ
>
> Says some smart dialogue.

> NILES
>
> Unbelievably dumb retort!

> FRASIER
>
> Says some smart dialogue.

> ROZ
>
> Oh, Frasier!

> NILES
>
> You guys are pigs!

> FRASIER
>
> Says some smart dialogue. Says some smart dialogue.
> Says some smart dialogue.

> ROZ
>
> Oh, Frasier! (SITS) Witty retort.

> NILES
>
> Anyone for coffee?

FADE OUT.

END OF ACT TWO

"Friends"

"Friends" is usually about 50 pages long and is made up of a teaser, two acts, and a tag. Scenes run roughly A through Z or 26 scenes. The

"Friends" script format sample follows and is reprinted with permission of the software program Final Draft, Inc. All dialogue should appear double spaced.

1.
(A)

TEASER
SCENE A

FADE IN:

A   INT. COFFEE HOUSE - AFTERNOON (DAY 1)   A

(Chandler, Monica, Phoebe, Ross)

ACTION. WHEN SOMEONE ENTERS LIKE JOEY, THE CHARACTER IS UNDERLINED.

                        CHANDLER
          Dialogue.

                        MONICA
          (AFTER A MOMENT) You, know, blah, blah, blah, blah.

AND ACTION STILL GOES ON RIGHT HERE.

                        PHOEBE
          No, I won't join with this 'blah, blah' stuff. I want to
          say something interesting!

                        ROSS
          Yeah, right! Blah, blah . . .

                                        FADE OUT.

<u>ACT ONE</u>

<u>SCENE B</u>

<u>FADE IN:</u>

B   <u>INT. JOEY AND CHANDLER'S APARTMENT - DAY</u>   B

(Rachel, Monica, Phoebe, Joey, Chandler, Ross)

ACTION GOES HERE LIKE THIS.

JOEY

Snappy, dumb dialogue. (SITS) More snappy, dumb dialogue.

<u>DISSOLVE TO:</u>

<u>SCENE C</u>

C   <u>INT. MONICA AND RACHEL'S APARTMENT - NIGHT</u>   C
(Rachel, Monica, Phoebe, Joey, Chandler, Ross)

ACTION.

JOEY

Dialogue would go here.

MORE ACTION HERE.

JOEY (CONT'D)
(SITS) Stage direction goes within the dialogue.

FADE OUT.

END OF ACT ONE.

"Episode Title Here"–First Draft   4.
(II/D)

ACT TWO

SCENE D

FADE IN:

D INT. HALLWAY/ INT. MONICA AND RACHEL'S APARTMENT - D
   DAY (2)

(Rachel, Monica, Phoebe, Joey, Chandler, Ross)

ACTION

FADE OUT.

END OF ACT TWO

"Episode Title Here"–First Draft   5.
(E)

SCENE E

TAG

FADE IN:

INT. JOEY AND CHANDLER'S APARTMENT - DAY (3)
(Rachel, Monica, Phoebe, Joey, Chandler, Ross)

ACTION GOES HERE, AS DOES THE USUAL COOKIE STUFF THESE
PEOPLE DO, JUST LIKE THIS.

> ROSS
>
> The end, huh?

> JOEY
>
> And so soon, too!

> MONICA
>
> Well . . . (SIGHS) That's the way . . .

> RACHEL
>
> . . . the cookie crumbles.

FADE OUT.

END OF SHOW

Film Format for Current Comedy Series

If the series is shot on film, then the format is very much like a feature
film script with single-spaced action and single-spaced dialogue; however,
every act is on a separate page. This is a sample format from the hour series
"Ally McBeal."

"Ally McBeal"

"Ally McBeal" is split up into four acts. The scenes are lettered A
through J and run about 10 scenes or more. Scripts read about 50 to 55 pages.
The "Ally McBeal" script format sample follows and is reprinted with permission of the software program Final Draft, Inc.

<u>ALLY MCBEAL</u>

<u>SCENE A</u>

<u>FADE IN:</u>

<u>INT. LYNE AND FANBROE LIBRARY - DAY</u>

Ally is doing some intense research.

                    VOICEOVER
        I wish I was a faster reader. These law books are bor-
        ing . . . Come to think of it, law is boring.

Books start falling, Richard is no doubt to blame. If you see any
SCRIPT NOTES, they contain useful information, view them; this is
one right here. Action is standard sitcom format, and looks exactly
like this.

                    VOICEOVER (CONT'D)
        I knew it.

                    ALLY
        How do you know just which buttons to push?

                    RICHARD
        I don't know . . . practice?

                    ELAINE
        How about timing?

<u>INT. BATHROOM - CONTINUOUS</u>

Ally and Billy have a flirtatious heart to heart.

>   ALLY
> This isn't going to work.

>   BILLY
> You mean us?

>   ALLY
> No, this flirtatious B story line.

After selecting transition to put in FADE OUT, hit Ctrl+9 to select end/start of act. Then type END OF ACT I and simply hit Enter, which will take you to a new page and the start of a new act. Type ACT II and hit the Enter key and type FADE IN. Then hit Enter again, and you're at the start of a new slug line.

                                                    FADE OUT.

                        <u>END OF ACT I</u>

"Ally McBeal"–Date   2.

                        <u>ACT II</u>
                        <u>SCENE B</u>

<u>FADE IN:</u>

<u>EXT. BEACON HILL APARTMENT - MORNING</u>

Ally and Renee bicker over the gas bill.

>   RENEE
> I've done enough work around here to pay off two
> gas bills.

ALLY
Shut up! Just cut the check.

INT. FISHMAN'S OFFICE - DAY

All the members of the firm stand around in a semicircle.

RICHARD
This is great!

FISHMAN
I've just one witty Fishism for all of you.

Everyone disbands, leaving Fishman looking sheepish.

FADE OUT.

END OF ACT II

"Ally McBeal"–Date   3.

ACT III

SCENE J

FADE IN:

EXT. STATE STREET - DAY

A cold Massachusetts-based wind blows. People are walking around
miserable. Typical day in Boston.

BILLY
I love these types of days.

                    ALLY
    Do you!

                    BILLY
        But Ally . . . I . . .

Cold wind blows both across the street.

                BILLY (CONT'D)
    Ally!!!!!!!!

Both Ally and Billy are blown away up into a tree.

                                    FADE OUT.

                THE END

Cast and Set Lists

When episodic comedy scripts are ready for production, producers usually work up cast and set lists to identify which characters are needed and what sets will be used in each scene. Those lists are *not* used if you're writing for television films or features. Dan Wilcox, one of television's most knowledgeable writer-producers, cautions against putting in your own cast and set list. It will look amateurish, as if you are trying to convince us the show is actually in production.

For the sake of production budgets, it's a good idea to limit sets to the ones regularly used in the series; otherwise, producers will have to budget in a "swing" set or new locale for the episode. Dan Wilcox found that three sets are ideal—one main set and two others. He has also successfully written up to five sets for some of his productions.

Sample Cast and Sets List from "Frasier"

A sample "Cast and Sets" is shown as follows. It is from a "Frasier" script entitled "Hot Pursuit," first draft written by Charlie Hauck, reprinted with permission of Richard D. Lindheim, Paramount TV Group. Because the main characters have been cast, their names are listed. Guests and extras are listed, but not yet identified. Following the "Cast and Set List" is a "Breakdown of Acts and Scenes" to be shot.

FRASIER
"HOT PURSUIT"
#40570-163

CAST

FRASIER CRANE	KELSEY GRAMMER
MARTIN CRANE	JOHN MAHONEY
DAPHNE MOON	JANE LEEVES
NILES CRANE	DAVID HYDE PIERCE
ROZ DOYLE	PERI GILPIN
DONNY DOUGLAS	SAUL RUBINEK
KENNY DALY	TOM MCGOWAN
STANLEY REDMAN	LARRY BRANDENBURG
EMPLOYEE	
EDDIE	MOOSE

SETS

INT. FRASIER'S LIVING ROOM/KITCHEN

INT. HOTEL ROOM

EXT./ INT. VAN

FRASIER – "HOT PURSUIT"
#40570-163

ACT ONE

Scene A   (1)

INT. FRASIER'S LIVING ROOM – DAY   DAY/1

(Frasier, Martin, Daphne, Roz, Niles, Donny)

RESET TO:

INT. KITCHEN – CONTINUOUS   (16)

RESET TO:

INT. LIVING ROOM – CONTINUOUS   (17)

Scene B

INT. HOTEL ROOM – NIGHT   (19)

(Frazier, Roz)   NIGHT/1

END OF ACT ONE

<u>ACT TWO</u>

Scene C

<u>EXT. VAN – NIGHT</u>   (24)

(Martin, Niles, Stanley)   NIGHT/1

CUT TO:

<u>INT. VAN – CONTINUOUS</u>   (24)

Scene D   (32)

<u>INT. HOTEL ROOM – NIGHT</u>   NIGHT/1

(Frazier, Roz, Employee)

Scene E   (36)

<u>INT. VAN – NIGHT</u>   NIGHT/1

(Martin, Niles, Stanley)

Scene H   (43)

<u>INT. HOTEL ROOM – NIGHT</u>   NIGHT/1

(Frazier, Roz, Kenny)

<u>END OF ACT TWO</u>

Sample Tentative Production Schedule from "Becker"

When the show is close to production, a producer sets up a "tentative production schedule." A sample "tentative production schedule" is shown as follows. It is from a "Becker" script called "One Angry Man," first draft written by Dan Wilcox, reprinted with permission of Richard D. Lindheim, Paramount TV Group.

<u>BECKER</u>
<u>"ONE ANGRY MAN"</u>

TENTATIVE PRODUCTION SCHEDULE: February 9–15, 2000

**PLEASE NOTE: ALL TIMES APPROXIMATE.

FINAL CALLS TIMES PER CALL SHEET ONLY**

<u>Wednesday, February 9</u>	<u>COOPER CONFERENCE ROOM</u>
11:30 AM–12:00 PM	Production Meeting
12:00 PM–1:00 PM	Table Read
1:00 PM	Network Notes
1:00 PM	Rehearse

<u>Thursday, February 10</u>	<u>STAGE 31</u>
9:30 AM–1:00 PM	Rehearse
1:00 PM–1:30 PM	Lunch
1:30 PM	Rehearse
T.B.A.	Producer Run-Thru

Friday, February 11	STAGE 31
9:30 AM–1:00 PM	Rehearse
1:00 PM–1:30 PM	Lunch
1:30 PM	Rehearse
1:00 PM	Network Run-Thru

Monday, February 14	STAGE 31
9:00 AM–1:00 PM	Camera Block
1:00 PM–2:00 PM	Lunch
2:00 PM	Camera Block
T.B.A.	Run-Thru

Tuesday, February 15	STAGE 31
12:00 PM–3:00 PM	Rehearse
3:00 PM–4:00 PM	Producer Run-Thru
4:00 PM–7:00 PM	Meal/Hair/Makeup/Wardrobe
7:00 PM	Shoot Show

ENDNOTES

1. Andrew Horton, *Laughing Out Loud,* Berkeley, University of California Press, 2000.

2. Andrew Horton, *Writing the Character-Centered Screenplay,* Berkeley, University of California Press, 1994.
3. Evan Smith, in *Writing Television Sitcoms,* New York, Perigee, 1999, 14–18.
4. Ibid., 18.
5. Jurgen Wolff, *Successful Sitcom Writing: How to Write and Sell for TV's Hottest Format,* Revised Edition, New York, St. Martin's Press, 1996.
6. Sol Saks, *Funny Business: The Craft of Comedy Writing,* Second Edition, Los Angeles, Eagle Publishing, 1991.

12

How to Write Professional Scenes in Sitcoms

Sitcom Characters and Dialogue

In sitcom, the comedy has to focus on the lead characters in the series. Comic dialogue must match the characters we've come to know and love. The "A" story must set up a driving force for the main characters, with some susceptibility, to face a crisis. Comedy lies in an effective setup and pay-off of the action and dialogue for the characters. The "B" story might deal with other secondary leads in the series. Producers are particularly finicky about the familiarity of characters to set up the comedy to work properly.

Sample from "Frasier"

Let's look at a "Frasier" script, entitled "Hot Pursuit." This is a first draft written by Charlie Hauck. Each of the lead characters—Frasier, Niles, Martin, Daphne, and Roz—have rich and appropriate predictable dialogue and reactions to the action in the scenes. In the "A" story, the driving force is set up for Frasier, who is convinced by Roz to go to an annual broadcasters convention, which will turn into a sure sexual conquest. But the place is packed, and Frasier can't get a room. They must sleep in the same hotel room. In the "B" story, Martin is recruited by Donny to do a stakeout to take pictures of a dumpster rental king having an affair.

To see how Act One from that "Frasier" script episode is written, see the following Act One Scene A excerpt, reprinted with permission of Richard D. Lindheim, Paramount TV Group. All dialogue should appear double spaced.

<u>FRASIER</u>

"HOT PURSUIT"

#40570-163

<u>ACT ONE</u>

<u>A</u>

FADE IN:

<u>INT. FRASIER'S LIVING ROOM - DAY - DAY/1</u>

(Daphne, Niles, Frasier, Martin, Donny, Roz)

AS <u>DAPHNE</u> SETS OUT SNACKS ON THE DINING ROOM TABLE, THERE'S A KNOCK ON THE DOOR. SHE OPENS THE DOOR AND <u>NILES</u> ENTERS WITH A VIDEOTAPE.

> DAPHNE
> Dr. Crane.

> NILES
> Hello, Daphne. Is that Jungle Gardenia I smell?

> DAPHNE
> That's quite a nose you've got.

> NILES
> That's quite a nice little nose you've got yourself.

DAPHNE, FLATTERED, TOUCHES HER NOSE SELF-CONSCIOUSLY.

> NILES (CONT'D)
> (NOTICING FOOD) What an elegant spread. I take it Frasier's back from Boston.

> DAPHNE
> Not quite. He called from the airport in a foul mood and asked me to fix him a little something.

NILES
Yes, brioche toast, salmon roe, and Truffle—comfort food. (THEN) Where's Dad?

DAPHNE
He's out with Donny.

NILES
Again? Where are they today?

DAPHNE
They went to the tractor pull.

NILES
Oh. (BEAT) What is that, exactly?

DAPHNE
As I understand it, they attach a large weight to the tractor and see how far they can pull it through the mud.

NILES OPENS HIS MOUTH TO SAY "WHY."

DAPHNE (CONT'D)
The answer to your next question is, It beats the hell out of me.

NILES
I hope he's back soon. We're supposed to watch a movie together.

DAPHNE
(NOTICES VIDEOTAPE) Oh . . . "Spartacus." Such a sad story. Two lovers who are torn apart by fate.

NILES
Dad likes the part where gladiators are torn apart by lions.

3.

(A)

NILES CROSSES TO THE KITCHEN. THE FRONT DOOR OPENS AND
FRASIER ENTERS WITH LUGGAGE. HE SPORTS A NEW FULL
BEARD.

> FRASIER
>
> Hello, Daphne.

> DAPHNE
>
> Oh, Dr. Crane, I see you've grown yourself a crumb
> catcher.

> FRASIER
>
> Spare me your jocular euphemisms. I just spent a
> week listening to Freddy and his precocious friends
> call it my chin sweater, my face fuzz, and my hickey
> hider. What is it about growing a simple beard that
> brings out the phrasemaker in everyone?

NILES CROSSES BACK IN.

> NILES
>
> Frasier, nice beard.

> FRASIER
>
> Thank you, Niles.

> NILES
>
> Or should I say soup strainer?

DAPHNE CROSSES OUT TO HER BEDROOM.

> NILES (CONT'D)
>
> What prompted you to grow it?

> FRASIER
>
> I just wanted to shake things up a little bit.

4.
(A)

NILES
Did you have a nice time with Freddy?

FRASIER
Yes, a delightful time with him. But not with Lilith.
She's in a torrid new relationship. She showed no end
of delight in flaunting it in my face. His name is
Marcul. He's twenty-eight and performs with the
Cirque de Soleil as a contortionist.

NILES
She's dating French circus folk?

FRASIER
He's perfect for Lilith. He has no apparent spine and
she can wrap him around her finger. That smug sat-
isfaction and shameless double entendre were pretty
hard to bear. Especially given how long it's been since
the circus came to my town.

THE FRONT DOOR OPENS AND <u>MARTIN AND DONNY ENTER</u> IN
HIGH SPIRITS. DONNY IS HOLDING A JOHN DEER CAP. THEY AD
LIB GREETINGS.

DONNY
(OFF THE BEARD) It's Grizzly Crane.

MARTIN
Nice mug rug, Fras.

FRASIER
Thank you.

MARTIN
It looks good, Fras.

NILES
So, Dad, did you enjoy the tractor pull?

MARTIN

Oh, it was great. (THEN, SEEING VIDEO) Oh, right—
we were going to watch "Spartacus" today, weren't
we?

DONNY

It's my fault, Niles. I had these passes I thought
Martin would enjoy.

NILES

It's all right. But you might have asked me along to
the tractor pull.

MARTIN

You're right, Niles. I should have thought of that. (TO
FRASIER) So, how's my grandson?

FRASIER

In great form, Dad. He loved the baseball mitt you
sent.

NILES

Didn't you just give Freddy a baseball mitt for
Hanukkah?

MARTIN

This is different. It's a catcher's mitt.

NILES

Aren't they all used for catching?

MARTIN

You wouldn't have enjoyed the tractor pull, son.

DONNY

So, where's Daphne? It's our anniversary this week
and I've got a present for her.

6.
(A)

NILES

A John Deere cap?

SFX: DOORBELL

FRASIER CROSSES TO OPEN THE DOOR.

DONNY

No. I'm just going to make her pretend to like it before
I give her the bracelet.

DONNY EXITS. FRASIER OPENS THE DOOR TO ROZ, WHO ENTERS
WITH AN ENVELOPE. THEY AD LIB GREETINGS. NILES AND
MARTIN EXAMINE THE VIDEOTAPE BOX AS ROZ CROSSES TO
FRASIER.

ROZ

Frasier. Cool beard.

FRASIER

Thank you.

ROZ

(HANDS HIM THE ENVELOPE) Okay, here's your directions, hotel confirmation, ferry pass, and ticket for the
big cocktail party tonight.

FRASIER

Excuse me?

ROZ

The broadcast conference.

FRASIER

I thought that was next week.

ROZ

It starts tonight. I'm on my way now.

FRASIER

I just got back from a trip. Can't I get out of it?

ROZ

Fine, Frasier, if you don't care about the industry you work in, keeping current, and staying competitive, then I'll go by myself.

FRASIER

All right, all right. I'll get up early tomorrow and make it in time for the panels.

ROZ

And miss the party tonight? That's the only reason to go to these things. By tomorrow, everyone will be paired up.

FRASIER

Now that I think about it, last year's kickoff party did get a bit raucous. I wondered why no one was at my nine a.m. seminar, "Reaching Your Maximum Audience."

NILES

Perhaps this is the boost you need after a week with Lilith and her pretzel boy.

FRASIER

I remember a particularly stunning blonde from last year. Rush Hour Rita—Laramie's eye in the sky.

ROZ

Yes, I remember her. Traffic was bumper to bumper outside her room.

                         FRASIER
Meow, Roz.

                           ROZ
I'm sorry. I'm just sick of listening to guys drool over
hot blondes. It's like one flash of blond hair instantly
turns all men into panting idiots.

                          NILES
That's an unfair oversimplification.

MARTIN NODS IN AGREEMENT.

                         FRASIER
To suggest that all men become panting dogs at the
sight of a blonde is sexist negative stereotyping and
outright male bashing of the worst order.

                           ROZ
Sorry. (THINKS) Wait a minute. You went nuts over
that blond waitress at Nervosa last week.

                         MARTIN
Mimi's back?

                          NILES
I'll have to stop in.

ROZ REACTS.

                         FRASIER
Seems like a good time for me to go and pack for the
lodge.

DAPHNE ENTERS TO CLEAR THE SNACKS AWAY.

> FRASIER (CONT'D)
> Daphne, I trust my silk pajamas are back from the cleaners.

WITH A KNOWING LOOK AT NILES, HE EXITS. DONNY ENTERS TALKING ON HIS CELL PHONE.

> DONNY
> (INTO PHONE) Davey, come on. I understand it's your kid's first communion, but doesn't that mean there'll be a second, and a third? Couldn't you catch one of those? All right! (HE HANGS UP) My surveillance guy canceled for tonight, just when I need him for this divorce case.

> DAPHNE
> Oh. The dumpster rental king.

> DONNY
> Stanley Redman. (TO THE OTHERS) He controls most of the dumpsters in this city. This is a big money case. His wife thinks he's been taking out the wrong kind of trash. If I can get the photos, the case is mine.

> NILES
> Why would a respectable dumpster king cheat on his dumpster queen?

> DONNY
> Yeah, but you should see his girlfriend—gorgeous, leggy, blonde . . .

> NILES
> (FOR ROZ'S BENEFIT) Ah, well then.

ROZ
(DISGUSTED) Goodbye.

ROZ EXITS.

DAPHNE
Donny, could you use Officer Stoltz to do your surveillance? He was interested in part-time work.

DONNY
I thought of him. He's still in jail. Wait a minute! Does everybody see the lightbulb over my head?
Marty, you were a cop. You must've done stakeouts?

MARTIN
Sure, all the time.

DONNY
Why don't you work for me tonight? It's forty-five dollars an hour.

NILES
I'm sure Dad isn't interested. We're going to watch "Spartacus" tonight.

MARTIN
Forty-five dollars?

DONNY
Okay, fifty. And if you get a picture of Redman and the girl, there's a five-hundred-dollar bonus.

MARTIN
(IMPRESSED) Five hundred dollars?

DONNY
All right, it's seven hundred. You're killing me.

NILES

Dad, this is not at all a good idea. (TO DONNY) Where
would this stakeout take place?

DONNY

At the girlfriend's apartment building, in Belltown.

NILES

That's a damn sketchy neighborhood. A church was
busted for illegal bingo there just last week.

MARTIN

Niles, I used to be a cop, remember?

NILES

Used to be. You're older now, and you have a bad hip.
You're not fit for sitting long hours and staring.

MARTIN

What do you think I'd be doing if we watched
"Spartacus"? I got a chance to pick up a nice piece
of change here.

NILES

If you need money, I'll give you money.

MARTIN

Well, that makes me feel just swell. Why don't I go
with you when you leave. You can drop me off at the
cemetery and get it over with.

NILES

Dad—

MARTIN

I'm taking the job, Donny.

DONNY

Great. I'll drive you over to pick up the van and the camera.

MARTIN

I'll get a jacket.

MARTIN EXITS TO HIS ROOM.

NILES

Well, thank you, Donny, for recruiting my father into your goon squad.

DONNY

What? He's sitting in a van, taking pictures.

NILES

It's dangerous and unnecessary.

DONNY

Hey, the man used to be a cop.

NILES

Yes, a police officer, upholding the law, not running a cheesy shyster scheme to trap a dumpster king with a little hottie.

DONNY

Niles, I don't think you're aware of it, but I could take that as a negative reflection on my work.

MARTIN ENTERS IN HIS JACKET.

13.
(A)

> MARTIN
> I'll have to pick up some stakeout gear. Binoculars, notepad, an old mayonnaise jar, some—

> DAPHNE
> What's the mayonnaise jar for?

THE MEN LOOK AT HER.

The characters are appropriately set up and ready for the payoff. At the end of Act One, Frasier has no choice but to stay with Roz because the whole island is booked. She's afraid that he may cramp her style, but Frasier reassures her that they are two attractive people on the prowl at a conference that turns into a bacchanal every year. Neither will be in the room overnight. In the next act, we learn that they both were turned down. And they must stay in their hotel room, susceptible, alone, and horny. They drink, and comic sparks are forced to fly.

In Act Two, the opening is a scene of Martin in his van, doing undercover work, and bored, as Niles enters with clam chowder. Niles appropriately feels guilty about putting down Martin's undercover work. Martin goes for Mallomars, and Niles takes over with proud affect. Then the perpetrator knocks on the window, and Niles lets him in to make a phone call to his girlfriend. Niles finally reveals he's a psychiatrist and the perpetrator discusses his stress. The scene is filled with appropriate comic dialogue from them all. The perpetrator pours his heart out to Niles, and when Martin returns, he is very surprised. At the end of the scene, Niles takes a picture of the adulterer so Martin can earn his reward.

Sample from "Becker"

Now, let's look at another sitcom, "Becker," episode titled "One Angry Man," from a first draft script, by Dan Wilcox. In the "A" story, the setup and driving force for John is when Linda is called to jury duty. He proudly tells her how he escaped from serving. She tells the jury selection committee about how he escaped jury duty. John is called to serve again. She is accepted. He is dismissed because he's too smart. He's jealous of Linda and angry at the jury system. Finally, he "outsmarts" them and is called to duty. He finds himself in competition with a gushing Linda, who is elected jury

Foreman. The payoff is executed with the deft, dark quick wit of John, playing against Linda's complete naivete. John fancies himself to be jury leader of the "12 Angry Men," but everyone agrees with him.

The "B" Story deals with characters at the diner. Margaret tries to make Reggie's coffee better with chicory, and finally succeeds. Bob tries to give Jake, a blind man, a seeing-eye dog. It has flatulence problems, and the dialogue is appropriately gritty and funny.

In Act Two, John finally succeeds at getting on a jury. To see how that scene is written, see the following script pages, reprinted with permission of Richard D. Lindheim, Paramount TV Group. All dialogue should appear double spaced.

"One Angry Man" 2/9/00

36.
II/M

SCENE M

INT. DINER - DAYS LATER (DAY 5)
(John, Reggie, Margaret, Linda, Jake, Bob)

REGGIE'S AT THE COUNTER WAITING ON A LINE OF CUSTOMERS. MARGARET'S ALSO THERE. JOHN BURSTS IN, TOTING A LEGAL PAD, A PEN, AND A BUNCH OF PAPERS.

> JOHN
> I did it! I fooled them! I got on a jury! And wait till you guys hear about this case I'm on. It's— (NOTICING CROWD) Hey, what's going on? There are customers in here. Was there a bomb scare across the street again?

> MARGARET
> They're here for the coffee.

> JOHN
> No, really.

> MARGARET
> It's true. Word spread about how good it is.

> JOHN
> (TO REGGIE) Your coffee?

MARGARET LOOKS AT REG, WAITING.

REGGIE

(BEATEN) Yes.

MARGARET

And why is that?

REGGIE

(FLAT) It's smoother and more flavorful.

MARGARET

And why is <u>that</u>?

REGGIE

(HATES TO ADMIT) Because . . . I added chicory.

MARGARET

And whose suggestion was that?

REGGIE

(BLOWS) Oh, all right. Yours! It was yours! You get
all the credit! Okay? Happy now?!

MARGARET

(PLEASANTLY) Well, you know me. Anything I can
do to help.

REGGIE

(SOTTO, TO JOHN) God, how can you work with her?

JOHN

I gave in to the chicory thing, like, six years ago.
(BEAT) All right, Reg, bring me coffee and keep it
coming.

JOHN SITS AND SPREADS HIS PAPERS OUT ON THE COUNTER.

REGGIE
What are you doing?

JOHN
I don't think my trial's going to take very long, so I
figure I'd better start preparing my final argument.

REGGIE
Your final argument?

JOHN
Yeah, if those mouth breathers I'm serving with try
to convict, they're not going to know what hit them.
I'm going to be organized. I'm going to be precise. I'm
going to be correct. Remember "Twelve Angry Men?"
Well, I'm going to be Henry Fonda! (BEAT) This guy
is so innocent. You see what happened was—

MARGARET
Whoa, whoa, Hank, I don't think you're supposed to
talk about the case.

JOHN
Okay, fine. But I think I'm going to have a fight on
my hands, and I'm going to do everything I can to
turn that jury one man at a time with the facts of
this case. Well, there's one lady I could turn with a
candy bar—but, by the end, they will see what I see.
And I don't care how long it takes.

REGGIE
Does that mean Margaret's going to be hanging
around here even longer?

LINDA ENTERS, EXCITED

LINDA

My case is so cool! Muffin to go, please, Reg. I know I'm not supposed to discuss it, but this guy is so guilty. First, there's the shape of his forehead. And then there's his lawyer's outfit. I mean, "Hello, the Eighties called, they want the suit back." Well, gotta go. Juror #4—not his real name—asked me on a date tonight.

SHE TAKES HER MUFFIN AND EXITS.

JOHN

See what I'm up against? I'm going to be making my case to eleven Lindas.

JOHN GOES BACK TO HIS NOTES. BOB ENTERS FROM THE MEN'S ROOM AS JAKE ENTERS WITH THE DOG.

BOB

So, Jake, how'd it go with the dog?

JAKE

Well, I think the problem is solved.

REGGIE

Good.

JOHN

Jake, you got a seeing-eye dog? But you always said—

BOB

Yeah, yeah, we know what he said. But the pooch was a gift from Bob and he loves it, so don't rock the boat.

JAKE

The vet gave him some medicine and he's pretty sure it's going to work.

AS JAKE CONTINUES, ONE BY ONE, PEOPLE'S HEADS START TO TURN. THE OTHER CUSTOMERS LEAVE THE DINER QUICKLY.

> JAKE (CONT'D)
> . . . All I have to do is put these tablets in his food twice a day and give him lots of water. The vet said it was a fairly common problem and . . . (IT HITS HIM) Damn!

> JOHN
> What the hell is that!?

> REGGIE
> Oh, God.

> JAKE
> (HOLDING OUT LEASH) Bob, he's all yours.

> BOB
> (TAKES IT) Bob understands. He also understands what killed Old Man Czerny.

> MARGARET
> (GASPING) He's dead. He's lucky.

> BOB
> I'll take Rocky back to his grandkids. They live in Jersey, they'll never know the difference.

BOB EXITS WITH THE DOG.

> JOHN
> Well, all those people are going to remember this place, but I'm not sure it's going to be for the coffee.

> MARGARET
> You know what would help? If you lit a few candles.

> REGGIE
> Yeah, that's just what I need around here—an open
> flame.

DISSOLVE TO:

The comedy plays effectively for each of the characters.

13

Animation, Interactive and New Media, and Nonfiction Entertainment

Writing for Animation Series

In an article entitled "Writing for The Simpsons," Executive Producer Michael Scully agrees with the Hollywood wisdom of not sending a spec script to the same series you're trying to write for.[1] If you're considering doing a spec script for a half-hour animation sitcom, then don't submit a spec script to "The Simpsons." Scully suggests sending one somewhere else, like "King of the Hill" or "Family Guy."

Scully advises writers not to confuse the "edge" of the characters. He describes Homer as "the quintessential American," asserting that many spec scripts depict Homer as uncharacteristically mean. He feels that pitfalls like mistaking Homer's nature are reasons for not submitting scripts to "The Simpsons."[2]

In another interview with Matt Groening and David X. Cohen, creators and executive producers of "The Simpsons" and "Futurama," they disclose how the "Simpsons" was created. Groening initially wrote them as "bumpers" for Jim Brooks' Gracie Film's "Tracy Ullman Show." The series became a phenomenal primetime hit. Responding to controversy about Bart Simpson's charisma and dialogue, Groening argued that "since it was in primetime, we couldn't possibly be aiming these jokes at kids."[3]

Writing the series remains a grueling process, contend Groening and Cohen. "We literally write in a padded room," says David X. Cohen, about the sound chamber that makes up their dorm-style quarters. Matt Groening explains that 17 writers work with them. "It's a collective process of very hard-working people."[4] He reveals that the storylines are often developed

195

in a group. Rewrites are done in a kind of tag-team approach. "Also, it's almost impossible for one person to get the pace that our staff puts together in that concentrated period of time. So, don't be afraid to throw stuff out, and keep punching things up repeatedly."

Finally, he advises: "Don't think that, just because it's animated, you have leeway to make a string of crazy things happened. Really try to build a solid story as your basis. And if you really look at our shows, it's almost always with a strong "A" storyline. So keep your writing and the story organized."[5]

This is how Cohen views the tone, characters, and stories for "Futurama": "Even in 'The Simpsons,' we don't pull any gross violations of the laws of physics, so working in the future, we had to place some kind of limits on it. Matt and I agreed that we could put the characters in crazy situations, but they had to respond in real, human ways. We had to have sympathy for these people and their predicaments. That was a lot of the challenge, ultimately—to try to make it real, regardless of the fantastic situations, and that gives both series a lot of grounding."[6]

WGA Animation Writers Caucus and Animation Contract

If you're developing projects for interactive, animation, or new media, then get in touch with the WGAw, Department of Industry Alliances, 7000 West Third Street, Los Angeles, CA 90048-4329; Website: www.wga.org/; phone: 323/782-4511; fax: 323/782-4511; e-mail: industryalliances@wga.org. The department furthers the cause of writers who work in fields other than traditional movies and television shows, with particular emphasis in four areas: interactive, nonfiction entertainment, animation, and informational films.

Be sure to contact the Animation Writers Caucus at WGAw, 7000 West Third Street, Los Angeles, CA 90048-4329; Website: www.awn.com; phone: 213/782-4511; fax: 213/782-4807. It pursues strategies toward improvement of terms and conditions of employment for animation writers.

To qualify for membership, applicants have to have been hired to write one-half hour of produced animation. Members are eligible to receive all WGA associate membership benefits. The annual membership service fee is $75 for non-Guild members. Membership is free to current WGA members. The Animation Writers' Directory lists AWC members and their credits and is mailed to producers, production companies, studios, distributors, and networks.

Brochures detail how to ask for a Guild animation deal, and the Animation Writers Writing Code of Ethics are available from the Animation Writers Caucus. To order publications or the Animation Writers Caucus application form, send your request to the WGAw, 7000 West Third Street,

Los Angeles, CA 90048-4329; Website: www.awn.com; phone: 213/782-4511; fax: 213/782-4807.

Format Samples for Current Animation Series

Here are sample animation series formats from Final Draft, Inc. These TV script format samples are reprinted with permission of the software program Final Draft, Inc. The script notes for the shows are reprinted as text before the format sample.

"King of the Hill"

"King of the Hill" is split into three acts. In "King of the Hill," words that demand attention are placed in boldface. The "King of the Hill" script format sample follows and is reprinted with permission of the software program Final Draft, Inc.

"TITLE HERE"–DATE   1.

ACT ONE

FADE IN:

INT. HILL HOUSE - UTILITY ROOM

We open with a shot of Peggy sitting at a little desk jammed against the water heater in a narrow utility room.

> HANK (OS)
> (TIGHTLY) Peggy?

> PEGGY
> I'm in my office!

> HANK (OS)
> Peggy! Uh . . . Peggy, I've got a problem here.

Peggy jumps up, concerned.

INT. HILL HOUSE - LIVING ROOM - CONTINUOUS

Peggy hurries out of the utility room.

> PEGGY
> What's up? Is it your back again?

He takes another step and **winces**.

> PEGGY (CONT'D)
> Why don't you sit down.

> HANK
> Don't tell me what to do, woman.

> PEGGY
> (EXPLODING) Woman! Why Hank Hill, I never.

> HANK
> And so you shouldn't.

EXT. HILL HOUSE

> BILL/DALE
> You got to set her straight. Damn straight.

> BOOMHAUER
> Yeah, man, I tell you what, you got that there women's
> lib, out of the kitchen, into the streets . . . Man, and
> sisters are doing it for themselves, man . . . better
> than having them barefoot and pregnant, burning bras
> . . . read it all in Cosmo.

Peggy walks up, distressed.

                         PEGGY
            Hank, I can't get the words out.

                          BILL
            Aw, you didn't come to . . .

                          HANK
            Stay out of this.

ANGLE ON HANK

He starts to speak, but stops.

                          HANK
            Peggy, I'm sorry.

Choose transition by typing ctrl+6, then hit enter, which will take
you to a new page and the start of a new act. Simply hit enter
after typing your act number (act one). Then enter again to take
you to slugline!

                                               FADE OUT.

                     END OF ACT ONE

"TITLE HERE"–DATE   4.

                      ACT TWO

EXT. ESTABLISHING - HILL HOUSE

INT. HILL HOME - BATHROOM

Closeup of Peggy, staring at a book, eyes wide in shock.

> PEGGY
> Oh my . . . (FLIPS PAGE) Oh Lord. For goodness sakes!

ANGLE REVEALS THE BOOK: "Final Draft, The Users Manual."

> HANK
> What's wrong?

> PEGGY
> Oh my! Oh Lord!!

> HANK
> Peggy, stop profaning the Lord like that.

Hank looks down and notices the book's title.

> HANK (CONT'D)
> MY GOD!!! What are you reading THAT for?

> PEGGY
> Instruction. I bought this software, and I can't use
> the damn thing!

> > > > CUT TO:

INT. BOBBY'S ROOM - LATER

Bobby is reading the same book manual.

> BOBBY
> Boring. COOOL. Boring. Huh?

> > > > FADE OUT.

END OF ACT TWO

ACT THREE

EXT. ESTABLISHING - STRICKLAND PROPANE

INT. STRICKLAND PROPANE - DAY

Hank is sitting at his desk talking on the phone.

> HANK
> C'mon, Bobby. You're coming to work with me.

> BOBBY (OS)
> O.K.

> HANK
> Fine, come over now.

FADE OUT.

END OF ACT THREE

CREDIT TAG

FADE IN

EXT. COMMON ALLEY

Hank is on his riding mower in the yard.

> HANK
> If you ask me, no one is better than . . . I mean . . .
> Oh, just write something witty for me to say.

He drives off on the mower.

FADE OUT.

END OF SHOW

"The Simpsons"

"The Simpsons" is split into two acts. "The Simpsons" script format follows and is reprinted with permission of the software program Final Draft, Inc.

Episode# Revision# Date Page 1.

<u>TITLE GOES HERE</u>

by

A. N. Other

<u>ACT ONE</u>

FADE IN:

INT. SIMPSON HOUSE - KITCHEN - MORNING   **SCENE 1**

Action goes here, as do **sound effects**, which are shown in bold. The whole thing reads like a movie. The only thing that leads us to believe it's a sitcom is the double-spaced dialogue.

HOMER enters.

                    HOMER
          Stupendously stupid line.

                    MARGE
          A perfect response.

Episode#   Revision#   Date   Page 2.

HOMER
(IN A LOW MOAN) Mmmm, dialogue.

And action continues here like this.

LISA
Witty, pithy remark!

BART
A gross reply.

HOMER
And he continues.

MARGE
As does Marge.

Action goes here.

What you might find is this . . . (**ANIMATOR'S NOTE:** This allows you, the writer, to convey what something should look like.)

HOMER
And so it goes.

MARGE
More dialogue here.

HOMER
And more of the same.

MARGE
More dialogue here.

Homer bangs his head on the kitchen table.

> HOMER
>
> Doh!

> LISA
>
> Blah, blah, blah blah blah.

> BART
>
> Blah!

> MARGE
>
> Blah, blah, blah blah blah.

On the television, KENT BROCKMAN is giving the details of a news story.

> KENT BROCKMAN
>
> Springfield is panic-stricken. Blah, blah, blah blah blah. Blah, blah, blah blah blah. Blah, blah, blah blah blah. Blah, blah, blah blah blah. Blah, blah, blah blah blah. Blah, blah, blah blah blah. Blah, blah, blah blah blah. Blah, blah, blah blah.

And action surprisingly melts into scenes without transitions, like this. The scene numbers increment upward as the scenes progress.

INT. DONUT SHOP - DAY   **SCENE 2**

The Springfield police are having a donut break.

> CHIEF WIGGUM
>
> Blah, blah, blah blah blah.

Episode# Revision# Date Page 4.

INT. SIMPSON HOUSE - KITCHEN - DAY

Action goes here.

> HOMER
> Blah, blah, blah blah blah.

FADE OUT.

Episode# Revision# Date Page 5.

ACT TWO

FADE IN:

INT. QUICKIE MART - DAY   **SCENE 3**

Apu, Homer, and some customers are going through the motions of shopping.

> APU
> Get away from those magazines, you naughty extras!
> (NOTICES HOMER) Hello Mr. Simpson, sir.

> HOMER
> Hey, Apu, blah, blah blah.

> EVERYONE
> (AND EVERYBODY STARTS LAUGHING)

FADE OUT.

END OF ACT TWO

"South Park"

   "South Park" is split into three acts. The "South Park" script format follows and is reprinted with permission of the software program Final Draft, Inc.

EXT. SCHOOL BUS STOP - MORNING

STAN, IKE, KYLE, AND CARTMAN—the act's characters are introduced in ALL CAPS; the rest of action is mixed case throughout the script.

                           KIDS
                        (Singing)
            Enter dialogue here.

Action here.

                           KYLE
               Enter dialogue here.

Action here.

                           IKE
               Enter dialogue here.

                           KYLE
               Enter dialogue here.

                           IKE
               Enter dialogue here.

                          CARTMAN
               Enter dialogue here.

2.

INT. CARTMAN'S BEDROOM - DREAM SEQUENCE

CARTMAN

                        CARTMAN
          Enter dialogue here.

Action here.

INT. ALIEN SHIP - DREAM SEQUENCE

                        <u>ACT II</u>

INT. SCHOOL - DAY

TEACHER

                        TEACHER
          Enter dialogue here.

Action here.

INT. SCHOOL CAFETERIA - DAY

STAN, CARTMAN

                        CARTMAN
          Enter dialogue here.

                        STAN
          Enter dialogue here.

3.

                        CARTMAN
      Enter dialogue here.

Acts are not started on a new page.

                                    ACT II FADE OUT.

FADE IN:

INT. SCHOOL - DAY

KYLE, CARTMAN

                        CARTMAN
      Enter dialogue here.

Action here.

                        KYLE
      Enter dialogue here.

                        CARTMAN
      Enter dialogue here.

                                    ACT III FADE OUT.

Writing for Interactive and New Media

Written By magazine has a monthly column called "Alt.Screenwriters," which discusses developments, issues, and strategies as they relate to writers on the digital frontier. As an example, this information appears on Brilliant Digital Entertainment (www.bede3d.com), which has the first multipath Movies on the Internet—KISS: IMMORTALS. Guild members Jeff

Sullivan and Bruce Onder wrote the new entertainment format. According to Onder, the story starts as the KISS band members are "transported to an alternate dimension where the personae they act out on Earth are reversed as super-powerful demigods who will now one day overthrow the evil, malicious ruler, Tempest. The only problems: They don't know how to harness their newfound godliness, and all the beauty wanted to do is go home."[7] For screenwriters who will be writing these projects, Sullivan advises that "you need to be familiar with what's been done, what failed, what succeeded, and even what's coming next—if you can see it."[8]

Executive producer Lisa Eisenpresser explains what she looks for in writers: "I look for writers who understand that the Web is not the fall-back plan for TV or film scripts they wrote. I look for concepts that would be better on the Web than on TV and for writers who have spent some time thinking about the medium, and are excited about the new possibilities it offers."[9]

If you're developing projects for interactive, animation, or new media, then get in contact with the WGAw, Department of Industry Alliances, 7000 West Third Street, Los Angeles, CA 90048-4329; Website: www.wga.org/; phone: 323/782-4511; fax: 323/782-4511; e-mail: industryalliances@wga.org.

Industry Alliance coordinates organizing efforts and implements new media policies and activities. While working closely with the New Media committee (formerly the Creative Media and Technologies Committee), the Department researches multimedia, including Internet activities, provides the *Directory of Interactive and Informational Writers*, and structures seminars and industry events.

If you are a writer in new media, a primary marketing tool for current contacts is *Hollywood New Media Directory* (HCD, 3000 Olympic Boulevard, Suite 2525, Santa Monica, CA 90404). It lists Website designers and developers, software developers, interactive TV companies, new media agents, and others. It is also available at www.hcdonline.com.

Multimedia Script Format

Multimedia scripts can range in scope and content, depending on the complexities of the project. The software program Movie Magic 2000 has superb multimedia script samples and interactive formats in its software package. The following is a Sample Multimedia Script Sample from the screenwriting software, ScriptThing, which is reprinted with permission of ScriptPerfection Enterprises, Inc. ScriptThing merged with Screenplay Systems and is now known as Movie Magic Screenwriter 2000.

<u>MULTIMEDIA DEMO SCRIPT</u>

an original script

by Ken Schafer

contact: Anne McDermott

Coast to Coast Talent Group

phone number

(1) ROCKY COURTYARD

It is a rock-hewn courtyard, old and decaying, but clearly having once been elegant.

To the north is the imposing edifice of a temple, to the west is a gaping chasm, completely impassible.

South of us is a gate, an apple orchard just beyond it.

➤ GO TO GATE (2) Pg: 1

➤ GO TO TEMPLE (3) Pg: 1

➤ GO TO CHASM (4) Pg: 1

(2) ORCHARD GATE

➤ IF YOU TRY TO OPEN THE GATE THEN

➤➤ IF YOU HAVE THE <KEY TO THE ORCHARD GATE> THEN

The gate creaks open

➤ GO TO THE ORCHARD (5) Pg: 2

^^   OTHERWISE

The gates rattle but you can't get through.

<<   ENDIF

<   ENDIF

➤ GO TO ROCKY COURTYARD (1) Pg: 1

(3) TEMPLE

The temple is elegant, bas-relief images of strange animals covering the walls.

You can go around the temple to the left or right.

➤ GO TO RIGHT AROUND TEMPLE (7) Pg: 2

➤ GO TO LEFT AROUND TEMPLE (6) Pg: 2

(4) CHASM

An uncrossable chasm at your feet.

> IF YOU JUMP THEN

➤ GO TO YOU'RE DEAD (16) Pg: 5

> ENDIF

➤ GO TO ROCKY COURTYARD (1) Pg: 1

(5) ORCHARD

Congratulations! You're in. Eat an apple while you're here.

➤ GO TO ORCHARD GATE (2) Pg: 1

(6) LEFT AROUND TEMPLE

Broken columns litter your path as you walk around the temple, finally opening up and leaving you at the inner buildings.

➤ GO TO INNER BUILDINGS (8) Pg: 2

(7) RIGHT AROUND TEMPLE

Broken columns litter your path as you walk around the temple. Midway around, you'll find an open door.

>   IF YOU ENTER THE DOOR THEN

➤ GO TO TEMPLE ROOM (13) Pg: 4

<   ENDIF

The walkway continues around, finally opening up and leaving you at the inner building.

➤GO TO INNER BUILDINGS (8) Pg: 2

(8) INNER BUILDINGS

➤ IF <CLOCK IS SET> THEN

➤ GO TO BACK OF TEMPLE (10) Pg: 3

<   ENDIF

A large ornate door blocks your way, a lion-headed knocker on the front door.

>   IF YOU USE THE KNOCKER THEN

It hits the door with a loud booming sound, but no one opens it.

<   ENDIF

>   IF YOU LOOK UP THEN

You will see more carvings and a sign over the door, held up by two clocks.

>> IF YOU EXAMINE THE SIGN THEN YOU'VE <EXAMINED SIGN> AND

It says:

Interactive Program Contract

The Interactive Program Contract (see Figure 13-1) is a user-friendly, one-page agreement that secures Pension and Welfare coverage, while providing writers with the opportunity to obtain Guild membership. You can get a copy from the WGAw or at its Website. The WGAw also developed an Internet contract for writers, available at their website.

Nonfiction Entertainment

The Writers Guild of America provides a helpful pamphlet to assist writers and producers and their representatives to understand their specific needs. Ask for *Guidelines for Hiring WGA Writers in Non-Fiction Entertainment*, WGAw, 7000 West Third Street, Los Angeles, CA 90048-4329; Website: www.wga.org; phone: 323/782-4511; or WGA, east, 555 West 57th Street, New York, NY 10019; phone: 212/767-7800.

The Writers Guild of America has established new guideline and rates (effective, May 2, 1999–May 1, 2000) for hiring WGA writers in nonfiction entertainment. Nonfiction entertainment includes documentaries, news, nondramatic programming and programs, minimal writing, and reality shows. Included within these categories are magazine shows, "making of" shows, travelogues, "how-to" shows, certain talk shows, certain children's shows, and infomercials.

Informational Program Contract

For a sample Informational Program Contract, see Figure 13-2.

INTERACTIVE PROGRAM CONTRACT
Letter of Adherence • Single Production Only

Company: _____ Phone: ( )_____
Street Address:_____
City:_____ State:_____ Zip:_____

FINANCIAL STRUCTURE

    Corporation: ☐   Partnership: ☐   10% or more owner: ☐

    Joint Venture ☐   Sole Owner: ☐   DBA: ☐

If corporation, name of state in which Corporation is registered:_____
If corporation, names of officers and principal owners:_____
List names of Partners or Joint Ventures:_____

TITLE OF PRODUCTION:_____
COMPENSATION (Writing and/or Designing Services):_____
LENGTH OF PROGRAM (In Minutes):_____

WRITER(S) EMPLOYED UNDER THIS CONTRACT
Name: _____ SS#:_____
Name: _____ SS#:_____

On behalf of the writers(s) employed on the above-named Interactive Program, the undersigned Interactive Program Producer hereby agrees to make contributions to the Producers-Writers Guild of America Pension Plan("Plan") and the Writers Guild-Industry Health Fund ("Fund") as set forth in Article 17 of the 1998 Writers Guild of America Theatrical and Television Basic Agreement ("the 1998 WGA MBA"), by reference incorporated herein and available on request. Producer agrees to be bound by the terms and conditions of the Plan Agreement and the Fund's Trust Agreement. No other terms of the 1998 WGA MBA shall apply to the employment of such writer(s). Currently, the contribution rates set forth in Article 17 are six percent(6%) of gross compensation for writing services to the Plan and six and one-half percent (6.5%) of gross compensation for writing services to the Fund.

Accepted and Agreed:

_____   _____
        (Company)   (Date)

By:_____   _____
        (Signature)   (Print Name and Title)

**WRITERS GUILD OF AMERICA, WEST, INC. on behalf
Of itself and its affiliate, WRITERS GUILD OF AMERICA, EAST, INC.**

By:_____

---FOR OFFICE USE ONLY---
Accepted this ___day of _____, 19____, Producers-Writers Guild of America Pension Plan and Writers

Guild Industry Health Fund. By: _____ Title_____

RETURN COMPLETED FORM TO: FOR QUESTIONS CALL:

Dept of Industry Alliance   Southern California: (323) 782-4511
Writers Guild of America, West, Inc.   Northern California: (408) 323-1898
7000 West Third Street, Los Angeles, California 90048

Figure 13-1
"Interactive Program Contract," reprinted with permission of the
Writers Guild of America, west, Inc., Department of Industry Alliances.

INFORMATIONAL PROGRAM CONTRACT
Letter of Adherence • Single Production Only

Company: _____ Phone: ( )_____

Street Address: _____

City: _____ State: _____ Zip: _____

FINANCIAL STRUCTURE

    Corporation: ☐   Partnership: ☐   10% or more owner: ☐

    Joint Venture ☐   Sole Owner: ☐   DBA: ☐

If corporation, name of state in which Corporation is registered: _____

If corporation, names of officers and principal owners: _____

List names of Partners or Joint Ventures: _____

TITLE OF PRODUCTION: _____

COMPENSATION (Writing and/or Designing Services): _____

LENGTH OF PROGRAM (In Minutes): _____

WRITER(S) EMPLOYED UNDER THIS CONTRACT

Name: _____ SS#: _____

Name: _____ SS#: _____

On behalf of the writers(s) employed on the above-named Interactive Program, the undersigned Interactive Program Producer hereby agrees to make contributions to the Producers-Writers Guild of America Pension Plan("Plan") and the Writers Guild-Industry Health Fund ("Fund") as set forth in Article 17 of the 1998 Writers Guild of America Theatrical and Television Basic Agreement ("the 1998 WGA MBA"), by reference incorporated herein and available on request. Producer agrees to be bound by the terms and conditions of the Plan Agreement and the Fund's Trust Agreement. No other terms of the 1998 WGA MBA shall apply to the employment of such writer(s). Currently, the contribution rates set forth in Article 17 are six percent(6%) of gross compensation for writing services to the Plan and six and one-half percent (6.5%) of gross compensation for writing services to the Fund.

Accepted and Agreed:

_____   _____
         (Company)   (Date)

By:_____   _____
          (Signature)   (Print Name and Title)

         **WRITERS GUILD OF AMERICA, WEST, INC. on behalf
of itself and its affiliate, WRITERS GUILD OF AMERICA, EAST, INC.**

     By: _____

            ---FOR OFFICE USE ONLY---

Accepted this ___day of _____, 19____, Producers-Writers Guild of America Pension Plan and Writers

Guild Industry Health Fund. By: _____ Title_____

RETURN COMPLETED FORM TO: FOR QUESTIONS CALL:

Signatories Department   (323) 782-4514
Writers Guild of America, west, Inc.
7000 West Third Street, Los Angeles, California 90048

Figure 13-2
"Informational Program Contract," reprinted with permission of the
Writers Guild of America, west, Inc., Department of Industry Alliances.

Documentary Format

A *double-column format* is often used for documentary scripts, news-oriented programs, commercials, and other projects requiring a running narrative, such as public service announcements.

This format breaks the script into two columns. One is for video, the other is for audio. Generally, every camera direction, scene description, and stage direction is capitalized. Only the dialogue remains in lowercase letters.

ENDNOTES

1. Alexander Kippen, "Writing for The Simpsons," *Creative Screenwriting*, November 1999, 66–68.
2. Ibid., 66.
3. John W. Kim, "Interview: Matt Groening and David X. Cohen: Keep Them Laughing," *Scr(i)pt*, September 1999, 38–41.
4. Ibid., 41.
5. Ibid., 40.
6. Ibid.
7. Terry Borst and Deborah Todd, "Excuse Me While I Kiss the Web," *Written By*, December/January 2000, 70.
8. Ibid., 72.
9. Ibid.

14

Television Drama Format

Writing Spec TV Drama Scripts

The same wisdom about not writing a spec script for the sitcom you want to work for holds true about writing spec scripts for a different current drama series than the one you write want to for. The series producers know the production crises and past, present, and future needs of the show, so don't write for them The only production company that is currently willing to look at scripts written directly for it is "Star Trek: Voyager."

Choose a one-hour show from any similar dramatic series. Watch the series regularly and analyze the leads, dramatic crisis, and pacing. Tape the show to find the right creative choices and act structure. And get sample produced dramatic television scripts from sources like *Script City*, or *Larry Edmunds Books* (see Chapters 8 and 11 for more information).

When you're writing a dramatic spec script, keep the scenes focused around the lead characters, and the right dramatic pacing in your pages. Keep the dialogue sounding like the lead characters.

Act Structure in TV Drama

Many dramatic 60-minute television scripts are broken down into a teaser and four acts of about equal length. Script length should run up to 60 pages.

Television movies of the week or TV features are broken down into seven acts, all of which are about equal length, totaling 90 pages for one-and-a-half hours, or 110 to 120 pages for a two-hour film.

TV Drama Format

If you're writing a script for an episodic drama, miniseries, or television film, then the format is the same as for a motion picture screenplay (see Chapters 8 and 9).

Format Samples for Current TV Drama Series

Here are sample TV formats from current dramatic 60-minute series. These TV script format samples are reprinted with permission of the software program Final Draft, Inc. The script notes for the shows are reprinted as text before the format sample.

"ER"

"ER" is made up of a teaser and four acts. Note how interior scenes are not prefixed with "INT." This is not the case for exterior scenes, which are prefixed with "EXT." The "ER" script sample follows and is reprinted with permission of the software program Final Draft, Inc.

ER—"Episode Name Here"   Date   1.

ER
"DAYS LIKE THIS"
TEASER

FADE IN:

ER/ADMISSIONS AREA

GREENE pushes through the crowd and walks over to CARTER, as action happens in wonderfully descriptive prose.

                                                      (CONTINUED)

CONTINUED:

                    GREENE
Says some smart dialogue. Says some even more outrageously smart dialogue, intermixed with thick medical jargon.

                    CARTER
Comes out with some huge, long medical term.

                    GREENE
Says some smart dialogue. Says some even more outrageously smart dialogue.

                    CARTER
Continues.

And action goes here.

                                        CUT TO:

ER/ADMISSIONS AREA

CHARACTERS go here in ALL CAPS, as does the pushing of gur-
neys past aimless extras, nurses, and doctors.

MORGENSTERN, BENTON, WEAVER arrive and discuss incoming
patients.

                    MORGENSTERN
Comes out with some huge, long medical term.

                    BENTON
                (to Weaver)
Smartass reply.
                                        (CONTINUED)

CONTINUED:

                                MORGENSTERN
                               (to Benton)
Continues.

                                BENTON
Continues.

                                WEAVER
Blah, blah.

Benton exits, as does Morgenstern.

                                GREENE
And he continues with a wonderful speech about saving lives.

Off Weaver's look—   SMASH CUT TO:

MAIN TITLES.

FADE OUT.

<u>END OF TEASER</u>

ER–"Episode Name Here"   Date 2.

<u>ACT ONE</u>

FADE IN:

ER/MAIN HALLWAY - 9:45 AM

Action goes here describing a huge foul-up in the hallway.

                                                  (CONTINUED)

CONTINUED:

ADMISSIONS DESK

Characters walk past and action continues. Weaver walks over to
Greene, who is talking to a patient.

> WEAVER
>> Blah, blah.

> GREENE
>> Blah, blah. Blah, blah.

FADE OUT

<u>END OF ACT ONE</u>

ER–"Episode Name Here"   Date   3.

<u>ACT TWO</u>

FADE IN:

DOCTORS'/NURSES' STATION

The doctors congregate and discuss an important patient.

> BENTON
>> Medical terms . . .

> GREENE
>> Observant reply.

EXT. BASKETBALL COURT - NIGHT

Action continues: Ross walks over to Greene, who is about to shoot
a basket.

> ROSS
>> Blah, blah.

"Law & Order"

"Law & Order" consists of a teaser and four acts. The "Law & Order" script format sample follows and is reprinted with permission of the software program Final Draft, Inc.

<u>1.</u>

<u>LAW & ORDER</u>

<u>"TITLE OF YOUR EPISODE"</u>

<u>ACT ONE</u>

FADE IN:

INT. MCCOY'S OFFICE - DAY

McCoy and Ross are watching the five o'clock news on TV—A senator is giving a statement.

> SENATOR (ON TV)
> Here we go again. Another one of these "script samples."

If you see any script notes, they contain useful information, so view them; this is one right here . . . Action is standard one-hour TV format, and looks like this:

McCoy turns off the TV.

> MCCOY
> Unbelievable!

> ROSS
> How can they do it?

> MCCOY
> All those cool templates?

When hitting the end of an act, choose End of Act by holding down the Control Key and pressing the number (8). Type in whatever act number it is, then simply hit Enter, which will take you to a new page and the start of a new act. Then, hit the Enter key, which will insert a "fade in" for you. Then hit Enter again, and you're at the start of a new slugline.

FADE OUT

END OF TEASER

2.

ACT ONE

FADE IN:

INT. PRECINCT - INTERVIEW ROOM - DAY

Mrs. Cahan sits at the table looking shell-shocked. Van Buren enters and gently closes the door.

VAN BUREN
Did you know that your son is creating nine new templates to add to another growing collection of TV templates?

MRS. CAHAN
I know . . . He told me he was a genius . . .

VAN BUREN
Modesty apart, what other plans does he have?

MRS. CAHAN
Ahh, now that would be telling.

Schiff enters and stands next to Van Buren.

                        SCHIFF
          Is she spilling the beans?

Notice how the character's dialogue, when broken up by action, is
not followed by a (CONT'D).

                    SCHIFF (CONT'D)
          Ask her what she said . . .

                                                        CUT TO:

INT. COURTROOM, CIVIL TERM - DAY

The judge raises his gavel.

                    JUDGE BARCLAY
          This court is adjourned until tomorrow morning.

Off his gavel—   FADE OUT

                    END OF ACT ONE

                        3.

                    ACT TWO

FADE IN:

INT. HOSPITAL CORRIDOR

Curtis is talking with a doctor, when Ross comes up behind him.

                        ROSS
          Blah, blah.

                         CURTIS
        Blah, blah, blah . . .

Off his dirty look—   CUT TO:

INT. INTERROGATION ROOM – DAY

Briscoe and Curtis are chatting with two Intelligence Division
Detectives, WATSON and HOLMES.

                         WATSON
        We got the guys who blew up the World Trade Center.

                         HOLMES
        It was elementary, really . . .

                         BRISCOE
        Nice to know you guys are doing such a great job.

                         CURTIS
        Yeah, we can all rest easy in our beds, right?

                                            FADE OUT

                    END OF ACT FOUR

"NYPD Blue"

    NYPD Blue is split up into four acts. Notice how the main titles barely
interrupt the flow of Act One. The "NYPD Blue" script format sample
follows and is reprinted with permission of the software program Final
Draft, Inc.

NYPD BLUE   "Episode Name Here"   First Draft 1.

<u>ACT ONE</u>

FADE IN:

INT. INTERVIEW ROOM - MORNING

When introducing regular characters, there is no need to put them in all caps. Only new characters, such as DENNY WHITE—black, forties, suburban, frazzled.

If you see any script notes, they contain useful information. Double-click the ScriptNote symbol to view it.

> SIMONE
> Says some smart dialogue. Says some even more outrageously smart dialogue.

> WHITE
> Equally loud and snazzy reply.

> SIMONE
> An even smarter reply.

> SIPOWICZ
> Monosyllabic utterance.

White gives a sheepish nod of acknowledgment.

> MARTINEZ
> Blah, blah.

                                                      CUT TO:

NYPD BLUE   "Episode Name Here"   First Draft   2.

INT. OBSERVATION ROOM - SAME MOMENT

Martinez and Medavoy are watching all this with a mix of professional duty, personal admiration, and sheer merry entertainment.

> WHITE
> I don't know her name.

> SIMONE
> (taking notes)
> What did she look like?

> WHITE
> Nice looking, dark-skinned black. You know . . . pretty.

Off Sipowicz, getting a load of this guy—   CUT TO:

INT. SQUAD ROOM - DAY

And the action continues in the squad room.

> MARTINEZ
> Earthy remark.

> MEDAVOY
> (laughs)
> Pithy reply.

Off them, chuckling—   SMASH CUT TO:

MAIN TITLES

EXT. ALLEY - DAY

As they enter the alley—

NYPD BLUE   "Episode Name Here"   First Draft   3.

SIMONE
And the tough language continues . . .

SIPOWICZ
And continues.

Action split up his dialogue, and notice the (CONT'D). Final Draft in version 4.1.1 puts it in automatically for you.

SIPOWICZ (CONT'D)
And the tough language continues.

SIMONE
And continues.

FADE OUT

END OF ACT ONE

"Star Trek: Voyager"

Voyager is split into a teaser followed by five acts. The "Star Trek: Voyager" script format sample follows and is reprinted with permission of the software program Final Draft, Inc.

VOYAGER: "Name of Episode"   Date   TEASER   1.

STAR TREK: VOYAGER

"NAME OF EPISODE"

TEASER

FADE IN:

(CONTINUED)

VOYAGER: "Name of Episode"   Date   TEASER   2.

CONTINUED:

EXT. SPACE - VOYAGER (OPTICAL)

in orbit of a planet.

                    JANEWAY (V.O.)
          Captain's Log, Stardate 49655.2. We're presently in
          orbit around Final Draft, a small planet in the B.C.
          quadrant.

EXT. PLANET SURFACE

In a sun-dappled glade, PARIS and NEELIX are picking flowers.

                    NEELIX
          Smell that, Tom. Isn't it exhilarating?

Neelix walks over to some flowers and plants.

                    NEELIX (CONT'D)
          Don't you think these are beautiful, Tom?

                    PARIS
          I wouldn't go that far.

OFF Neelix—   CUT TO:

EXT. SPACE - VOYAGER (OPTICAL)

still in orbit . . .

INT. BRIDGE

                                                  (CONTINUED)

VOYAGER: "Name of Episode"   Date   TEASER   3.

CONTINUED:

PARIS is sitting at the bridge console. JANEWAY enters and goes
over to TUVOK, stationed at the science console.

> JANEWAY
> Problem, Mr. Tuvok?

> TUVOK
> There seems to be a small cloud off to our port bow,
> Captain.

> JANEWAY
> Port bow?

> TUVOK
> Yes . . . it's to the left!

FADE OUT

END OF TEASER

VOYAGER: "Name of Episode"   Date   ACT ONE   4.

ACT ONE

FADE IN:

INT. TRANSPORTER ROOM

Moments later. Kim and Kes step up to the transporter pad.

> KES
> Warm sweet line.

(CONTINUED)

VOYAGER: "Name of Episode"   Date   ACT ONE   5.

CONTINUED:

                          KIM
          Replies bravely.

Kim steps up onto the Transporter pad.

                     KIM (CONT'D)
          When a character continues after action, (CONT'D) is
          not required.

                   JANEWAY'S COM VOICE
          Have a nice trip.

They all smile.

                          KES
          And the dialogue continues.

                          KIM
          And continues.

                          KES
          Blah, blah, blah . . .

And more action goes here.

                          KIM
          Blah, blah, blah.

                                        FADE OUT

                    END OF ACT ONE

VOYAGER: "Name of Episode"   Date   ACT TWO   6.

<u>ACT TWO</u>

FADE IN:

INT. BRIDGE

Janeway, Kim, Paris, Neelix, Chakotay, Tuvok, Kes react to the end of the show. They all turn to camera, and wave.

                         KES
          And they all share a warm story.

                         KIM
          Chips in with a wry observation.

                       CHAKOTAY
                        (smiles)
          Let's get back to work!

And he moves off to the science station.

                        PARIS
          Lets rip with a pithy one liner.

                        TUVOK
          Doesn't get it.

                       JANEWAY
          Rounds off the discussion with a wonderful, com-
          passionate speech about peace, love, and under-
          standing.

They all share a moment . . .

                                        FADE OUT

VOYAGER: "Name of Episode"   Date ACT ONE   7.

CONTINUED:

END OF ACT TWO

THE END

"The X-Files"

   "The X-Files" starts with a teaser. "The X-Files" script format sample follows and is reprinted with permission of the software program Final Draft, Inc.

1.

TEASER

EXT. OREGONIAN FOREST - NIGHT

We see a bright light, which is illuminating the forest quite well considering how dark a forest can get, but the source of the light is not visible—it is hidden by the trees. There is a fierce wind that is beginning to bend everything in its path. From off in the distance, we see a figure running at a speed so fast that if it hit a tree, the tree would be uprooted.

As the figure gets closer, we see that the figure is a girl, most likely in her teens, and she is covered by some sort of sticky goo. As she darts past the camera, taking a few small branches with her, we see why she is running. Two uncommonly statuesque figures are pursuing her. And although they are moving as fast as the girl, perhaps even a little faster, they don't appear to be running at all. They are gliding, and they are definitely gaining on the young girl.

GIRL
(out of breath, but screaming anyway)
Somebody help me! Somebody help me, please!

Just then, in true helpless, horror-movie-victim fashion, she trips on a branch that is part of a tree trunk growing out of the ground. She falls and hits her head on another tree on the way down, and lands on her stomach. She is injured but not yet unconscious, as we switch to:

GIRL'S P.O.V.

Everything is slightly darker than our original perspective, and things are going in and out of focus. The girl looks at her arms and hands, which are now covered with leaves, which have apparently stuck to the goo she is covered in. We see the girl roll over, and the two statuesque pursuers suddenly fill our view. They seem even larger than before, being so close. Just as things go into sharp focus again, we see both of the pursuers begin to reach out for the girl as things begin to become blurry and fade as we:

<u>END TEASER</u>

2.

<u>ACT ONE</u>

EXT. OFFICE BUILDING - DAY

We are outside looking at a large office building wondering where we are as a title comes across the bottom of the screen:

FBI HEADQUARTERS - WASHINGTON, D.C.

Since nothing is going on outside the building, we cut to:

INT. FBI HEADQUARTERS - DAY

Mulder and Scully are walking down a long hallway inside FBI headquarters. At the end of the hall, they come to a door marked "Agent Skinner." They open the door, and we are:

INT. SKINNER'S OFFICE - MORNING

Skinner is sitting in his chair with his back to the door. Upon hearing the door open, he spins, sees Mulder and Scully, and rises to his feet.

                    SKINNER
              (coming around desk)
    Agents Mulder and Scully, come on in.

                    MULDER
    What's up, sir?

                    SKINNER
    Well, it looks like you two are going back to Oregon
    again.

                    SCULLY
    What is it this time?

Well, we think you get the point. We've included a small list of characters for this show, since the recurring characters are few and far
between, and Deep Throat and Mr. X are both dead. There is, of
course, Mulder and Scully, the main characters, and their superior,
Skinner. Other recurring characters include the elusive Kyrcek (also
known as Ratboy by many), Cancer Man (Cigarette Smoking Man,
if you prefer), and the editors of The Lone Gunman, Byers, Langly,
and Frohike. Also, Max Fennig, from the Fallen Angel episode, whom
Chris Carter said might return (perhaps you could influence him
on this matter). Also included are common sluglines, such as the
FBI building, and others such as:

INT. MULDER'S APARTMENT - DAY

And

INT. MULDER'S APARTMENT - NIGHT

Or

INT. SCULLY'S APARTMENT - DAY

Also

INT. SCULLY'S APARTMENT - NIGHT

Other than those, the show takes place in so many different locations that there aren't really any standard locations. Well, that about covers it. Good luck, and remember:

<u>THE END</u>

15

How to Write Professional Scenes in TV Drama

Action, Characters, and Dialogue in TV Drama

In TV drama, the scenes are written much like films or motion picture screenplays. Every scene has rich visualization, describing specific visual action, character action, and reactions. The scenes are part of a visual sequence that builds the pacing of the script.

Dramatic action series have their own lead characters, which have their own unique dialogue patterns and reactions. Think about the different characters and dialogue in series such as "ER," "NYPD Blue," "Law & Order," "The X-Files," and "Star Trek: Voyager." The characters must maintain that uniqueness and credibility all through the script.

Pacing starts quickly in the teaser, or at the beginning of Act One, and builds dramatically in each act. The acts are well structured, with the action building throughout.

Sample from "Star Trek: Voyager"

Let's look at a shooting script from "Star Trek: Voyager," entitled "Life Line," story by John Bruno and Robert Picardo, teleplay by Robert Doherty and Raf Green. The "Star Trek: Voyager" script is reprinted with permission of Richard D. Lindheim, Paramount TV Group.

The "A" story is set up early in Act One when the Doctor learns that Louis Zimmerman, a father of modern holographic technology, who invented the matrix that made his program possible, is acutely ill. The Doctor's driving force is quickly set up to save the man who created him. But there are problems getting there, and Zimmerman, himself, is too self-centered to get help from the Doctor—a most difficult patient.

The teaser and Act One follow and are reprinted with permission of Richard D. Lindheim, Paramount TV Group.

VOYAGER: "Life Line"   2/3/00   TEASER   1.

<u>STAR TREK: VOYAGER</u>

<u>"LIFE LINE"</u>

<u>TEASER</u>

FADE IN:

1   EXT. SPACE - JUPITER STATION (OPTICAL)   1

A large Federation complex in orbit of the massive, swirling gas giant.

2   NEW ANGLE (OPTICAL)   2

A small Starfleet SHUTTLECRAFT flies into view . . .

3   INT. SHUTTLECRAFT   3

REG BARCLAY is at the helm, dressed in a Starfleet uniform. (NOTE: This is a RE-USE of our existing Shuttlecraft set.)

                    BARCLAY
                    (to com)
      Shuttlecraft Dawkins to Jupiter Station.

                    COM VOICE
      Go ahead.

                    BARCLAY
      This is Lieutenant Reginald Barclay . . . requesting
      permission to dock.

                                        (CONTINUED)

VOYAGER: "Life Line" 2/3/00 TEASER 2.

3 CONTINUED: 3

> COM VOICE
> Granted. (BEAT) How are you, Reg? It's me . . . Bob.

> BARCLAY
> How are you, Bob?

> COM VOICE
> Well, thanks. Long time no see.

> BARCLAY
> All work and no play.

> COM VOICE
> What brings you to this part of the solar system?

> BARCLAY
> Oh . . . just . . . visiting an old friend.

OFF Barclay . . . his expression tells us that something is troubling him . . .

CUT TO:

4 AN IGUANA 4

sitting on a desktop cluttered with PADDs, tricorders, a desk-top monitor, etc. (As we'll learn, this lizard is holographic, but it looks perfectly real at the moment.) We hear a door CHIME. A beat, then it CHIMES again.

> ZIMMERMAN (O.C.)
> What? What is it?

> BARCLAY'S COM VOICE
> It's . . . it's me, sir . . . Reg Barclay.

(CONTINUED)

VOYAGER: "Life Line" 2/3/00 TEASER 3.

4 CONTINUED: 4

> ZIMMERMAN (O.C.)
> Yes, yes, yes . . . come in.

REVEAL we are in—

5 INT. JUPITER STATION - HOLOGRAPHIC RESEARCH LAB 5

A state-of-the-art Starfleet research facility, with a smattering of unusual touches—the lizard, artwork, a couple of lab coats draped over a work station, an antique chair, etc. This room is the domain of Dr. Zimmerman, an eccentric holo-engineer. The doors slide open and Barclay ENTERS. It's been several months since he's been here, and he's a little nervous. He stops when he sees someone off-camera.

> BARCLAY
> Doctor Z.

6 NEW ANGLE - DOCTOR LOUIS ZIMMERMAN 6

An intense, irritable but brilliant holo-engineer—a dead inger for Voyager's Doctor. (NOTE: This character is played by Bob Picardo.) At the moment, he looks gaunt and unshaven, and he has streaks of gray in his hair. He eyes Barclay.

> ZIMMERMAN
> (wry)
> Nice of you to finally drop by.

> BARCLAY
> (awkward)
> I've . . . I've been extremely busy . . . the Pathfinder Project.

(CONTINUED)

6   CONTINUED: 6

                         ZIMMERMAN
        Are you still searching for that ship? What's it called
        . . . Pioneer?

                         BARCLAY
        Voyager.

                         ZIMMERMAN
        Any luck?

                         BARCLAY
        Actually . . . we're on the verge of a breakthrough
        . . . a communications link . . .

                         ZIMMERMAN
        Congratulations!
                         (sarcastic)
        The first transgalactic phone call.

        A beat . . . then Barclay takes a step toward him, concerned . . .
        not sure how to broach the subject.

                         BARCLAY
        Any . . . word from Starfleet Medical?

                         ZIMMERMAN
        Doctors! I've been scanned and probed and injected
        a hundred times . . . and they still can't tell me what's
        wrong!

                         BARCLAY
        I'm . . . I'm sure it's only a matter of time before
        they—
                                              (CONTINUED)

VOYAGER: "Life Line"   2/3/00   TEASER   3.

6   CONTINUED: 6

                          ZIMMERMAN
                    (cuts him off, irate)
          I'm dying, Reg! It doesn't take Jonas Salk to tell me
          that! And there's nothing anybody can do about it!

OFF the moment . . .

                                                      FADE OUT

                        END OF TEASER

VOYAGER: "Life Line"   2/3/00   ACT ONE   4.

                          ACT ONE

FADE IN:

     (NOTE: Episode credits fall over opening scenes.)

7   EARTH (OPTICAL)   7

     The familiar big blue marble. We HEAR a complex series of
     TONES—what we'll learn is a DATA STREAM being transmit-
     ted by Starfleet Command.

                                                      CUT TO:

8   EXT. SPACE - THE MIDAS ARRAY (OPTICAL)   8

     A large relay station hanging in space (as seen in the episode
     "Pathfinder"). We HEAR the DATA STREAM from Earth. As the
     array LIGHTS UP with POWER . . . the data stream gets
     LOUDER, and the tonal modulations become more rapid . . .

                                                      CUT TO:

9   EXT. SPACE - A PULSAR (OPTICAL)   9

A bright, compact SPHERE of ENERGY spinning rapidly, surrounded by swirling gas and dust. Again, we HEAR the DATA
STREAM . . . and now it RISES in PITCH . . .

                                                    CUT TO:

10   EXT. SPACE - VOYAGER (OPTICAL)   10

In the far distance, moving toward us. As the ship draws closer
. . . we can HEAR the high-pitched DATA STREAM, which is
now heavily FRITZED . . .

                                                    CUT TO:

11   INT. ASTROMETRICS LAB   11

SEVEN OF NINE is working at a station. A quiet moment, then
. . . beep-beep-beep . . . beep-beep-beep! A console sounds an
alarm. Seven moves to the main controls, works. A beat, then
we HEAR the DATA STREAM, fritzed and crackling. Seven eyes
the readings . . . reacts.

                        SEVEN OF NINE
                        (taps combage)
            Seven of Nine to Bridge.

INTERCUT:

12   INT. BRIDGE   12

JANEWAY, CHAKOTAY, TUVOK, PARIS, KIM, N.D.s at their
stations.

                                              (CONTINUED)

VOYAGER: "Life Line"   2/3/00   ACT ONE   6.

CONTINUED: 12

> JANEWAY
> (to com)
>
> Go ahead.

> SEVEN OF NINE
>
> We're receiving a transmission . . . from Starfleet.

Reactions.

> JANEWAY
>
> Route it here.

Seven works a beat . . .

13   INCLUDE - THE DOMESCREEN (OPTICAL)   13

It COMES ALIVE with a CHAOTIC JUMBLE of images, alphanu-
merics, graphics—all of it fragmented and fritzing.

> SEVEN OF NINE
>
> It's not a comlink, Captain . . . it appears to be a com-
> pressed data stream . . . badly degraded.
> (works)
> I'm clearing it up, now.

> JANEWAY
>
> On my way.

Janeway glances at Chakotay and they head for the door. OFF the
image of the DATA STREAM on the Domescreen . . . fritzing and
scrolling . . .

CUT TO:

14   INT. BRIEFING ROOM (VPB)   14

Janeway addressing the crew—Chakotay, Tuvok, Paris, Kim, TORRES, the DOCTOR, NEELIX, and Seven of Nine. There's a sense of excitement in the air. Janeways sets a PADD on the table.

                        JANEWAY
        Good things come in small packages.
                      (re: PADD)
        Seventy-four megaquads of data, to be exact. That's
        all Starfleet could send us . . . until next month.

                        TORRES
        Next month?

Chakotay taps a control by the wall monitor, which displays a GRAPHIC of a PULSAR seen earlier.

                        CHAKOTAY
                      (re: monitor)
        They're using a cyclic pulsar to amplify a signal from
        the MIDAS Array . . . but the cycle only peaks every
        thirty-two days.

                        JANEWAY
                      (off that)
        Once a month, we'll be able to receive a short burst
        of information . . . and we'll only have seventeen
        hours to respond.

                                        (CONTINUED)

14   CONTINUED: 14

Reactions—this is big news.

> JANEWAY
> I want to caution you against getting too excited . . .
> this process is highly experimental . . .

A beat as she studies their faces. She can't help but smile.

> JANEWAY
> (lightly)
> What the hell . . . get excited.

There's a spontaneous eruption of enthusiasm:

> EVERYONE
> (overlapping)
> It's about time! . . . What'd they say? . . . Any let-
> ters? . . . I can't believe it . . . One step closer . . .
> etc.

> CHAKOTAY
> (cutting in, to all)
> So far, we've gotten tactical upgrades . . . letters from
> home . . . news about the Alpha Quadrant . . .

> KIM
> I don't suppose they found us a shortcut home?

> CHAKOTAY
> It doesn't look that way.

                                        (CONTINUED)

VOYAGER: "Life Line"   2/3/00   ACT ONE   9.

14   CONTINUED: (2)   14

                    PARIS
                 (with humor)
        Any Holodeck programs?

                  CHAKOTAY
        We'll know soon enough.

He glances at Seven.

                SEVEN OF NINE
                  (off that)
        I'll need several hours to process the remaining data.

                   JANEWAY
                   (to all)
        We don't have much time to prepare a response . . .
        and we'll have to keep it short. But I want to give
        everyone an opportunity to send something . . . even
        if it's only a brief note. Inform the crew.

                  EVERYONE
                (overlapping)
        Aye, Captain . . . Yes, Ma'am . . . Right away . . . etc.

Janeway eyes her people.

                   JANEWAY
        The Pathfinder Project . . . Lieutenant Barclay . . .
        they didn't give up on us.
                   (light)
        When you write those letters . . . you might want to
        thank them.

                                          (CONTINUED)

VOYAGER: "Life Line"   2/3/00   ACT ONE   10.

14   CONTINUED: (3)   14

As everyone swings into action . . .

                                                        CUT TO:

15   EXT. SPACE - VOYAGER (OPTICAL)   15
     at impulse.

16   INT. SICKBAY   16

     A short time later. The Doctor is working at a station when
     Neelix ENTERS, holding a small stack of PADDs.

                          NEELIX
         Mail call!

The Doctor turns. Neelix hands him a PADD.

                          DOCTOR
                        (surprised)
           A letter . . . for me?

                          NEELIX
           It's got your name on it. "Voyager EMH."

                          DOCTOR
                        (delighted)
         Who's it from?

                          NEELIX
           I'm not sure. Why don't you read it and find out.

The Doctor looks pleased, taps a control on the PADD . . . starts
reading.
                                                   (CONTINUED)

VOYAGER: "Life Line"   2/3/00   ACT ONE   11.

16   CONTINUED: 16

> DOCTOR
> (off PADD)
> It's from Lieutenant Barclay . . .

He reads further . . . reacts with dismay.

> NEELIX
> Bad news?

> DOCTOR
> Louis Zimmerman . . . apparently, he's seriously ill.

> NEELIX
> Zimmerman?

> DOCTOR
> He's the father of modern holographic technology . . .
> he invented the matrix that made my program
> possible . . .

> NEELIX
> (re: PADD)
> What's wrong with him?

> DOCTOR
> (reads)
> ". . . suffering from acute subcellular degradation. The
> doctors here are having trouble finding the cause,
> much less a treatment. I was hoping you could exam-
> ine this medical data and give us a second opinion. I
> know it's a long shot . . . but maybe your unique expe-
> rience could provide some insights."

(CONTINUED)

VOYAGER: "Life Line"   2/3/00   ACT ONE   12.

16   CONTINUED: (2)   16

They take this in, troubled.

                         NEELIX
          Shame.
                         (beat)
          Did you know him?

                         DOCTOR
          No . . . I've never met the man.

The Doctor looks a little shell-shocked. Neelix prompts him
gently . . .

                         NEELIX
          The Captain needs everyone to submit their responses
          by nineteen hundred hours.

                         DOCTOR
                         (nods)
          I'd better get started.

                         NEELIX
          Good luck.

Neelix turns to go. As the Doctor moves to a console and starts
working . . .

                                                  CUT TO:

17   EXT. SPACE - VOYAGER (OPTICAL)   17

          at impulse.

18   ON LOUIS ZIMMERMAN (VPB)   18

A photo-image on a MONITOR of the man during healthier times,
surrounded by various medical data, including a graphic of CELL
STRUCTURES. REVEAL we're in—

19   INT. SICKBAY - MEDLAB (VPB)   19

The Doctor is working at the monitor, intent. Seven of Nine
ENTERS . . . hands him a PADD.

                        SEVEN OF NINE
          The information you requested.

                        DOCTOR
          Thank you.

He studies the PADD with interest. Seven glances at the monitor.

                        SEVEN OF NINE
          Any progress?

                        DOCTOR
          I've found a slight abnormality in his cell membranes
          . . . it might be due to a defective protein sequence
          . . . or exposure to some unusual form of radiation.

He studies the PADD.

                                            (CONTINUED)

VOYAGER: "Life Line"   2/3/00   ACT ONE   14.

19   CONTINUED: 19

> DOCTOR
> (re: PADD)
> I was hoping these Borg regeneration techniques would provide a temporary means of restoring his cell structures.

He continues working. Seven eyes the image of Zimmerman.

> SEVEN OF NINE
> You bear a striking resemblance.

> DOCTOR
> He used his own physical parameters as a model for my holo-matrix.
> (light)
> Can't say I blame him . . . a doctor needs to inspire confidence in his patients. Compassionate eyes and a strong chin can go a long way.

Seven shoots him a look. The Doctor works the monitor.

> DOCTOR
> (off monitor)
> I wish I knew his (TECH) membrane ratios. I need to run a new series of scans . . .

> SEVEN OF NINE
> That might be difficult.

(CONTINUED)

> DOCTOR
> You're telling me.
> (frustrated)
> I can only do so much . . . I can't treat a patient I
> can't examine!

> SEVEN OF NINE
> Perhaps you could examine him . . .

He looks at her.

At the beginning of Act Two, the Doctor has problems to overcome. Seven of Nine informs him that his program is too big to handle all his mindset, and that Dr. Zimmerman requires only medical insight, not his sensitivity. But the Doctor insists on maintaining his individuality, although there may be some degradation. In Engineering, Janeway and Torres work separate consoles, and Seven activates the transceiver.

We see the visual entry from space in optical illusion. Then we see the Doctor zimmer into space in optical illusion for a time cut. In Jupiter Station, we see Zimmerman with an assistant, Hannah, who is a hologram. The Doctor zimmers into view, eager to see and help his creator. But Zimmerman wants nothing to do with him.

Soap, Talk Show, and Variety

Writing Soaps

One of daytime television's best-known writers, Thom Racina, discusses how to break into and thrive in the soap market.[1] Racina was Head Writer of "General Hospital," "Days Of Our Lives," "Another World," "Generations," and "Santa Barbara," and is now writing thriller novels. He mentions how important it is to know the history of every show. "I did "General Hospital," and I learned pretty quickly, but when I was done there and went to "Days of Our Lives," I had two weeks to learn the show. Sometimes you get writers not knowing certain things about the characters."[2] He says that he learns a new show by reading documents given to the Head Writer about the history of the show, as well as by discussing it with fans.

When asked what advice he has for someone who wants to get into writing soaps, Racina recalls his advice to students at a seminar at UCLA: "Are you all crazy . . .Why do you want your words flushed down the toilet? . . . Get rid of your egos; get rid of loving anything you do. My first advice is to run, go somewhere else . . . You'll be a lot happier, a lot more creative. But if you love soaps, if you grew up on them, if they're in your blood . . . then you should do it, because you might be able to make a really great living."[3]

Format Samples for Current TV Soaps

Here are sample TV formats from current soap series. These TV script format samples are reprinted with permission of the software program Final Draft, Inc. The script notes for the shows are reprinted as text before the format sample.

"Days of Our Lives"

"Days of Our Lives" scripts have three transitions here with triple spaces between them. Type in the text, then go up to TEXT to SPACE BEFORE. The "Days of our Lives" script format sample follows and is reprinted with permission of the software program Final Draft, Inc. Dialogue should appear double spaced.

TEASER

FADE IN:

MARLENA'S HOUSE – NEW DAY, ABOUT 8 A.M.

(NOTE THAT ALL ACTION TAKES PLACE IN PARENTHESES AND IS IN ALL CAPS. WE USE THE ACTION ELEMENT AND MANUAL TYPING IN THE PARENTHESES.)

MARLENA

Dialogue is always double spaced in Days of Our Lives

scripts.

(DEFIANT)

And any action between dialogue is also in parethe-

ses, left justified.

STEFANO

You always have to be a stickler for details.

MARLENA

But this helps the writer, Stefano. And we know how

much you love to help people.

STEFANO

Except you.

(STEFANO LAUGHS AND STARES AT HER IN ALL HIS EVIL.)

CUT TO:

PARK

(YOU CAN USE EITHER THE SLUG LINE OR ACT AND SCENE HEAD-
ING ELEMENTS TO START A SCENE. WE HAVE SET UP THE ACT
AND SCENE HEADING TO AUTOMATICALLY JUMP TO A NEW PAGE,
SO IT MAY BE EASIER TO USE THIS ELEMENT. FURTHERMORE, WE
HAVE SET UP THIS ELEMENT TO BE THE DEFAULT ELEMENT
AFTER THE END OF EACH SCENE BY JUST HITTING 'RETURN.'
SINCE "DAYS OF OUR LIVES" DOESN'T USE SCENE NUMBERS, IT
MAY BE EASIER TO USE INSTEAD OF SLUG LINE.)

(NOTE THAT WE HAVE ALSO SET IT UP SO THAT WHEN YOU HIT
'ENTER,' YOU AUTOMATICALLY GO TO THE ACTION ELEMENT. IF
YOU WANT TO GO TO SLUG LINE AT THE BEGINNING OF A NEW
ACT, MANUALLY GO TO SLUG LINE BY HITTING 'CONTROL' AND
(1). IF YOU NEED A PRINTED SCENE REPORT, HOWEVER, PLACE
ALL SCENE HEADINGS IN THE SLUG LINE ELEMENT.)

(SAMI AND AUSTIN SIT ON A BENCH)

                    SAMI

    I have some dialogue here.

                    AUSTIN

    And I have a response here.

(IF YOU SEE ANY 'SCRIPTNOTES' THEY CONTAIN USEFUL INFOR-
MATION, VIEW THEM; THIS IS ONE RIGHT HERE . . . .)

FADE TO: BLACK

FOR: HOUR GLASS INSERT   (:32)

AND: COMMERCIALS 31 AND #2

                    ACT ONE

FADE IN:

BRADY LIVING ROOM

(ACT NUMBERS IN THE HEADER ARE DENOTED BY ROMAN
NUMERAL. EACH TIME A SCENE CHANGES, PLACE THE CURSOR
AT THE TOP OF THE PAGE AND GO TO THE DOCUMENT MENU TO
'ATTACH HEADER LABEL.' TYPE IN THE ACT NUMBER AND SCENE
NUMBER, THEN CLICK OK. YOU WILL SEE THE NUMBER NEXT TO
THE PAGE NUMBER AT THE TOP RIGHT OF THE PAGE. FOR EXAM-
PLE, THIS PAGE IS MARKED I – 3.)

ERIC

I'm talking to myself here.

(LOOKING AT PICTURE)

. . . and reminiscing.

(SCRIPTS CAN RUN TO ABOUT 75 PAGES OR SO WITH SEVEN ACTS PLUS THE TEASER.)

CUT TO:

BO AND HOPE'S BEDROOM

(BO AND HOPE ARE IN THE MIDST OF A PASSIONATE KISS)

HOPE

(PULLING AWAY) We do a lot of this on daytime.

BO

That's what everyone wants to see.

(THERE ARE GENERALLY ABOUT THREE OR FOUR SCENES PER ACT. AT THE END OF THE EPISODE, WE . . .)

FADE TO: BLACK

CLOSING: UP ON HOUR GLASS

THEME:

MATTTE: CRAWL

"General Hospital"

The General Hospital script format sample follows and is reprinted with permission of the software program Final Draft, Inc. Dialogue should be double spaced.

TEASER

FADE IN:

[A] TOWNHOUSE LIVING ROOM: NEW DAY. AM TO AFTERNOON.

ACTION IS ALL CAPS, AND NOT IN PARENTHESES.

IONA

Dialogue here.

KATHERINE

(EMOTION) Parenthetical emotions are placed on the

same line as dialogue, so the Parenthetical element

is not used, it is created in Dialogue and typed in All

Caps.

DISSOLVE TO: MAIN TITLE

COMMERCIAL #1

ACT 1

FADE IN:

[A] FELICIA'S APARTMENT: IMMEDIATE PICKUP.

COLTON

(EMOTION) Parenthetical emotions are placed on the
same line as dialogue, so the Parenthetical element
is not used, it is created in Dialogue and typed in All
Caps.

ACTION IS ALL CAPS, AND NOT IN PARENTHESES.

FADE OUT:

COMMERCIAL #2

ACT II

FADE IN:

[A] ROBERT'S OFFICE: SHORT TIME LAPSE.

ACTION IS ALL CAPS, AND NOT IN PARENTHESES.

FELICIA

(EMOTION) Parenthetical emotions are placed on the
same line as dialogue, so the Parenthetical element
is not used, it is created in Dialogue and typed in All
Caps.

                                         ANNA
        Dialogue here.

ACTION IS ALL CAPS, AND NOT IN PARENTHESES.

FADE OUT:

COMMERCIAL #7

GENERAL HOSPITAL

CLOSING CREDITS

Talk Show and Variety Format

Talk shows and variety shows are often taped before an audience with a full complement of video cameras for editing. In late-night shows such as "Saturday Night Live," "The Late Show with David Letterman," and "The Tonight Show with Jay Leno," scenes are referred to as *segments*. Each segment is paced carefully for timing. The script conveys the talent requirements, stage blocking, and dialogue for comedy sketches and music.

Because segments are shot in continuity, each is written as a separate unit. SEGMENT ONE appears at the top left-hand corner of the page. SEGMENT TWO follows on a new page when the previous one is over.

Sample Song Segment "The Late Show with David Letterman"

Here's what a sample song segment might look like for a musical segment on "The Late Show with David Letterman." Dialogue should appear double spaced.

                   SAMPLE SONG SEGMENT:
              LATE SHOW WITH DAVID LETTERMAN

                      SEGMENT TWO:
          JASON B. SINGS "WHAT'S THE SENSE"©

(DAVID HOLDS UP JASON'S NEW CD FOR THE AUDIENCE TO SEE, GETS AUDIENCE APPLAUSE. JASON PICKS UP HIS GUITAR, CROSSES

TO THE MAIN SET, AND PLAYS THE OPENING LICKS. PAUL AND
THE BAND BACK HIM UP.)

JASON

(SINGING)

What's the sense of talking

If your talking ain't real talking

And if you don't mean anything you're sayin'?

What's the sense of meaning

If your meaning is deceiving

And your actions don't believe in what you're sayin'. . .

(PAUL SMILES AT THE GREAT GUITAR WORK, CLAPS LOUDLY, AND
THE AUDIENCE BREAKS INTO APPLAUSE.)

© "What's the Sense," music and lyrics by R. Blum, Laurelton Music
& Entertainment. All Rights Reserved.

ENDNOTES

1. Tony Ross, "Writing in Soap: An Interview with Thom Racina,"
   Creative Screenwriting, March/April 2000, 59–63.
2. Ibid., 61.
3. Ibid., 64.

17

How to Create New Television Series

How TV Series Concepts are Developed

Developing new series has been described as television's oldest crapshoot. In the heyday of network programming, the logic—if it could be called that—was to bombard the network with thousands of ideas, and somehow one or two would make it to pilot.

When network executives were aiming for the largest possible audiences, it was logical to ask why they didn't break away from trends rather than imitate them. In the early days of network dominance, a classic theory was proposed by program executive Paul Klein. It was called "L.O.P."—"Least Objectionable Programming." The idea was simple. If a show didn't offend anyone, then it would appeal to the widest possible audience. If ABC came out with a show about a group of singing termites—and if that show went through the roof of ratings' homes—then NBC and CBS would have similar shows in development faster than you could call an exterminator.

But as audiences defected to competitors like Fox, and more heavily to the glitzier, grittier shows on HBO and Showtime, the networks—ABC, CBS, NBC, Fox, UPN, and Warner Bros.—had to pay more attention to smaller, low-budget demographic targets, as well as to specific weaknesses in time periods.

A program development executive receives thousands of submissions each year—in verbal pitches, in written concepts, and in fully detailed presentations. He or she is responsible for bringing new ideas into the network or cable company. Once the show actually gets on the air, then another department takes over—current programming. That department is concerned with time slots, competition, demographic appeal, lead-in and lead-out programs, and other factors that affect ratings performance.

At the networks, job security is about as stable as the changing decimals on the overnight ratings. So, understandably, some executives view innovative program concepts as a threat rather than a challenge. Jobs literally depend on generating ideas that are greeted with enthusiasm by senior management, advertisers, and the whimsical public. If the show is inexpensive and modeled after a highly successful show, then the personal risk is minimized. The executive can always blame the unpredictable tastes of the viewing public.

Does this mean you have to create the same kind of formula programs you see every night? In one sense, yes. In another sense, no. Let me explain. Television is an imitative medium. It thrives on successes and spits out a slew of spinoffs in an effort to reach the same target audiences. We've all experienced the competitive glut of sitcoms, reality-based shows, police dramas, and law shows.

That doesn't mean that new ideas or innovative concepts won't make it to the screen. Each television season brings many examples of shows that break new ground. Consider "X-Files," "Ally McBeal," "The Simpsons," "Law & Order," "NYPD Blue," "ER", and earlier hits such as "Cheers," "Seinfeld," "All in the Family," "Star Trek," and "Miami Vice." The fact is, once the ground is broken, the *imitation syndrome* runs rampant, and we quickly forget that one show was the forerunner of the current trend.

After analyzing the program development deals, this is how *Variety* summed up the trends back in 1993: "Reality-based programming, action hours, and the ghetto as a radical chic locale are all part of the pilot landscape. In addition, nearly every net is casting about for a hit sitcom. The phrase 'next season's "Home Improvement"' was perhaps the most tiresome phrase that tumbles off the tongue of studio execs."[1]

In developing a new concept, it is important to think about the specific target audience that a show can appeal to—program executives will try to fill those demographic voids. For example, in 1993, NBC broke from its long-standing hold on adults ages 18 to 49 by signing development deals with comic John Larroquette, former star of "Night Court." CBS had a strong lineup of "female-skewed" shows, including a second comedy from "Murphy Brown" producers Diane English and Shukovsky Entertainment. One-hour action-adventure shows had more appeal than softer drama series. ABC built up its action lineup for men with Steven Bochco's "NYPD Blue" and Tom Fontana's "Philadelphia Heat." Fox did a complete turnaround from its reliance on younger demographics to develop cop shows, fantasy shows, and Westerns like "The Adventures of Briscoe County, Jr." and "Darkman."

"Put" Pilots

By 1999, because of continued extensive competition among the six broadcast networks and increasing diversity and competition from cable TV venues, a new phenomenon occurred in series development—the "put" pilot. Writers and producers could get a guaranteed commitment for a pilot, without a pilot script. As detailed in *Variety*, "In the TV biz, puts are standard when negotiating for a superstar thesp or writer along the lines of Steven Bochco, Chris Carter or Bruce Helford ("The Drew Carey Show"). NBC raised few eyebrows last week when it inked a blind series deal with Castle Rock to produce six segs of a new laffer produced by a trio of ex-"Seinfeld" writers and starring former "Seinfeld" sidekick Michael Richards. But this season, network bean counters are getting heartburn from much less established players who are starting to snag guaranteed pilots."[2]

NBC Entertainment President Garth Ancier voiced the frustration of all six network entertainment executives at a Hollywood Radio & TV Society panel. He bemoaned the fact that talent now pitches projects "by saying, 'I don't want to develop, I just want to make it.'" As he points out, "The problem with that is that we all have a certain budget to make our shows with, and once you put 'put' pilots out there, you're out of money. . . . I'm very concerned this year that a lot of people won't get a shot to write scripts."[3]

As Ancier adds, "The abundance of puts means less coin to spend on scripts, reducing the chances of finding that unknown voice for a bold new concept. It also sets up a precedent that could be hard to break in the future years."[4]

Series Concepts, Presentations, and Series Bibles

Industry jargon is rife with terminology for series concepts, presentations, and bibles. The terms are often used interchangeably and can be confusing. In this chapter, we'll define them as follows:

- The *concept* is the blueprint for the arena/setting, characters, and conflicts. It is the skeletal premise for the show. It serves as the foundation for the more detailed presentation.
- A *series presentation* is a more developed concept. It includes the concept with arena/setting, characters, pilot story, and sample storylines.
- A *series bible* is the most detailed series information. It includes the fully developed pilot script, detailed character arcs for each lead character, and multipart storylines.

How to Create Marketable Television Series Concepts

To give you a sense of how marketable concepts are developed, here are some strategies that Richard D. Lindheim and I detailed in *Primetime: Network Television Programming*.[5] They have been revised here to incorporate some of the latest series trends. Television professionals acknowledge that ideas are as free as the breeze. The successful execution of ideas is what counts.

What Makes an Effective Series Concept?

These seem to be the key elements for effective series concepts: (1) *the desirability of the inherent idea,* (2) *the ability to sustain the concept over many episodes,* and (3) *internal conflict among series characters.*

The Desirability of the Inherent Idea

The first question usually asked of any new project is: "Why will people watch this show?" In network and cable programming, each series must carve itself a sufficient audience to survive. Networks, especially, demand large audiences, numbering tens of millions, to achieve competitive ratings. New series must be inherently desirable and appealing to draw those potential viewers. Any idea for a series must demonstrate desirability. Specifically, this means a concept should answer affirmatively at least one of the following questions:

1. Is the basic storytelling arena interesting?
Is the idea set in a desirable and exotic locale (e.g., Florida, Hawaii, San Francisco, or the Caribbean)? Does it feature interesting occupations (e.g., deep-sea diver, astronaut, racecar driver, mystery writer, policeman, trial attorney, TV journalist, TV comic, or bar owner)? Does it have the ability to use unusual and fascinating machinery or technology (e.g., special cars, weapons, or high-tech equipment)? Does it lend itself to an interesting visual approach?

2. Does the concept represent some form of wish fulfillment?
In our turbulent society, there are few places where people can turn to satisfy the frustrations of everyday life. Many long-running television series trade upon this frustration by showing a more comforting world, or by focus-

ing on characters we would like to believe exist. We can fantasize about the lifestyle of characters like those in "Touched by an Angel," and on game shows where contestants may win a fortune. "Ally McBeal" deals with quirky personal fantasies, as does the HBO comedy "Sex and the City." Other examples of fantasy shows include "Baywatch," or the classic "Love Boat."

3. Is the concept relatable?

Does the idea feature characters and circumstances we can accept as real? Television series provide us with a sense of verisimilitude, or the appearance of reality. Under these conditions, we accept Mulder and Scully as leads who are justifiably suspicious of the FBI and will do anything to investigate the "X-Files" for the truth out there. We accept the characters in "ER" as a medical team who will do anything to save their patients. We believe "NYPD Blue" is an inside look at real police work in New York, and "Law & Order: SVU" is an inside look at a special victims unit in New York. We believe the "Sopranos" family is filled with rage and self-anger as a quirky Mafia family in New Jersey. We believe the Solomon family members are aliens from the "3rd Rock from the Sun," who will do anything to learn what it's like to be human and to protect their identities. We accept "Coach" as a susceptible character in midlife, who will do anything to succeed. We could accept "Seinfeld" as a standup comic with zany next-door neighbors, and "M*A*S*H" as a realistic war comedy. We accept relatable shows as a mirror of life.

The Ability to Sustain the Concept Over Many Episodes

One of the prime causes of failure in television series is the inability to sustain the premise over the three to five years necessary for financial success. Too often, a network commissions a pilot that seems innovative, only to discover later that it lacks the elements necessary to sustain itself over time.

Frequently, network programmers are attracted to a pilot story that is a *premise pilot*, which shows how the characters get together. It sets the stage for the rest of the series. Unfortunately, it may be a poor indicator of what the series will be. Network development executives want assurances that the expensive pilot they commission will represent the series to come. At NBC and ABC, a rule of thumb was that the first half of the pilot establishes the premise, but the remainder represents a "typical" episode. CBS almost always rejected *premise pilots* in favor of *midcut pilots*. That story is written as if it were being produced for the middle of the series.

Internal Conflict Among Series Characters

An often overlooked but essential ingredient of both drama and comedy series is *internal conflict.* Ally McBeal is a susceptible, emotional over-achiever, who has fantasies of love and is set up for clashes with the other leads. The same is true for lead characters in "The Practice." Murphy Brown was an emotional powerhouse who clashed with anyone in her way.

The necessity for internal conflict fulfills important dramatic needs. Conflict is the simplest way for characters to express their opposing feelings and attitudes. If all of the continuing characters love one another, then all they can do is smile and support each other. That can be boring and saccharine. It fails to provide dramatic tension and fails to provide viewers with insights into the inner life of lead characters.

As discussed in "Plot Patterns" in Chapter 3, the strongest series concepts tend to feature individuals who are trapped in a Group and Family Ties story pattern. Those leads are forced to interact with each other by circumstance. It creates wonderful ongoing internal conflicts for characters featured in shows such as "Malcolm in the Middle," "Friends," "Everybody Loves Raymond," "3rd Rock from the Sun," "The Drew Carey Show," "Ally McBeal," "The Practice," "ER," "Chicago Hope," "Law & Order," "Law & Order: SVU," "NYPD Blue," "Frasier," "Coach," "Veronica's Closet," "90210," and "Melrose Place." It was a classic sitcom setup for "Seinfeld," "Cheers," "Taxi," "Murphy Brown," and "M*A*S*H."

Sample Concept from "Coach"

Let's analyze the series concept for "Coach," which was created by Barry Kemp. Richard D. Lindheim and I discussed the development process for "Coach" and "Law & Order" in our book *Inside Television Producing,* which is now out of print.[6] This concept for "Coach" is reprinted with permission of Richard D. Lindheim. We are planning to write a new book entitled *Law & Order: The Inside Story,* which will detail the development of the pilot.

THE CONCEPT FOR "COACH"

Coach Hayden Fox (Craig T. Nelson) heads the athletic department at Minnesota State University. In his early forties with a perennially losing football team, he recognizes, but is not willing to admit, that the forward progression of his career has ended. His only hope is to meld the disparate team into an effective unit. His only help in this task are the assistant coaches, Luther (Jerry Van Dyke) and Dauber (Bill Fagerbakke). Dauber is also a member of the team and holds the record for being a student at the university for the most number of years.

Coach Fox has been divorced for many years and has had little, if any, contact with his daughter Kelly (Clare Carey). Recently, he has developed a relationship with Minneapolis newscaster Christine (Shelley Fabares).

In the pilot story, Coach Fox learns that his daughter is entering Minnesota State as a freshman. He feels uncomfortable as a father but desperately wants to reestablish a relationship with her. At the same time, he feels awkward about exposing Kelly to his emerging relationship with Christine.

The concept for "Coach" sets up unique character drives, strong potential dramatic conflicts for each of the lead characters, and is set within the setting/arena of a Midwest campus. The Coach is faced with the angst of midlife crisis, needing to succeed at all costs. He is going against his own grain to build nurturing relationships with Christine and Kelly. His girlfriend and daughter become pivotal additions to the potential conflicts in future episodes.

How to Write Original TV Series Presentations

A written series presentation details these elements: (1) *concept (arena/setting)*, (2) *characters*, (3) *pilot story*, and (4) *sample storylines*.

Concept (The Arena/Setting)

The first section of a written series presentation provides a description of the basic arena or setting for the series. Locations are often key elements in setting a TV series. Hawaii has been found to be charming and desirable. Florida is a hot spot. San Francisco has proven to be a favorite for several successful shows. New York is interesting, although expensive. New Orleans is a colorful favorite. Washington, D.C. is an interesting political backdrop (like "West Wing"). Other locales seem less appealing, probably because of production limitations. Chicago is attractive, but it is difficult to film there during the winter. Water (and underwater) shows are highly attractive (like "Seaquest") but very complex to execute on television budgets and schedules.

This is a sample of the concept for a dramatic TV series called "Beltway Bandits," which I created with Frank Tavares. See how it details the arena and setting of Washington, D.C.

BELTWAY BANDITS©

Washington, D.C.—Capital of the free world. Center of government for the richest nation on Earth. Surrounding this powerful city are dozens of suburbs—communities that house the tens of thousands who daily fight the heavy traffic on their way to offices in the federal metropolis—communities connected by hundreds of miles of local highways and expressways, and the infamous Washington Beltway. The Beltway circles the waist of the city, looping in and out of Maryland and Virginia suburbs. Small companies, many of them high-tech consulting firms, are located in towns close to Beltway exits. They avoid the high expense and congestion of the city, while easily accessing the corporations and government agencies in Washington.

With perseverance, luck, and occasional connections, the consulting firms that surround the city—the "Beltway Bandits"—compete for corporate and federal contracts to provide services and advice in every conceivable field.

Mark Cole, Tony Miller, and Renee Carlson are partners in one such suburban enterprise. Taking the bull by the horns, they've called their undertaking Beltway Bandits, Inc., figuring their creative posture will attract more clients than it will repulse. And so far, it's been working.

Characters

Program development executives have learned that continuing lead characters are the key element to any successful series. Series presentations contain detailed descriptions of lead characters, often including a biography that is rarely referred to in the pilot or series. Such detailed biographies provide valuable insight, especially for casting.

In preparing a presentation, it is not unusual for a writer or producer to contact talent agents to determine whether available known actors might be interested in the still-evolving concept. If the response is positive, then the leading character may be molded after that particular actor.

In almost all circumstances, a prototype or model for the leading character is identified. These are usually well-established film stars or personalities, who would never actually work in a series. Their names provide convenient images. A leading character may be described as an "Eddie Murphy type," a "Julia Roberts type," or a "John Travolta type."

This is an example of how characters are described in the series presentation for "Beltway Bandits."

THE CHARACTERS

MARK COLE, in his late thirties, is a small, well-built man who works hard to thwart the symptoms of approaching middle age. A James Spader type, he has a background in computer science and electrical engineering, and he spent twelve long years working for the Department of Energy. He is level-headed and conservative, always one to carefully think things through before making decisions. His midlife crisis was jump-started when his wife changed careers and filed for divorce just when he thought he was happily married. The divorce action has been dragging on much longer than anticipated, and in the interim he's been sharing an apartment with his old high school buddy, best friend, and business partner, TONY MILLER.

TONY MILLER, also in his late thirties, is rugged and athletic. Unlike Mark, he's a risk taker, always ready to try something new. A Tom Hanks lookalike, he has had a varied and adventurous career as a writer and investigative journalist. He's been an important source of support for Mark—and a source of angst, leading the intractable Mark into uncharted territory.

RENEE CARLSON, in her late twenties, is appealing, magnetic, a Sharon Stone lookalike. Her appearance belies years of intense training as an agent for a branch of the National Security Council, referred to only as "The Agency." Although still subject to call by the Agency, she is able to work as a free agent with Mark and Tony. Her covert experience and discipline are invaluable assets for the team. She loves the work they do, but Washington is not where she wants to be. Born and raised in the Southwest, Renee is a desert artist at heart and cherishes the time she is able to steal in the quiet studio abode she inherited from her father in Nevada. Her frequent travel between her Washington townhouse and desert home is a source of humor and frustration for Mark and Tony, who argue about the injustice of Renee having four times their closet space.

The temperaments and talents of the three Beltway Bandits are different, but their friendship is cemented in a shared experience— one that began as a result of a freelance writing assignment that Tony undertook with Mark along as a lark. Through this adventure, the two men met Renee in a dangerous exploit that permanently changed all of their lives.

Pilot Story

A series presentation almost always contains a brief description of the proposed premise story that begins the series. It sets the characters in place and provides the jumping-off point for the series. If the concept is accepted, then the premise story will be expanded to a detailed story outline and subsequently to a full-fledged pilot script.

This is the pilot story for the series "Beltway Bandits." It's written in a typical story treatment structure.

BELTWAY BANDITS

PILOT STORY

Mark Cole is a twelve-year veteran of the Department of Energy (DOE) in Washington. Recently separated, he's temporarily living with his buddy Tony Miller, a freelance journalist. The two plan a weekend adventure in Las Vegas to lift their spirits. Tony has a writing assignment near there, and Mark tricks the DOE computer— and his chain-smoking supervisor, Stanley—into assigning him a field survey of a Nevada solar energy project a few miles away.

They soon find themselves at a small motel bar in Elton, Nevada, populated by rowdy locals, some of whom work for Hazardous Salvage, Inc. (HSI), the company Tony will be visiting in the morning. HSI is a unique operation that salvages munitions debris from a government target range. One of the locals, an attractive young woman named Renee, befriends Mark and Tony, encouraging them.

Mark's visit to the Elton Project is anything but routine. He discovers that the energy project camouflages missile silos. He and Tony are questioned, then detained. The two attempt an escape, but they are recaptured and are considered enemy agents.

Mark and Tony are moved to a "secure" location. This time, a helmeted guard helps them escape, barely making it past a hail of bullets and pursuing military vehicles. The guard turns out to be Renee, who is working for an offshoot of the National Security Council. She reveals that the missiles hide even deeper secrets—virtual-reality laser weapons developed to destroy anything in orbit. The obsessive project leader, Colonel Ferguson, is convinced that nuclear warheads from the former Soviet Union will be sold to third-world terrorists. He plans to use the virtual-reality lasers and missiles in a first strike against Israel. That will force Israel into instant retaliation against former Soviet Union hidden missile sites.

The colonel has secured all communications, and there is no way to call for outside support. Renee has to rely on Tony to reach the HSI crew for help. She forces Mark to return to the project site with her, where she directs him to the missile silo as she heads to stop the colonel.

Renee is captured, but Mark and the trained HSI specialists attempt to disarm the missile. Time is too short. The missile fires. Mark and the crew race back into the complex, overpowering the colonel and rescuing Renee. She quickly elicits Mark's help and, using experimental virtual-reality lasers, they manage to divert the missile seconds before it hits.

The National Security Council moves quickly to cover up the story. No one will ever know what almost happened. Mark and Tony must remain quiet.

The two friends return home. Tony digs into another project, but Mark can't face the thought of returning to his depressing DOE office. He wants something different. He quits his job and proffers goodbyes to his bureaucratic boss. The events of the previous weeks have transformed him. He wants to be with Renee, the woman who changed his life. He offers to join her in Nevada, but she still has a job to do and puts a stop to those plans. It's better if he just stays in Washington with Tony, but perhaps there's some way they'll be able to work together again.

In the tag, Renee convinces her agency to provide Mark and Tony with seed money to start their own consulting business. That's the **least** they can do for the makeshift heroes. The bigwigs concur. They'll provide startup funds, provided they can tap into the boys' "expertise"—through Renee—whenever they want. Renee smiles.

"Beltway Bandits, Inc." is born, with promises of continued high adventure.

Sample Future Stories

The inevitable question raised by all concerned is how the series will sustain itself throughout the seasons. What kinds of stories can be told the second year? The viability of a concept is measured by its ability to sustain itself over many episodes without having to repeat storylines.

It is important to demonstrate the many avenues from which stories can be derived. About five or six new story ideas are usually included in the concept, each showing the uniqueness of the characters in conflict, without duplicating ideas.

These are sample future episodes from "Beltway Bandits."

FUTURE STORIES

1. Mark is hounded by calls from his ex-wife, then receives a call from Renee. She wants to see him right away. He's ecstatic, but the news is not good. She's going undercover, can't tell him more, she'll be in touch. She kisses Mark good-bye. This is serious. When he doesn't hear from her as planned, he convinces Tony to help track her down. The National Security Agency refuses to help. Finally, they acknowledge that she hasn't communicated with them, either. After many near misses, the boys finally find her—the quarry of a Mideast hit man. They swing into action to help her, and they just barely succeed. Renee—and the agency—are most grateful.

2. Mark is working at his computer in the small office of "Beltway Bandits, Inc." when the screen temporarily blanks out. It's not as benign as it seems. A computer virus threatens every interconnected computer in the Washington, D.C. area—including high-security mainframes at the Pentagon and the National Security Council. Through

journalistic probing, Tony uncovers a lonely computer hacker trying to undermine the bureaucracy he was once a part of. They convince him to disrupt and destroy the program he has worked on for the past five years.

3. Business is not very good, and the boys need some capital to make the bills. One large company calls, wanting them to set up a satellite communications link for international business ventures. In a plot reminiscent of "Sorry Wrong Number," Mark accidentally uncovers an investment conspiracy to gain control of the well-known company. Trying to find out more, he, Tony, and Renee discover that a murder is planned during an international flight on a corporate jet. Through their computer facility, investigative ploys, and quick action, Mark, Tony, and Renee prevent the crime.

4. Mark's ex-boss Stanley Ebert is furious. He's convinced that Mark is still plugging into Department of Energy computers. There are missing DOE files and others that have been tampered with. Ebert threatens Mark with retaliation. He'll close down their business. Beltway Bandits are stealing the Beltway blind. The more Mark protests, the more it seems he's guilty. With the help of his former secretary, and a somber Tony, evidence is finally uncovered to point to the real culprit, a former agency executive now running for state office in the Midwest. He agrees to return the documents only on the condition that no one knows he took them.

5. While doing routine research at the Pentagon, Renee discovers that three people have mysteriously died in their offices within a two-day period. Although officials try to keep it quiet, news travels fast, and employees fear for their own health. Renee drafts Mark and Tony, who help her unravel a complicated mystery involving contamination from a biological warfare project gone awry. The contamination is contained, but all involved know how lucky they have been, and how easily it could happen again.

The Art of Pitching Ideas

In *Primetime*, Richard D. Lindheim and I describe how to pitch ideas to the networks.[7] I've incorporated that discussion here, since the procedure varies little from network to network.

The process begins with a phone call to schedule the pitch meeting. Because network development executives are invariably busy, it may take a week or two for the actual meeting to occur. The phone call acts as a screening process for network development executives. Individuals without representation will often be rebuffed or referred to a subordinate. Networks are wary of discussing projects with people who are not properly represented (the fear of lawsuits prevails).

Just before the meeting, all of the participants assemble outside the office of the network development vice president. The roster of individuals varies but usually includes the creator of the concept to be pitched, the writer (if the creator is not a writer), and the creator's legal representation. If the creator works independently, then this person will usually be an agent. If the individual has a contract with a studio or production organization, then this person will be a studio development executive. The network will usually be represented by three people—the head of development, his or her assistant, and a junior member of the department who will sit silently with a writing pad to record notes about the project.

The meeting always begins informally. The development executive tries to make the nervous creative people feel at ease. There is a short period of casual conversation and jokes, while coffee and nonalcoholic drinks are served for those wishing it. Finally, the development executive tactfully brings the conversation to the business at hand.

Usually, the first person to speak is the agent or studio representative, who introduces the project in a general way, expresses confidence in the creative team and the concept, often indicating time periods on the network schedule where this show might be ideally placed.

Then the spotlight is focused on the creator, who proceeds with the verbal "pitch." First, the basic concept is described, with arguments supporting the idea's merit and uniqueness. The creator explains how this project is different from present and past shows on television. In addition, he or she describes how the concept allows many different types of stories to be told from week to week.

Now the principal characters are described in detail. Their biographies (which may never appear on screen) are revealed, along with their attitudes and character quirks. The prototype actor or actress will often be mentioned. Only the primary characters are presented in detail. The subsidiary ones may be referred to briefly or not at all. They are often dismissed with a comment like "and, of course, there are several other characters who will interact with our leads."

After presenting the basic idea and characters, the individual pitching the idea usually pauses. This is the time for the network executives to respond. This response can take several forms, including the following:

1. The network executive in charge may declare disinterest in the idea or inform the group that something similar is already in the works. If so, that is the conclusion of the meeting.
2. The network executive may ask questions. In this situation, the response is critical. If a developer is asked to discuss some of the potential stories for the series, then adequate preparation can spell the difference between acceptance and rejection.
3. The development executives will smile and thank the people for coming in and presenting the project. While projects are sometimes approved in the meeting, the network programmers usually maintain a placid countenance and end the meeting without stating a conclusion.

Following unwritten but established procedure, the development executives will mull over the proposal and subsequently meet to reach a consensus. One of them will then phone the project's representative (studio/production company or agent) and inform him or her of the decision. This accept/reject call usually occurs within 72 hours of the pitch session.

Personal Ingredients for Successful Pitching

Several key ingredients are necessary for a successful presentation of a television concept. Among them are *honest enthusiasm, abundance of detail, humor, conviction*, and *adaptability*.

Honest Enthusiasm

It would seem superfluous to state that the presenter should have enthusiasm about the project. This is expected. It is crucial, however, that this enthusiasm be real and not overstated. Network executives are constantly bombarded with sales pitches for "new, wonderful series." If the presenter lapses into hyperbole, then his or her credibility and that of the project will both suffer. The key element is realistic enthusiasm.

Abundance of Detail

Although some projects succeed because of slick salesmanship, the success record of such concepts is poor. A well-thought-out concept is rich in detail, covering most exigencies. The network programmers listen carefully for flaws in the concept and to ascertain that it has been carefully conceived.

Humor

What separates contemporary television and film from the past is humor. Examine the best of today's entertainment offerings, and you will discover a mixture of intense conflict and comedy, sometimes almost overlapping. Every contemporary concept, no matter how dramatic, should have humor, and levity in the presentation of any project is important as well. Network executives interpret the intensity and style of the pitch as a faithful indicator of the creator's stylistic intent for the program.

Conviction

This should not be confused with enthusiasm. The determination of the creator to have this project accepted and on the air is vital to the presentation. People who are firm in their beliefs command respect. Conviction may not guarantee acceptance, but lack of conviction will certainly encourage rejection.

It should be noted that it is preferable for a creator to present only one idea per meeting. Because network meetings can be difficult to arrange and have to be scheduled far in advance, there is the tendency to consolidate and pitch several ideas per meeting. This presents some problems, however. The network may interpret the bombardment of ideas as lack of conviction concerning any one concept. It also puts the executives in an uncomfortable position, choosing one idea over the others. Often, they will take refuge in simply rejecting them all.

Adaptability

In the meeting, a network development executive often has suggestions about modifying the concept in some way. Obviously, to admonish such advice with an unsuitable comment like "That's stupid," or "It won't work," or "I don't think so" is the quickest way to have the project rejected. The minimal response should be "That's interesting. Let me think about that."

An open mind is crucial in such situations. It does not take much psychological training to understand that accepting an executive's modification gives that person a stake in the project and increases its chances of acceptance. Moreover, development people are often concerned about the flexibility of the creative people. Because television is a collaborative effort, it is easier to work with someone who is thoughtful and accepting of ideas than with someone who takes any comment as criticism and a personal assault.

During the development process, some hard-nosed creators find themselves feigning amiability. Those with reputations for being extremely difficult often solicit network "input" at the formative stages of a project. If the show succeeds, they are the ones who receive the critical and remunerative rewards. They can safely turn from Dr. Jekyll to Mr. Hyde after the series has been ordered.

How to Create TV Series Bibles

A series bible includes a full description of the arena/setting, lengthy character descriptions, and the story arcs for each of the regular characters. That information is important for casting possibilities. The bible also includes the fully developed pilot script. After the pilot, the future sample storylines are presented to show the diversity of the series.

ENDNOTES

1. John Brodie, "Pilots' Code: Pitch to the Niche," *Variety,* February 15, 1993, 104.
2. Josef Adallian, "And 'Put Pilots' Force TV Networks to Fly Blind," September 27–October 3, 1999, 30.
3. Ibid., 30.
4. Ibid.
5. Richard A. Blum and Richard D. Lindheim, *Primetime: Network Television Programming,* Boston, Focal Press, 1987, 63–66.
6. Ibid.
7. Ibid., 72–75.

PART SIX

MARKETING AND SELLING YOUR SCRIPT

18

How to Sell Your Motion Picture Screenplay

What You Should Know Before Marketing

Marketing a spec screenplay requires strategy, determination, and a realistic understanding of the industry. The marketplace is extremely competitive, and even the best projects written by established professionals can end up on the shelf or forever lost in development hell. Still, an excellent original script, submitted to the right person at the right time, might suddenly break through the barriers. The key word is "excellent." It makes no sense to submit a script unless it is in its most polished, producible, and castable form (and even then it will be subject to countless rewrites).

Your script represents the highest caliber of your creative potential. You might think producers and agents are inclined to see the masterpiece lurking behind a rough-draft script. More likely, they'll focus on the weaknesses, compare it to top submissions, and generalize about the writer's talents. So, if you feel uncertain about a script's professional quality, producibility, or castability, then hold off on submitting it. Write another script to show you have the right stuff to execute ideas. Your next script might show you off to better advantage.

Selling scripts is an arduous task, and only intricate strategy and perseverance pay off. Here is how to get your script ready for the marketplace.

Register and Copyright Your Script

Before sending out any story or script, it is important to register it with the Writers Guild of America (WGA) and copyright it with the U.S. Copyright

287

Office. The WGA Registration Service is set up to assist writers in establishing the completion dates of pieces written for radio, theater, television, motion pictures, video cassettes/discs, and interactive media. They register more than 30,000 pieces of literary material annually. You don't have to be a member of the Guild to take advantage of this service. As of this edition's publication date, the registration fee for members is $10, and for nonmembers is $20. Registration is valid for a term of five years and may be renewed for an additional five years at the same rate.

On your script title page, print "Registered WGAw" or "Registered WGAE," but don't put the full registration number down because it might mark you as an amateur, who is afraid of being sued. Get in touch with the WGA Registration Service for current fees and requirements. You can contact the WGA Intellectual Property Registry Office, 7000 West Third Street, Los Angeles, CA 90048-4329; phone: 323/921-4500. In the East, you can contact the WGA Intellectual Property Registry Office, WGA East, 555 West 57th Street, New York, NY 10019; phone: 212/767-7800). The Guild plans to initiate online registration from their Website at www.wga.org in the future.

Know that WGA registration does *not* take the place of copyright. I strongly recommend that you also copyright your scripts with the U.S. Copyright Office, Library of Congress, 101 Independence Ave., S.E., Washington, D.C. 20559-6000; phone: 800/688-9889. A new copyright fee has been established for the year 2000, so contact the U.S. Copyright Office to determine the correct fees. Ask for "Short Form PA," which is used to copyright scripts and stage plays. If you want information, or to register online, the Copyright Office Website is http://lcweb.loc.gov/copyright. When you send your script out to the industry, you can put the copyright symbol (©) on the script, but you do not need too.

It can take several months for the copyright process to work through the bureaucracy. So, it can't hurt to protect your script with another online protection service. Firstuse is an international copyright registration service that permits you to register your screenplay at any stage of development, from a synopsis to final draft. There is a small $8 fee, which enables you to register your material as you create it. Registrations are stored for 10 years. Firstuse indicates that this step is an important precursor to copyright registration because it serves as ongoing verification of work in development. The Academy of Television Arts and Sciences endorses it. The Firstuse Website is http://Firstuse.com.

ProtectRite is another intellectual property protection system for writers, developed by the National Creative Registry. It permits protection for outlines, treatments, and rock drafts from any word processing system. Your work is immediately encrypted and saved in long-term storage that only you can access. You receive a courtesy e-mail with your confidential registration number and completion date of the original material. They charge $18.95 for a ten-year registration. ProtectRite can be reached at www.protectrite.com.

Joining the Writers Guild of America (WGA)

Membership rules are a bit confusing for the WGA west, and WGA East. The WGA is a labor union that represent writers in the motion picture, broadcast, and cable industries, as well as new technologies. The WGAw has approximately 8,500 members. It is affiliated with the Writers Guild America, East, and numerous organizations throughout the world, representing writers in a variety of ways, including traditional collective bargaining agreement efforts, and determining writing credits for feature films and television.

The WGA west is more expensive to join, but the West Coast is where most film and television action takes place. You pay a one-time membership fee of $2,500 and then 1.5 percent of gross earnings as a writer. For eligibility, you need to sell several projects to producers who have signed agreements with WGA, until you have 24 units of professional writing credit (as outlined in the WGAw requirements for admission). The contracts are automatically forward to the Guild, and you receive notice indicating that you are a member. Once you become a member, you cannot write for any producer who is not a Guild signatory.

If you are close to a script sale, get information about the Guild requirements nearest you. The WGAw is at 7000 West Third Street, Los Angeles, CA 90048-4329; phone: 323/921-4500; Website: www.wga.org. Writers residing in the East, contact the Writers Guild of America, East, 555 West 57th Street, New York, NY 10019; phone 212/767-7800; Website: www.wgaeast.org.

The Release Form or Submission Agreement

If you have an agent, then you don't need to bother with release forms. Your agent has the professional contacts and industry know-how to submit scripts. But, if you're going to submit a project to producers without an agent, then you may have to sign a release form—a submission agreement—in advance. Most production companies will return your manuscript if a submission agreement is not included. The waiver states that you won't sue the production company and that the company has no obligations to you. That may seem unduly lopsided, but millions of dollars are spent annually fighting potential lawsuits, and thousands of ideas are being developed simultaneously by writers, producers, studios, and production companies.

The waiver is a form of self-protection for a producer who wants to avoid unwarranted legal action. But it also establishes a clear line of communication between the writer and producer, so if legal action is warranted, it can be taken. A sample release form follows and is reprinted with permission of Done Deal, at www.scriptsales.com.

RELEASE FORM:

TITLE:

FORM OF MATERIAL:

DATE:

PRINCIPAL CHARACTERS:

BRIEF SUMMARY OF THEME OR PLOT:

WGA REGISTRATION NO.:   NO. OF PAGES:

1. I request that you read and evaluate said material.

2. I warrant that I am the sole owner and author of said material, that I have the exclusive right and authority to sumbit the same to you upon the terms and conditions stated herein; and that all of the important features of said material are summarized herein. I will indemnify you of and from any and all claims, loss, or liability that may be asserted against you or incurred by you, at any time, in connection with said material, or any use thereof.

3. I agree that nothing in this agreement nor the fact of my submission of said material to you shall be deemed to place you in any different positions than anyone else to whom I have not submitted said material.

4. I understand that as a general rule you consider literary properties through the established channels in the industry. I recognize that you have access to and/or may create or have created literary materi-

als and ideas that may be similar or identical material, which may have been independently created by you or have come to you from any other independent source. I understand that no confidential relationship is established by my submitting the material to you hereunder.

5. I have retained at least one copy of said material, and I hereby release you of and from any and all liability for loss of, or damage to, the copies of said material submitted to you hereunder.

6. I enter into this agreement with the express understanding that you agree to read and evaluate said materials in express reliance upon this agreement and my covenants, representatives, and warranties contained herein, and that in the absence of such an agreement, you would not read and evaluate said material.

7. I hereby state that I have read and understand this agreement and that no oral representatives of any kind have been made to me, and that this agreement states our entire understanding with reference to the subject matter hereof.

Very truly yours,

Address	Signature
City and State	Print Name
Telephone Number	SS#

Writing A Query Letter

When you prepare to send out your project, craft a concise one-page query letter that is addressed to a specific person at the agency, studio, or production company. Be personal and selective in your letters. First and foremost, find contacts in resources like the *Hollywood Creative Directory - Producers (HCD)* (Vol. 39, Spring 2000), which can be obtained by writing to 3000 Olympic Blvd., Suite #2525, Santa Monica, CA 90404;

phone: 800/815-0503, fax: 310/315-4815; e-mail: hcd@hcdonline.com; Website: www.hcdonline.com. *HCD* publishes more than 1,700 companies, 7,700 names, as well as producers, production companies, and television executives with sample credits. Another excellent Website for a list of motion picture and television production companies is Done Deal at www.script-sales.com.

Because the industry is so quixotic, if you're not sure who is in charge of development, then call the receptionist. If the answer is "Ms. So and So handles new projects," then ask how to spell the name. That courtesy minimizes the chance of embarrassment and maximizes the chance that the project will wind up at the right person's desk.

The query should be no longer than one page, professional, and intriguing. If your screenplay has won any awards, or is a finalist in a national competition, then be sure to mention that in the query. Don't mention that the project is perfect for a big star because that sounds amateurish. And don't discuss a budget, or imply that your project is under consideration by another production company, unless it is. There's no need to offer apologies for being an unsold writer, or to suggest that the next draft will be 10 times better than this one. If a cover letter starts off with apologies, what incentive is there to read the project? Be sure to include a phone number where you can be reached and a self-addressed stamped envelope (SASE) for a response.

The Annual Screenwriter Guide, 1999, reminds us that agents and producers need different information in the query letter.[1] Producers and agents want to be hooked right away, but producers look to the synopsis for more information about the story. When querying producers, a one- or two-page synopsis is required. Most agents find a synopsis helpful, but not necessary.

In the *Guide*, New York agent Lawrence Mattis of Circle of Confusion Ltd. notes that "overwriting is usually more of a problem than underwriting." His clients, Larry and Andy Wachowski, writers/directors of the feature THE MATRIX, were discovered through their one-paragraph query letter.

Because query letters are so important, I am including a helpful article on the subject, "Writing Effective Query Letters," by Kerry Cox, which appeared in the *Hollywood Scriptwriter: The Trade Paper for Screenwriters.*[2] Kerry Cox is a former editor of that trade paper. It is reprinted with permission of Lou Grantt, Editor of *Hollywood Scriptwriter: The Trade Paper for Screenwriters* (P.O. Box 10277, Burbank, CA 91510; phone: 818/845-5525; fax: 818/709-7540; e-mail: editor@hollywoodscriptwriter.com; Website: www.hollywoodscriptwriter.com). He presents two sample queries, with explanations.

WRITING EFFECTIVE QUERY LETTERS
by Kerry Cox

At least in the initial stages of your career as a screenwriter, your success or failure may very well depend more on your ability to write a compelling query letter than on creating a wonderful script.

The reason's simple: without a good query letter, your script may never get read. The vast majority of agents and producers want to see a letter of inquiry and/or synopsis before they'll spend time reading a complete script (a quick look at our Annual Agency Survey certainly confirms this!)

So, what follows are two query letters, one fictitious, and one I used for a script of mine that never sold, but did land me a couple of assignments. While neither is presented here as the most fabulous query letter every written, they should serve as clear examples of the kind of format and structure you want to aim for in your letter.

Joe Agent
Writers and Money Agency
1000 Beverly Blvd.
Hollywood, CA 90028

Dear Mr. Agent:

Imagine that an uncle you barely knew passed away, leaving you as the sole owner of a Las Vegas casino.

Okay, so maybe that kind of thing has happened to you before. And maybe you handled it just fine.

But when it happens to Freddy Gambini, 32-year-old professional student and world-class klutz—and when it turns out that the aforementioned deceased uncle became that way in the crossfire of a decidedly unfriendly takeover attempt—"fine" isn't the first word that springs to mind to describe the resulting chaos.

Right from Page 1, Freddy is embroiled in a race against time to save the casino, his life, the first woman he's had in 10 years, and whatever dignity he can still salvage as Mr. Lucky, suave kingpin of The Smiling Fortune casino.

ASK FOR MR. LUCKY is a feature-length comedy rife with cold-blooded killers, hot-blooded undercover agents, lethal lounge acts, acrobatic sex, and in the midst of it all, Freddy, an overeducated goofball who somehow shakes the dice and throws a perfect seven.

I'd like to send you ASK FOR MR. LUCKY. I've been a professional writer for 11 years, having written for Aaron Spelling Prods., The Disney Channel, and more. I've had a play produced about as far off-Broadway as you can get without having to swim. I've had two books published, I penned a humor column for three years in the Ventura Star–Free Press, and for the past 10 years I've published *The Hollywood Scriptwriter*, an international newsletter for screenwriters.

I've enclosed a self-addressed, stamped postcard for your reply. Thanks very much for your time and consideration.

Sincerely,

Kerry Cox

As you can see, in the previous query, I tried to emphasize the comedic nature of the script, and devoted little space to any description of the story. The idea was to establish the general tone, and make it clear to the reader that they would be seeing a broad, almost farcical comedy. In this kind of script, no one's really expecting a riveting plotline full of twists and rich with meaning—they're looking for a decent "hook" and lots of laughs.

The following, on the other hand, is a query for a completely different kind of script.

Josephine Agent
Great Writers Agency
1001 Beverly Blvd.
Hollywood, CA 90027

Dear Ms. Agent:

Thirteen years ago, J.T. Wheeler woke up at 5:30 a.m., showered, had a light breakfast, and savagely murdered his family of four. He then hopped into his Lexus and vanished from the face of the earth.

Or did he?

It's a question Susan Morgan, wife of prominent attorney Lawrence Morgan, has to answer fast. The chilling fact is, the more she learns, the more she realizes that Wheeler's killing spree not only wasn't his first . . . but it may very well not be his last either.

And she might be married to him.

BED OF LIES is a psychological thriller and dark mystery with a strong female protagonist, a deeply horrifying villain, and a series of disturbing surprises that build to an ultimate shocker of an ending. It is also a story of trust, betrayal, and the fine line that divides the two when secrets are buried between a husband and a wife.

I'd like to submit BED OF LIES for your consideration and possible representation. I've written professionally for television, radio, and print, including network TV credits and two published books. I've also worked extensively as a crisis intervention counselor, specializing in marital crisis managemnt.

I've enclosed a prepaid postcard for your reply. Thanks very much for your time and consideration.

Sincerely,

Kerry Cox

In this case, it's fair to say that you have an excellent idea of what the story is going to be about, and what the general tone of the movie will be. Hopefully, the query letter will be perceived as being well-written enough to reflect clearly that the reader won't be wasting her time if she requests the script.

Note also that I generalized my writing credits, as opposed to being specific as in the first letter. Since those credits reveal a body of work heavy in comedy, they wouldn't be helpful in convincing an agent I could write drama, and in fact might be deleterious. Better instead to bring up some "life experience" that would tend to show a familiarity with the subject matter of the script. If you don't have any such experience, then don't apologize or list a bunch of unrelated jobs you've held, or say that you've read extensively on the subject. Just tell your story, ask permission to send the script, and sign off.

The Synopsis

When you send a query, include a short synopsis. The synopsis expands your one-sentence logline into more detail about the plot and main characters. You have only one or two pages to hook them, tell the story, set up the main characters, and establish the tone of the film. The synopsis is needed when sending queries to producers and development executives. It may not be requested by agents, but if you do send it, then it can provide clues to the project's genre and marketability.

These are some helpful insights from agents and producers in the *Annual Screenwriter's Guide, 1999.*[3] Agent Lawrence Mattis of Circle of Confusion, Inc. says, "The synopsis can be helpful because sometimes if you're on the fence, you just want to see a little bit more about the story."[4] Producer Marcia Kirkely of Homegrown Pictures observes, "I know it's a bummer as a writer, because you can never really convey the tone of the script in one page. How can you really give your script justice? But for me, I'm trying to evaluate material. I like to see the whole story."[5]

Agent Bruce Bartlett of Above Line Agency remarks, "If a person can't write a letter, how in the world are they going to write 120 pages?"[6] The shorter the synopsis, the better. Bartlett reminds that a good synopsis includes relevant information about all three acts and establishes the main characters. "The synopsis isn't a scene breakdown. You wouldn't be able to do that in a page and a half." Riaz Patel, Director of Development for Bob Balaban's Chicago Films adds, "It's not supposed to be a long, detailed description of the plot; it's what is the essence of the script in two pages."[7] The goal is to tell the story quickly and succinctly.

Story Editor Brenda Taylor of Alex Rose Productions notes, "I have to know the characters. Is it strong enough writing that I can believe that the writer can transform that into a script? It is imperative that writers keep the style consistent from query to synopsis." Preferred Artists agent Kimber Wheeler says, "If I smile at the synopsis, I'll probably laugh at the script." Rebecca Bregman, V.P. of Development for Double A Films comments, "If we like the synopsis, then we'll call and ask for the script."[8]

As discussed in that *Annual Screenwriter's Guide, 1999*, the synopsis should include the main characters and then hit all of the major beats of the story. Only include the main characters that are essential in moving the story forward. The synopsis is the first writing sample a producer or agent will read, so make sure it reflects the tone and genre of the story. Describe the key events of the story. High-concept genres like adventure and comedy are easier to break down into a few short paragraphs. Agents and producers may allow a longer synopsis for genres that require more of a setup, such as thrillers, dramas, and untraditional, offbeat independent scripts.

How to Prepare Your Script for Submission

Your script should look professional, with the appropriate format and the right number of script pages, up to 120 pages. (For more information on proper screenplay format, see Chapters 8 and 9). Because scripts tend to be "misplaced" by production companies, it's a good idea to make a sufficient number of copies for multiple submissions.

Submission Status Reports

It's helpful to keep a submission status report, summarizing pertinent information about marketing contacts, dates, reactions, and follow-ups to each project. That information can be kept in a computer chart or on paper. The following log shows one way to set it up:

SUBMISSION STATUS REPORT			
PROJECT TITLE:			
DRAFT COMPLETED/REGISTERED:			
SENT TO:	*MAILED:*	*RESPONSE:*	*FOLLOW-UP:*
1.			
2.			
3.			
4.			
5.			

Under the first column (*SENT TO*) you can select the names and addresses of agents, producers, studio executives, directors, and actors who might be interested in your project. If the first person turns down the project or doesn't respond within a reasonable period (four to six weeks), then send it to the next person on the list. This preselected listing provides you with a planned strategy for an otherwise erratic marketplace.

The second column (*MAILED*) indicates when you forwarded—or plan to forward—the project to each person on the list. In the next column (*RESPONSE*) you can summarize reactions received (e.g., "Received letter from studio. They're not interested in this genre, but like my writing style. Asked to see more material."). The final column (*FOLLOW-UP*) leaves room for your initiatives (e.g., "If no word from studio, phone them," "Sent copy of another screenplay, per their request."). Submission status reports can help keep track of strategies, problems, and solutions on a day-to-day basis.

How to Get an Agent

If you have no agent representing you, then it's difficult to get projects considered by major producers. One of the best ways to make headway is to submit your work to an agent who represents a friend, a teacher, or a long-lost relative. If you are recommended by someone known to the agency, it makes you less of an unknown commodity.

If you have no contact, then the quest for representation can be handled effectively through another type of marketing strategy. The Writers Guild of America, west, publishes the *WGAw Agency List,* which lists Guild signatory agencies. The *WGAw Agency List* is available on the WGAw Website at www.wga.org.

The *WGAw Agency List* categorizes agencies into these specific classifications: (1) this agency has indicated it will consider new writers; (2) this agency has indicated it will consider writers only as a result of references from persons known by it; (3) a packaging agency represents a group of the major talent or star components of a television program or series or theatrical film receives a package commission from the employer/producer, as distinguished from the standard 10 percent commission from the representation of the writer's services or literary material; (4) society of author representative—signed through WGAE only; (5) letter of inquiry; or (6) if there are no symbols next to the agency, this agency will *not* accept unsolicited material.

This advice appears on the *WGAw Agency List* and is reprinted with permission of the Writers Guild of America, west, Inc.

We suggest that the individual first write or telephone the agency, detail their professional and/or academic credentials, and briefly describe the nature of the material they desire to submit. The agency then will advise the individual whether it is interested in receiving the material with a view to representing it. Most agencies, as a courtesy to writers, will return material sent to them if a self-addressed stamped envelope accompanies the submission. However, should material not be returned for any reason, the individual should be aware that the agency is under no obligation to return literary material to a writer seeking representation. The Guild cannot assist in seeking the return of the material. We regret we can offer no assistance in finding, selecting, or recommending an agent. The agencies that appear on this list have promised not to charge fees other than commission to WGA

*members. If you find that any of these agencies do charge fees,
then please contact the Guild at once. If you believe an agency is
signatory and you do not see it listed here, then please contact
the Guild's Agency Department at (323) 782-4502.*

From that list, work up a roster of potential agents for your project, and write a professional query letter. In *The Hollywood Scriptwriter*, an Annual Agent Survey reveals that "the query letter remains the preferred method among agents for initial contact. Each and every one of the agencies I talked with mentioned that they do not want to be contacted by phone, fax, or e-mail."[9] That same reporter recounts that agents receive from 25 to 50 queries per week, and "some of the instant query killers that agents mentioned are poor grammar, misspelled words, treatment-length letters, cast lists, and budgets. Keep it simple. Only 5 percent of queries pique enough interest among agents for them to ask for a script, so the need to labor over every word of your query should be obvious."[10]

Many of my students have been successful in sending out shotgun queries to agencies, especially if they've placed in national screenwriting competitions or won awards. There is nothing wrong with a limited, organized campaign that seeks representation for your project. A brief query letter might introduce you as a freelancer looking for representation on a specific project. If you don't get a response within six to eight weeks, then you can follow up with a phone call or letter, and submit the project to the next agent on your list. Don't be discouraged if you get no response at first. Just keep the project active. If the script is good enough, you might eventually wind up with some positive and encouraging feedback from the agency.

If an agency is interested in your script, they'll ask for exclusive representation on that project. If the script is optioned or sold, the agent is entitled to a 10 percent commission for closing the deal. If the work elicits interest but no sale, then you have at least widened your contacts considerably for the next project.

The larger agencies, such as William Morris Agency (WMA), International Creative Management (ICM), and United Talent Agency (UTA), are virtually impenetrable to new writers. They have a long list of clients in every field from variety and concerts to film, television, and the legitimate stage. They handle writers, producers, directors, actors, and even production companies. They also compete with large talent-management companies.

For that reason, a major agency can package top clients into a new project with a huge multi-million dollar price tag. If the package is appealing enough, then the script may sell at a very lucrative price for the writer. The package is a strong way to present an original script, but it is not without its drawbacks. The process may take as long as three or four months to set up, and may stretch out for some additional months before getting a reading from the buyer. The most erratic aspect of packaging is the marketplace response. An entire deal can be blown if a buyer dislikes any of the elements attached. If one actor is preferred over another by any executive, then months of waiting can explode into fragments of frustration. The project may never get off the ground.

The larger agencies offer an umbrella of power and prestige, but that advantage can be offset by the sheer size of the agency itself. Many clients may feel lost in an overcrowded stable, and newcomers can hardly break into that race. In contrast, a smaller literary agency might provide more personalized service, and might be more open to the work of new talent. Many of these agencies are exceptionally strong and have deliberately limited their client roster to the cream of the crop. In fact, many smaller agents have defected from executive positions at the major agencies. So, you'll have to convince them you're the greatest writer since Shakespeare came on the scene—and that your works are even more saleable.

How do you prove that you have the talent? It's all in the writing. If your projects look professional, creative, producible, and castable, then you're on the right track. Indeed, you can call yourself a writer. If the artistic content is also marketable and you back it up with determination and know-how, then you just might become a produced writer. Continue writing more scripts.

Analyzing the Marketplace

If you have a marketable, castable, producible script, then the next step you need to take is to get it to the right sources. Be creative and ingenious. You can read the trades, such as *Daily Variety*, *Hollywood Reporter*, and *Variety*, to find out what film projects are in production in similar genres, and which are planned for the future. Also read professional trade magazines designed specifically for screenwriters such as *Written By* (published by the WGAw), *Creative Screenwriting*, *Fade In*, *Hollywood Scriptwriter: The Trade Paper for Screenwriters*, *Scr(i)pt*, and *The New York Screenwriter*. Each publication has valuable and current marketing advice, and important interviews. Other magazines such as *Writer's Digest* provide occasional articles on screenwriting, and the *2000 Writer's Market* offers contact information in all areas of fiction and nonfiction writing.

You can also find invaluable market information online at Movie Bytes at www.moviebytes.com, which lists who's buying what in the film script marketplace and has the most comprehensive information on contests, updates, workshops, news, producers, and agents. Done Deal is another valuable and current marketing Website at www.scriptsales.com. You will also find current marketing trends at In Hollywood at www.inhollywood.com.

Major Studios and Production Companies

Get your agent to submit the screenplay directly to the head of feature development at a major studio or production company. Or, you can strategically market it yourself. Because industry contacts change regularly, check resources such as the invaluable *Hollywood Creative Directory - Producers (HCD)*, which lists more than 1,700 companies and 7,700 names, titles, phone and fax numbers, addresses, and credits for producers, studios, and network executives.[11] It is also available online, and it lists production companies with studio deals.

Sources for Top Grossing Films, 1998

According to a survey on the sources for the 50 top grossing films of 1998, *Variety* found that Hollywood's biggest hits derive from writer's pitches. Recycled ideas are on the rise, and fewer stories are being put into development. "The bad news is that we've seen, or read, most of them already. Only 20 of the 50 pics were based on original scripts or pitches. The remaining 30—that's 60%—were culled from novels, plays, TV series, previous pics, or other published material."[12]

Some other findings of that *Variety* survey were as follows:

- "Pitches, which were often criticized as being the lazy executive's best friend, accounted for only 10% of the 50 pics—yet three of the top four films released in '98 were pitch-based. Though they were only five, they were an impressive five: 'Saving Private Ryan,' 'Armageddon,' 'The Waterboy,' 'The Wedding Singer,' and 'Urban Legend' together amassed $700 million in domestic grosses, making pitches the biggest money-making category of the lot."
- "Original screenplays (specs acquired on the open market or studio writing assignments) barely edge out books as the lead category, with 15 specs comprising 30% of the top 50 grossers."
- "Only 20% of the top 50 pics were sequels, remakes, or spinoffs. However, given the town's growing interest in film libraries, that figure is sure to increase in coming years."

- "In terms of genre, there was no clear victor. Action, drama, and romantic comedy were the most popular, with eight pics each. There were seven sci-fi pics, seven comedies, six thrillers, four horrors pics, one war film, and one foreign language acquisition."
- "The lion's share of the 50 titles, even where the studio claimed to have completely reinvented the wheel, were based on icons or ideas that had huge preexisting awareness—among them 'Dr. Doolittle,' 'The Mask of Zorro,' and 'Mighty Joe.' Most believe that Hollywood will stick to rehashing well into 2000, given its current predilection for cost cutting."

Spec Screenplay Trends

What is Hollywood looking for in spec scripts? Whatever is hot at the box office this week. As producer Howard Meibach notes, "Whatever is doing well at the box office is hot. And these days, comedy is cleaning up at the box office, with hits like 'South Park,' 'The Spy Who Shagged Me,' 'Big Daddy,' and 'American Pie,' and comedy sales are dominating the marketplace."[13]

Another resource for current spec script trends is *The Literary Report*, which is published quarterly in *Scr(i)pt* magazine. *The Literary Report* is also published on the Website InHollywood.com. It analyzes spec script sales by studio, by genre, and by source material. It also lists markets and recent sales. You'll find a wealth of current marketing trends and contacts online at Websites like InHollywood.com, Done Deal at www.scriptsales.com, and Hollywood Lit Sales at www.hollywoodlitsales.com.

To help analyze the spec screenplay trends for 1999, I have included *The Literary Report's* "Sales by Studio," "Sales by Genre," and "Sales by Source Material." The reports are reprinted with permission of Jason Agard, Webmaster, InHollywood.com, at www.inhollywood.com.

Script Sales by Studio, 1999

As an example of marketing trends available on the Web, Figure 18-1 shows *The Literary Report's* analysis of "Script Sales By Studio, 1999" It is reprinted with the permission of Jason Agard, Webmaster, InHollywood, at www.inhollywood.com.

Script Sales by Genre, 1999

The Literary Report's "Sales by Genre - 1999" is printed in Figure 18-2. Note how comedies were box office winners for that period. Also examine how the different genres compare to previous years.

Script Sales by Studio - 1999

In a year when only three of the top ten box office grossers - RUNAWAY BRIDE, THE MATRIX, and BIG DADDY - came from spec scripts, Hollywood's faith in the spec market appears to have been shaken. Nerves were further rattled by the such unquantifiable smashes as THE BLAIR WITCH PROJECT and THE SIXTH SENSE, each of which defied all expectations to prove the old cliche that when it comes to movie-making, "Nobody knows anything." As a result, the literary market was off some 40 purchases from its 1998 level. Whether this is the beginning of a larger trend remains to be seen, as does the impact that the Internet will ultimately have on the film business.

Warner Wins Again	Sales By Studio

For the second year running, Warner Bros. has emerged as the studio most willing to nab new material, with their own subsidiary, New Line, arriving a step behind. The next spots are occupied by Sony and Disney, both of which took only small steps back from their sales levels of last year, unlike Fox, which picked up less than half the new material they sprung for in 1998. After a more aggressive 1998, DreamWorks returned to the conservative stance it has chosen since it's inception. Miramax, on the other hand, showed a new interest in the spec market that might result from its continuing shift towards younger demographics.

** Includes 20th Century Fox, Fox 2000, Fox Family, and Fox Searchlight.
***Includes Miramax and Dimension.
**** Includes Touchstone Pictures, Walt Disney, Disney Animation, and Hollywood Pictures.

	Literary Market Share	Literary Sales		
	1999	1999	1998	1997
20th Century Fox*	9%	24	52	54
DreamWorks SKG	4%	11	32	10
MGM/UA	7%	18	17	22
Miramax**	6%	16	10	7
New Line	14%	36	43	14
Paramount	11%	28	30	20
Sony	12%	31	27	40
Universal***	8%	22	36	47
Walt Disney***	11%	29	33	41
Warner Bros.	17%	45	58	44

Figure 18-1

Script Sales by Genre - 1999

Kings of Comedy	Sales By Genre

Half of the year's top 20 box office winners were comedies, eclipsing all other genres, and this fact was clearly not lost on Hollywood's executive ranks. Moreover, those films boast a profit margin far exceeding those of their successful counterparts from the Action-Adventure, Thriller and Science Fiction worlds. As a result, the long-standing rivalry between Drama and Comedy for the top of the genre heap was no contest at all this year. Of all the new purchases made this year, nearly one in three was a Comedy, and of the rest, nearly one in eight was a Romantic Comedy.

Genre	Literary Market Share	Literary Sales		
	1999	1999	1998	1997
Action-Adventure	9%	32	37	37
Animated	1%	3	4	1
Black Comedy	5%	17	24	23
Children	0%	1	6	4
Comedy	32%	117	90	81
Drama	21%	76	88	85
Fantasy	0%	1	7	4
Horror	2%	6	7	21
Musical	1%	2	2	0
Romance	4%	14	10	16
Romantic Comedy	9%	34	48	32
Science Fiction	3%	11	20	28
Thriller	16%	47	70	77
War	2%	6	1	2
Western	0%	1	0	0
Total		368	414	411

Figure 18-2

Script Sales by Source Material, 1999

The Literary Report's "Sales by Source Material - 1999" is in Figure 18-3. It breaks down projects sold according to pitches, spec scripts, fiction, nonfiction, articles, treatments, and remakes. It also compares the source material with the previous year.

Sales by Source Material - Third quarter, 1999

Fiction.	Sales By Source Material

1999 Out of 368 new projects...	1998 Out of 414 new projects...
• **148 scripts** sold, accounting for a full 40% of the sales.	• **132 pitches sold,** totaling over 32% of the market.
• **111 pitches** sold, totaling 30% of the market.	• **115 spec scripts sold,** accounting for a full 28% of the sales.
• **79 works of fiction** sold, for 21% of the action.	• **91 works of fiction sold,** for 22% of the action.
• **21 nonfiction**, making up under 6% of the scene.	
• **13 comic books** sold.	• **23 nonfiction pieces were picked up,** making up 5.6% of new projects.
• **11 articles** were nabbed.	• **12 were articles and 12 were comic books,** each notching under 3% of the scene.
• **6 remakes and 6 treatments** were picked up.	

Figure 18-3

The Million-Dollar Spec Script

The million-dollar spec script phenomenon is detailed in an informative book, *The Big Deal: Hollywood's Million Dollar Spec Screenplay Market,* by Thom Taylor (William Morrow & Co., 1999). Taylor's book is excerpted in the April 1999 edition of *Written By.*[14] As Taylor points out in that article, "In today's studio environment, a writer's material must wind its way through a massive labyrinth of noise and confusion that can often drown out the screenwriter's voice. But an original spec screenplay remains the easiest path into Hollywood's game, and can lead to a gratifying bidding war and huge pay days."

If your agent sends your script out to competitive companies, and you receive positive feedback, then hopefully you can create a "buzz." If you're very lucky, that's when your agent can heat up the million-dollar bidding war.

Pitching

Before a pitch meeting, be thoroughly prepared. Write out copious notes about the story and character arcs. Know them intimately. It can't hurt to practice and rehearse with a friend, spouse, or colleague. Be personal and enthused about the story and characters. At the beginning of the meeting, set up the title, genre, and theme, and grab the producer's interest. Be an effusive storyteller. (Refer to "The Art of Pitching Ideas" in Chapter 17.) Be in control of the meeting: Know your story and character arcs inside and out, but leave your notes at home.

Successful writer-producer Robert Kosberg was interviewed about the art of pitching in *Hollywood Scriptwriter,* and offers these practical revelations: "No one should expect to sell an idea for $1 million. That's not going to happen. But you can make anywhere from $25,000 to $150,000 from an idea. [New screenwriters] need to recognize that their first efforts are a way into the business, which leads to bigger and better deals, because deals are built on precedent."[15]

Kosberg tends to like to pitch comedies because "it's much easier to walk into a room and throw out a couple of funny, high-concept comedies and get a great reaction than any other genre."[16]

Asked if he fits the pitches into a standard formula, Kosberg confesses:

They're similar. Most of my pitches are high-concept, with the strong emphasis on the plot. Most pitches I keep short—anywhere from two minutes to five or six minutes. Most pitches are very simple to understand. Act 1, Act 2, Act 3. Pitching is not reinventing the wheel; it's giving the studio the structure they are used to. Most people make the mistake of going into way too much detail. The rest of pitching is cosmetic. Of course, the pitch also depends on being articulate, enthusiastic, humorous, being a good storyteller, all of which you can't really learn; anymore than you can learn to be a professional comedian. . . . I like "performing" in a room, and I pitch the movie as if I had seen it last night.[17]

Another successful "pitch king," Bo Zenga, was interviewed in *Creative Screenwriting*.[18] Zenga was an unknown in the early 1990s, then on the basis of his storytelling and ideas, studios waged bidding wars over his high concepts. He made deals with Dimension/Miramax, DreamWorks, MGM Paramount, and Warner Bros. In 1997, he started a bidding war between Paramount and Warner Bros. for TIME JUMPERS, in which he wrested back rights, and is rewriting for Steven Spielberg. To retain control, Zenga stays attached as producer of his projects.

When asked if he has a written pitch, he responds:

That's an oxymoron. Something is either written or you have a pitch. I write a ten-page treatment or outline and I memorize that. And it evolves and becomes something more dramatic. People often ask if I can leave something behind, and I won't even let them know that those ten pages exist—they'd get mad and think you're trying to be difficult. But in my opinion, the only thoughts that sell in this town are pitches and scripts. I don't think anybody sells treatments—maybe one a year or something.[19]

Zenga offers these other insights in the article:

You have to believe in a pitch and care about the characters. When I speak to writers' groups, it always sounds so English 101, but I have to be because so many people come to me and they don't have a pitch. They just start off "A guy's rushing down the beach and a spaceship lands," and I say, "Hold on. What's your title, what's your genre, and what's your theme"—the three most important things.[20]

Development Trends in Theatrical Motion Pictures, 1999–2000

For the longest time, all film projects had to have clear premises that could be pitched in loglines, with a traditional story structure. Audiences expected that familiarity. But, "after two decades of formula comedy, feel-good tales, and big-budget he-man adventures, the mass audience seems much more willing to embrace movies that astonish them, even in unsettling ways, and use fresh storytelling techniques to upend their expectations."[21]

According to Terry Press, chief of marketing at DreamWorks, "The idea was that if you can't tell the story in two lines, don't make the movie because audiences won't get it. That has literally taken 20 years to die, but it's finally dead." Adds Joe Roth, former president of Walt Disney Studios, "It doesn't have to have a dark edge, but the idea of a surprise is the crucial point. . . . The audience is way more sophisticated. . . . We're at the point now, where if you come at the audience in the traditional way, they're way ahead of you . . . but if the public hears about something fresh and new, they're onto it immediately."[22]

Lasse Halstrom, director of THE CIDER HOUSE RULES, partially attributes this change to an increase in media outlets: "People are finding so many interesting and sophisticated things on cable television and the Internet that it is opening them up to a different experience."

Ron Howard, actor-director and co-founder of Imagine Entertainment, observe: "What I have noticed is that the audience is much more interested in an unexpected twist, even if it's a downbeat twist. . . . If something is a little bit shocking or unexpected, it has a better chance of attracting people. I think there's just a broadening of tastes, a broader acceptance of these tones."[23]

No one claims that these films dominate the mainstream, "but just that there has been a persistent shift in that direction. Genre films and those relying on more traditional storytelling techniques are still being made and often do quite handsomely at the box office. It's just not a sure thing anymore, and that makes movie executives nervous."[24] Some people see the trend as a return to the sophisticated cinema of the 1970s, whereas others see it as the impact of independent filmmaking of the Sundance Film Festival in the 1990s.

Skeptical screenwriters and producers argue that studios are not about to abandon the old formulas for a riskier form of storytelling. Marc Norman, screenwriter for the Oscar-winning script SHAKESPEARE IN LOVE, with Tom Stoppard, noted:

I haven't yet noticed a major difference in the taste of the studios. I think we're in a period where there isn't anything in the studios' mind that is as surefire and risk-free as the Arnold or Sly action movies used to be. But it doesn't mean that they're abandoning formulas. It's that the studios are kind of in-between. If we're getting more adventurous movies at the moment, it's only because they are looking for the next formula, the next sure thing.[25]

Obviously, it is difficult to generalize about something as amorphous as audience taste. Bill Mechanic, chairman of Fox Film Entertainment, points out: "The problem is that sometimes audiences accept movies like that and sometimes they don't."[26]

Dan Jinks and Bruce Cohen, producers of the Academy Award-winning AMERICAN BEAUTY, written by Alan Ball, have no doubt that the success of their film was driven by this craving for surprise and originality. Cohen says, "Audiences are tired of seeing the same movies over and over again. . . . They also don't want to have movies jammed down their throats. They want to discover them. There have always been dark movies, but what's different now is that the storytelling is a little bit different, not as formulaic." Jinks adds: "The thing we kept hearing when we were preparing 'American Beauty' is that teenagers just won't go to see a movie unless it has nothing but teenagers in it."[27] But they were wrong. The film was hugely successful with teens and also connected to broad general audiences.

The emergence of the script-driven movie is having an impact on the industry. "It's not only shaking up the industry, it's turning a generation of screenwriters into pricey stars."[28] As Amy Pascal, chairwoman of Columbia Pictures, admits: "In some cases, the screenwriter invented it. . . . 'Malkovich' wouldn't have existed without Charlie Kaufman."[29]

And with increased recognition come increases in "clout, credit, and cash. (Ball, who got $350,000 for 'Beauty,' is expected to get $600,000 for his next script.)" "There's more of an awareness that the writers have a vision," explains AMERICAN BEAUTY director Sam Mendez. "It's wonderful to be part of a year where so much great work came directly out of the writer's brain."[30]

Hollywood is still studio-controlled, and still a place "where writers are often barred from sets, screwed on credits, and forced to sacrifice idiosyncrasy for commerciality." But there is some clear shift. As John McLean, executive director of the Writers Guild of America, west, observes, "you only have to look at the five films nominated for best picture. . . . Each either had a director who directed his own script, or closely collaborated with the writer. . . . Studio execs addicted to assembly line writing are dooming films before the director calls 'Action.'"[31]

Sample Going Rates for "Star" Screenwriters, 1999–2000

These are the going rates for these new "star" screenwriters as reported in *Entertainment Weekly.*[32]

- *Adam Herz* (AMERICAN PIE): going rate is $750,000 for AMERICAN PIE, $900,000 for EASTBOUND, $2 million from Universal to write and direct his own feature.
- *Jim Uhls* (FIGHT CLUB): going rate is an estimated $600,000.
- *Alexandra Payne and Jim Taylor* (ELECTION): going rate is $2 million to write and direct SIDEWAYS for Artisan.
- *Ehren Kruger* (ARLINGTON ROAD, SCREAM 3, and REINDEER GAMES): going rate is an estimated $800,000, remaking romantic comedy and new comedy-adventure scripts.
- *Alan Ball* (AMERICAN BEAUTY): going rate for next script, THE GIRL LEAST LIKELY, could reach $6,000,000, and he is negotiating to write and direct an HBO pilot.
- *Susannah Grant* (ERIN BROKOVITCH): going rate is undisclosed, but with 28 DAYS, she's joining the trend to take lower upfront fees in return for 2 percent of the gross.
- *Wes Anderson and Owen Wilson* (RUSHMORE and BOTTLE ROCKET): going rate is $1 million.

Business Deals and Contracts for Spec Screenplays

If a producer is interested in a project, then he or she will offer you a deal. If you don't have an agent yet, this is the time to get one. Any agent will gladly close the deal for the standard 10 percent commission. An attorney would be equally effective. The need for counsel depends on the complexity of the proposed deal and the counterproposals you wish to present.

If you're dealing with a producer who is a signatory to the Writers Guild (most established producers are), then the contract will adhere to the terms of the schedule of minimums negotiated by the Writers Guild of America.

Portions of the *WGA 1998 Theatrical and Television Basic Agreement Schedule of Minimums,* applicable during the period 5/2/00–5/1/01, are reprinted with permission of the Writers Guild of America, west, Inc., in Appendix A. If you have any questions regarding the application of these provisions or minimums, or relating to categories of minimums not included in the schedule, or if you have a question about the interpretation of the Basic Agreement, then contact the Guild.

Writer's Theatrical Short-Form Contract

A sample theatrical screenplay short-form contract is reprinted in Figure 18-4 with the permission of the Writers Guild of America, west, Inc. It is also available at www.wga.org.

Rules of Spec Contracts

To help navigate the rules of spec contracts, here is information provided by the WGAw Contracts Department, in "Navigating the Spec Waters" in the April 1999 edition of *Written By.*[33]

Options

Generally, an option is a right given in exchange for something of value (such as money) to subsequently purchase a literary property at an agreed-upon price and terms, within a specified time period. Often, companies try to get a "free option" and keep a writer's original material off the market without paying for the right.

The Writers Guild Minimum Basic Agreement (MBA) regulates options. Other than a limited exception in television for so-called "if-come" deals (see following section), if the writer is a "professional writer" as defined in the MBA (or the writer's individual contract provides that the writer shall be treated as such), then a company may not take a writer's completed work, "test the waters," and have the right to set it up, without having paid at least WGA minimum for such a right.

For theatrical motion pictures, the company must pay not less than 10 percent of the applicable minimum due upon the sale of such material, for each option period of up to 18 months; for television, the company must pay not less than 5 percent of the applicable minimum due upon the sale, for the first option period of up to 180 days, and 10 percent of the minimum for each period of 180 days thereafter (minimums may be verified using the Schedule of Minimums, which is available from The WGA). All of these minimums may be credited against the purchase price, unless such crediting is prohibited in the writer's individual contract.

Therefore, material from a professional writer may not be optioned for $1.00 or $10.00, or any amount less than the Guild Minimum. (Of course, writers may always negotiate for compensation above the minimum rates.)

WRITERS THEATRICAL SHORT-FORM CONTRACT

DATE : _____

1. NAME OF PROJECT:_____ ("PROJECT")

2. NAME/ADDRESS OF COMPANY:

       _____("COMPANY")

       _____

       _____

3. NAME OF WRITER: _____("WRITER")

       SOCIAL SECURITY NUMBER _____

4. WRITER'S REPRESENTATIVE:_____

5. CONDITIONS PRECEDENT:
    ❑ W-4   ❑ I-9   ❑ OTHER, IF ANY

6. COMPENSATION:
    A. GUARANTEED COMPENSATION (SEE 11, BELOW): $ _____
    B. CONTINGENT COMPENSATION (SEE 11, BELOW): $ _____
    C. PROFIT PARTICIPATION: IF SOLE WRITING CREDIT, ____% OF (NET/GROSS) PROCEEDS;
    REDUCIBLE FOR SHARED CREDIT TO ____% (SEE 27, BELOW)

7. SPECIFIC MATERIAL UPON WHICH SERVICES ARE TO BE BASED, IF ANY (A COPY WILL BE SENT TO WRITER UNDER SEPARATE COVER):

8. OTHER WRITERS EMPLOYED ON SAME PROJECT OR FROM WHOM MATERIAL HAS BEEN OPTIONED/ACQUIRED, AND DATES OF MATERIAL, IF ANY:

9. COMPANY REPRESENTATIVE AUTHORIZED TO REQUEST REVISIONS:

10. COMPANY REPRESENTATIVE TO WHOM/PLACE WHERE MATERIAL IS TO BE DELIVERED:

Figure 18-4 *(continued)*

11. SERVICES TO BE PERFORMED, INCLUDING NUMBER OF STEPS *(e.g., story and first draft, two rewrites and a polish)*:

        A. FOR STEP 1:   ❑ GUARANTEED

                              ❑ OPTIONAL

            WRITING PERIOD: _____ WEEKS

            READING PERIOD: _____ WEEKS

            PAYMENT DUE: $_____

            (50% DUE ON COMMENCEMENT, 50% ON DELIVERY)

      B. FOR STEP 2 (IF APPLICABLE): ❑ GUARANTEED

                              ❑ OPTIONAL

            WRITING PERIOD: _____ WEEKS

            READING PERIOD: _____ WEEKS

            PAYMENT DUE: $_____

            (50% DUE ON COMMENCEMENT, 50% ON DELIVERY)

      C. FOR STEP 3 (IF APPLICABLE): ❑ GUARANTEED

                              ❑ OPTIONAL

            WRITING PERIOD: _____ WEEKS

            READING PERIOD: _____ WEEKS

            PAYMENT DUE: $_____

            (50% DUE ON COMMENCEMENT, 50% ON DELIVERY)

      D. FOR STEP 4 (IF APPLICABLE): ❑ GUARANTEED

                              ❑ OPTIONAL

            WRITING PERIOD: _____ WEEKS

            READING PERIOD: _____ WEEKS

            PAYMENT DUE: $_____

            (50% DUE ON COMMENCEMENT, 50% ON DELIVERY)

      E. FOR STEP 5 (IF APPLICABLE): ❑ GUARANTEED

                              ❑ OPTIONAL

            WRITING PERIOD: _____ WEEKS

            READING PERIOD: _____ WEEKS

            PAYMENT DUE: $_____

            (50% DUE ON COMMENCEMENT, 50% ON DELIVERY)

Figure 18-4 *(continued)*

F. ADDITIONAL STEPS (IF APPLICABLE):

_____

_____

12. COMPANY SHALL PAY THE ABOVE GUARANTEED AMOUNTS DUE IF READING PERIODS PASS AND COMPANY DOES NOT REQUEST SERVICES; HOWEVER, IF THERE HAS BEEN NO INTERVENING WRITER(S), SERVICES SHALL BE DUE, SUBJECT TO WRITER'S PROFESSIONAL AVAILABILITY, FOR A PERIOD NOT TO EXCEED _____ MONTHS.

13. BONUS:
   A. For sole writing credit: $_____

   B. For shared writing credit: $_____
      Shared credit bonus will be paid on commencement of principal photography if no other writer has been engaged; balance to be paid on determination of writing credit.

   C. For "green light" or engagement of an "element": $_____
      If Writer is writer of record or is most recent writer on the Project at the time the Project is given a "green light" by a studio or an element is attached on a pay-or-play basis, Writer shall be given a bonus of _____ Dollars ($_____) which may ❑ may not ❑ be applied against the bonus in A. or B., above.

14. CREDITS AND SEPARATED RIGHTS:
   Per WGA MBA.

15. EXISTING CREDIT OBLIGATIONS REGARDING ASSIGNED MATERIAL, IF ANY (SUBJECT TO WGA MBA):

16. VIEWING CUT:
   Per WGA MBA: Writer shall be invited to view a cut of the film in time sufficient such that any editing suggestions, if accepted, could be reasonably and effectively implemented. Writer shall also be invited to [_____] other screenings.

17. PREMIERES:
   If writer receives writing credit, Company shall ❑ shall not ❑ provide Writer and one (1) guest with an invitation to the initial celebrity premiere, if held, with travel and accommodations at a level not less than the director or producer of the project.

18. VIDEOCASSETTE:
   Per WGA MBA.

19. TRANSPORTATION AND EXPENSES:
   If Company requires Writer to perform services hereunder at a location more than ____ miles from Writer's principal place of residence, which is _____, Writer shall be given first class (if available) transportation to and from such location and a weekly sum of $_____ ($_____ per week in a high cost urban area).

Figure 18-4 *(continued)*

20. SEQUELS/REMAKES:

If separated rights,

- Theatrical sequels = 50% initial compensation and bonus; remakes = 33%.
- Series Payments: $ _____ per 1/2 hour episode; $ ____ per 1 hour episode; $ _____ per MOW (in network primetime or on pay television, otherwise $ _____ per MOW); $ _____ per sequel produced directly for the videocassette/videodisc market; $ _____ per product produced for the interactive market based on the Project; _____ [other, e.g., theme park attractions based on the Project].
- Spin-offs: Generic – 1/2 of above payments
  Planted – 1/4 of above payments
- If Writer is accorded sole "Written by" or "Screenplay by" credit, Writer shall have the right of first negotiation on all audio-visual exploitation, including, but not limited to remakes and sequels and MOWs, mini-series and TV pilots (or first episode if no pilot) for a period of seven (7) years following release.

21. NOTICES:

All notices shall be sent as follows:

TO WRITER: TO COMPANY:

22. MINIMUM BASIC AGREEMENT:

The parties acknowledge that this contract is subject to all of the terms and provisions of the Basic Agreement and to the extent that the terms and provisions of said Basic Agreement are more advantageous to Writer than the terms hereof, the terms of said Basic Agreement shall supersede and replace the less advantageous terms of this agreement. Writer is an employee as defined by said Basic Agreement and Company has the right to control and direct the services to be performed.

23. GUILD MEMBERSHIP:

To the extent that it may be lawful for the Company to require the Writer to do so, Writer agrees to become and/or remain a member of Writers Guild of America in good standing as required by the provisions of said Basic Agreement. If Writer fails or refuses to become or remain a member of said Guild in good standing, as required in the preceding sentence, the Company shall have the right at any time thereafter to terminate this agreement with the Writer.

24. RESULTS AND PROCEEDS:

Work-Made-For-Hire: Writer acknowledges that all results, product and proceeds of Writer's services (including all original ideas in connection therewith) are being specially ordered by Producer for use as part of a Motion Picture and shall be considered a "work made for hire" for Producer as specially commissioned for use as a part of a motion picture in accordance with Sections 101 and 201 of Title 17 of the U.S. Copyright Act. Therefore, Producer shall be the author and copyright owner thereof for all purposes throughout the universe without limitation of any kind or nature. In consideration of the monies paid to Lender hereunder, Producer shall solely and exclusively own throughout the universe in perpetuity all rights of every kind and nature whether now or hereafter known or created in and in

Figure 18-4 *(continued)*

connection with such results, product and proceeds, in whatever stage of completion as may exist from time to time, including: (i) the copyright and all rights of copyright; (ii) all neighboring rights, trademarks and any and all other ownership and exploitation rights now or hereafter recognized in any Territory, including all rental, lending, fixation, reproduction, broadcasting (including satellite transmission), distribution and all other rights of communication by any and all means, media, devices, processes and technology; (iii) the rights to adapt, rearrange, and make changes in, deletions from and additions to such results, product and proceeds, and to use all or any part thereof in new versions, adaptations, and other Motion Pictures including Remakes and Sequels; (iv) the right to use the title of the Work in connection therewith or otherwise and to change such title; and (v) all rights generally known as the "moral rights of authors."

25. WARRANTY AND INDEMNIFICATION:

A. Subject to Article 28 of the WGA Basic Agreement, Writer hereby represents and warrants as follows:

1. Writer is free to enter into this Agreement and no rights of any third parties are or will be violated by Writer entering into or performing this Agreement. Writer is not subject to any conflicting obligation or any disability, and Writer has not made and shall not hereafter make any agreement with any third party, which could interfere with the rights granted to Company hereunder or the full performance of Writer's obligation and services hereunder.

2. All of the Work (and the Property, if any) shall be wholly original with Writer and none of the same has been or shall be copied from or based upon any other work unless assigned in this contract. The reproduction, exhibition, or any use thereof or any of the rights herein granted shall not defame any person or entity nor violate any copyright or right of privacy or publicity, or any other right of any person or entity. The warranty in this subparagraph shall not apply to any material as furnished to Writer by Company (unless such furnished material was written or created by Writer or originally furnished to Company by Writer) or material inserted in the Work by Company, but shall apply to all material which Writer may add thereto.

3. Writer is sole owner of the Property together with the title thereof and all rights granted (or purported to be granted) to Company hereunder, and no rights in the Property have been granted to others or impaired by Writer, except as specified, if at all, in this Agreement. No part of the property has been registered for copyright, published, or otherwise exploited or agreed to be published or otherwise exploited with the knowledge or consent of Writer, or is in the public domain. Writer does not know of any pending or threatened claim or litigation in connection with the Property or the rights herein granted.

4. Writer shall indemnify and hold harmless Company (and its affiliated companies, successors, assigns, and the directors, officers, employees, agents, and representatives of the foregoing) from any damage, loss, liability, cost, penalty, guild fee or award, or expense of any kind (including attorney's fees (hereinafter "Liability") arising out of, resulting from, based upon or incurred because of a breach by Writer of any agreement, representation, or warranty made by Writer hereunder. The party receiving notice of such claim, demand or action shall promptly notify the other party thereof. The pendency of such claim, demand, or action shall not release Company of its obligation to pay Writer sums due hereunder.

B. Company agrees to indemnify Writer and hold Writer harmless from and against any and all damages and expenses (other than with respect to any settlement entered into without Company's

Figure 18-4 *(continued)*

written consent) arising out of any third party claim against Writer resulting from Company's development, production, distribution and/or exploitation of the Project.

26. NO INJUNCTIVE RELIEF:

The sole right of Writer as to any breach or alleged breach hereunder by Company shall be the recovery of money damages, if any, and the rights herein granted by Writer shall not terminate by reason of such breach. In no event may Writer terminate this Agreement or obtain injunctive relief or other equitable relief with respect to any breach of Company's obligations hereunder.

27. PROFIT PARTICIPATION:

Terms to be negotiated in good faith. If the parties fail to reach agreement within [ ] months after execution hereof, either party, upon 30 days notice to the other, may submit the matter to what is known as a "baseball arbitration," in which each party presents one profit proposal and the arbitrator is required to adopt one of the two proposals. The arbitrator shall be selected and the arbitration conducted pursuant to the Voluntary Labor Arbitration Rules of the AAA.

28. AGREEMENT OF THE PARTIES:

This document [including Attachment 1, if any] shall constitute the agreement between the parties until modified or amended by a subsequent writing.

By: _____   By: _____

[Name of writer] Title

cc: WGA Contracts Department

Figure 18-4 *(continued)*

ATTACHMENT 1

ATTACHMENT 1

ADDITIONAL PROVISIONS, IF ANY:

_____

_____
_____
_____
_____
_____

Figure 18-4

Spec Sales

Writers who qualify as professional or who are treated as such (as described previously) must be paid not less than the minimum for the sale of a high-budget ($2.5 million or more) original screenplay. This price does not include any additional services. Each rewrite and polish requires an additional payment of not less than WGA minimum.

Guaranteed Rewrite/Meeting

The writer of original material is guaranteed the right to stay involved in the project as follows (these rules apply only to an original script to which separated rights apply):

- Options: When a script for a theatrical motion picture or long-form television motion picture is under option, the company is obligated to employ the writer of the original material for the first rewrite of the material at not less than WGA minimum.
- Theatrical Motion Pictures: The first rewrite rule also applies to original material sold. In addition, for both employment and sales, if the company contemplates replacing the writers, then a senior production executive who has read the writer's material shall meet with the writer to discuss the company's view and give the writer a reasonable opportunity to discuss continued service on the project.
- The writer, who also wrote the original material and has performed the first rewrite, must also be given the opportunity to make an additional

set of revisions if there is a "changed element" (e.g., new director, principal actor) within three years (for material originally written after 1995) of the writer's latest writing, provided no other writer was engaged before the changed element is in place.

- Television Motion Pictures: In long-form television, it is important to determine whether the company is signed to Network MBA or the AMPTA MBA (call the WGA signatories department for this determination). Both agreements provide for the first rewrite to the writer who sells or options original material, as time permits; however, note the following differences:

- The Network MBA signed by the traditional networks (and many independent production companies) also provides that, for both long-form employment and sales, if the company contemplates replacing the writer, a senior production executive who has read the material and has decision-making authority shall meet with the writer to discuss the company's view and give the writer reasonable opportunity to discuss continuing services on the project.

- The AMPTP MBA (generally signed by the majors and affiliated companies) provides that if the company wishes to replace a writer employed to write an original long-form teleplay, it will inform the writer of the reason why the writer will not continue on the project.

"If-Come Deals"

An exception to the option requirements described previously is the "if-come" deal, which is applicable only to television motion pictures. The rule provides that money need not be paid to the writer for the period during which the company is actively seeking licenses, interest, or other financing. The writer's deal must be fully negotiated so that in the event the company efforts are successful (the "if" part), the writer will have his or her deal already in place (the "come" part) and be attached to the project. The consideration provided by the company for the "if-come" deal is the company's active efforts; specific time periods cannot logically apply. If the company's efforts have ended after four weeks, for example, then the company has no further rights to it thereafter; unless there are further negotiations, the company may not engage in development during the "if-come" timeframe, and writers (including the "if-come" writer) should not be employed. The company has only the right to obtain financing or to generate interest during this time.

"Shopping"

"Shopping" is the submission of literary material to a third party. Unlike an option, there is no exclusive right to shop and there is no guaranteed right of the company to buy property at a set price. The company may not shop television literary material to any third parties without first obtaining the writer's written consent to do so.

The company may not shop theatrical literary material to any third parties if the writer requests (again, in writing) that the script be shopped only to a designated third party, and the company must comply with this request. Therefore, to preclude companies from shopping to outside parties, a writer must request in writing that a company not do so.

Screen Credits and Arbitration

Screen credits equate to money in the bank. If you receive sole credit—WRITTEN BY—then you are entitled to full payment for the story *and* screenplay, and full residuals payment and benefits.

If a producer hires another writer to revise a project—which happens more often than not—then the credit problem is automatically referred to the WGA for arbitration. WGA members review all materials, anonymously. It's their job to decide who is entitled to what credit. If the final credit is sole story or screenplay by (STORY BY or SCREENPLAY BY), then the payment and residuals will be based on that contribution alone. If a credit is shared with another writer (STORY BY "A" AND "B"), then so are the payment and residual checks.

The issue of screen credits is so important and complex that many pages of legal definitions and regulations are included in the MBA. In an effort to stay on top of credit problems, the Guild requires the production company to send a "Notice of Tentative Writing Credits" to Writers Guild headquarters, and to all participating writers. If a writer protests the credits for any reason, then the project automatically goes into the arbitration process.

Writing Violence in Films

The subject of violence in films deserves special attention. The ethical issue of writing violence is frustrating for writers, who disdain censorship in any form. In a cover story a few years ago on the moral climate of screenwriting, *The Journal of the Writers Guild of America* interviewed professionals about their perceptions of violence in films.[34]

Oscar-winner Ron Bass (RAIN MAN, co-writer of THE JOY LUCK CLUB) doesn't think violent films result in violent acts, but he has this conviction about the artistic integrity of his own work: "Film frames issues in a way that impacts on large numbers of people. It frequently happens that we're talking about notes in a situation, and I'll say, 'Is this what we really want our film to say? Is that insensitive to these values? Or to women?'"[35] He recalls only one argument with Amy Tan (THE JOY LUCK CLUB) concerning a sex scene in the nightclub. She thought it was gratuitous, but he felt it was critical for the audience to understand how completely this woman was taken by the male character.

Thriller writer Dan Waters (DEMOLITION MAN, HEATHERS, and BATMAN RETURNS) places the writing process in this context: "I'm at a certain point in the chain, and I'd hate to be thinking, while I'm writing, about what the effect on society is going to be. If you try to ask me to think about social responsibility, it creates bad art." Justifying violent films as art is film writer Tim Metcalf (KALIFORNIA): "I think that great violent movies do exist. . . . And they have the same good effect on people that you would get from seeing a Rembrandt hanging on the wall. Maybe they have a bad effect on the wrong people, but an insane person can misuse a chainsaw."[36]

Are filmmakers and screenwriters responsible for the violence in our culture? That heated argument was debated in a special edition of *Written By* in 1999, in which, "Writers Of Conscience"—award-winning writers—explored this subject.[37] These are some of the opinions revealed.

Screenwriter William Mastrosimone had an epiphany about film violence when he was sitting in a packed theater watching NATURAL BORN KILLERS. He says he saw that:

Kids cheered every shot, stab, kick. . . . They were drunken Roman citizens watching humans thrown to the beasts in the Coliseum. A short time later, sitting at "Pulp Fiction," they rolled in the aisles when the gun went off accidentally and the kid was killed in the back seat of the car, fouling the upholstery. They weren't seeing black comedy. . . . Something snapped in me back then in '94 and I began to feel a sense of shame about belonging to the Hollywood community. And those movies are tame compared to others. But for me a saturation point had been reached. A line was crossed between artistry and social responsibility. . . . It was then I began to see that my shame was an

*epiphany about the pervasive and profound effect we writers
have on the world. . . . And there are hundreds of laboratory and
real-life studies that have to give pause to any writer with a functioning conscience. These studies are not theories. They are sci-
entific fact. Like it or not. . . . The evidence is overwhelming that
increased viewing of violence leads to increased acceptance of
aggressive behavior. . . . There is a core of writers, producers, and
actors who are traffickers in gratuitous violence—the crack deal-
ers of fantasy—who feel they must "push the envelope," as they
say. I offer this litmus test: If an act of violence is without
remorse or consequences and uses human suffering for "entertainment" it's wrong.[38]*

Writer-director George Lucas, at a PHANTOM MENACE press conference, expressed his views on film violence: "Life is violent, and to deny
that would be almost as dangerous as glorifying it and making it an obses-
sion. It really has to do more with the context. I definitely think that hurt-
ing people for fun, for enjoyment, is a central issue here."[39]

Writer Millard Kaufman perceives that:

*Too many movie heroes are frightening and destructive. To
empathize with them, as we the audience are encouraged to do,
is to applaud the defeat of reason by malice; to celebrate mind-
lessness as long as it is kinetic; to root for the advocates of stick-
and-slash aggression with just one more kick in the plums for the
jolly old hell of it. The perpetrators of all this criminality, and
the screenwriters who chronicle their mayhem, do it under the
guise of righteousness, and they've done it on stage and books
long before Hollywood made public its love affair with
turpitude.[40]*

Award-winning screenwriter Steven Zaillian offers this insight:

*If we believe we have any power at all as artists to positively
affect the world we live in, I think we must also accept the possibility that we have the power to damage it. And if that is the*

case, we should all start talking, if not to each other, at least to
ourselves, about personal responsibility. We are, in fact, at liberty
to write whatever we want. We are also at liberty to not write
what we don't want. We are completely in control of the content
of the films in our theaters and the television shows in our living
rooms. Directors don't have that kind of control. Producers don't.
Actors don't. Executives don't. Only we have that power.[41]

As a screenwriter, you might evaluate "gratuitous" violence this way: Ask yourself if the violent action is necessary for heightened dramatic storytelling. Does it tell us about the drives of characters? Does it move the story forward? If the violence sets up justifiable actions and reactions for the characters, and it is consistent with the character development and conflicts, then it is integral to the credibility of the film.

ENDNOTES

1. "Query Letters," *The Annual Screenwriter Guide, New York Screenwriter*, March 1999, 16–18, 21.
2. Kerry Cox, "Writing Effective Query Letters," *Hollywood Scriptwriter: The Trade Paper for Screenwriters*, August 1999, 16–17.
3. "The Synopsis: A Page or Two to Sell the Story," *The New York Screenwriter*, 1999, 30–31, 33; address: 655 Fulton Street, Suite 276, Brooklyn, New York 11217.
4. Ibid., 30.
5. Ibid.
6. Ibid., 31.
7. Ibid., 30.
8. Ibid., 31.
9. Tim Tonelli, "The Shotgun Query: Does It Ever Work?," *Hollywood Scriptwriter*, August 1999, 5.
10. Ibid.
11. *Hollywood Creative Directory - Producers (HCD)*, Vol. 39, Santa Monica, CA, Hollywood Creative Directory, Spring 2000.
12. Benedict Carver and Chris Petrikin, "Hollywood's Pitches Reap Riches," *Variety*, August 30–September 5, 1999, 1.
13. Howard Meibach, "Spec Watch," by *Hollywood Scriptwriter: The Trade Paper For Screenwriters*, September 1999, 11.

14. Thom Taylor, "The Big Deal: Hollywood's Million Dollar Spec Screenplay Market," *Written By,* April 1999, 33–37.
15. Michael Gill, "Robert Kosberg, The Pitch King," *Hollywood Scriptwriter: The Trade Paper for Screenwriters,* May 2000, 5.
16. Ibid., 6.
17. Ibid.
18. Elayne Taylor, "The Pitch King Produces: An Interview with Bo Zenga," *Creative Screenwriting,* September/October 1999, 60–62.
19. Ibid., 61.
20. Ibid., 62.
21. Rick Lyman, "A Movie Surprise Is in the Audience and on the Screen," *The New York Times, National,* Sunday, March 19, 2000, 1–3.
22. Ibid., 30.
23. Ibid.
24. Ibid.
25. Ibid.
26. Ibid.
27. Ibid.
28. Jeff Jensen, "The Write Stuff: Behind the Scenes," *Entertainment Weekly,* March 31, 2000, 18.
29. Ibid.
30. Ibid.
31. Ibid., 19.
32. Ibid.
33. "Navigating the Spec Waters," *Written By,* April 1999, 34–37. Reprinted with permission of the Writers Guild of America, west.
34. Catherine Seipp, "One from the Heart: Do Writers Affect the Moral Climate?," *The Journal of the Writers Guild of America West,* December/January 1994, 19).
35. Ibid.
36. Ibid.
37. "Writers of Conscience," *Written By,* June/July 1999, 30–48.
38. William Mastrosimone, "Confessions of a Violent Movie Writer," *Written By,* June/July 1999, 30–34.
39. F. X. Feeney, "The Phantom Menace in Littleton," *Written By,* June/July 1999, 47.
40. Millard Kaufman, "Character Is Action: Excerpts from Millard Kaufman's Plots and Characters," *Written By,* June/July 1999, 35.
41. Steven Zaillian, "Smoking Guns," *Written By,* June/July 1999, 37.

19

How to Sell Your Television Script

What You Should Know Before Marketing

If you are writing for television, the script is the most important writing sample you have. This is your calling card for a possible freelance writing assignment. Get your agent to submit your script to a producer of a similar-genre show. If it shows professional talent, then you might be invited to a pitch. Revise and tighten your script before submitting it anywhere. Be very objective and thorough in your revisions. Read Chapter 10, Script Revisions, and go through the script revision checklist, then polish it. This is the only chance you get to impress agents and producers.

Know that in television, the producer—or executive producer—is the creative king (or queen). He or she is usually a writer who created a successful series. That creative head of a series is called a *show runner*. Writers who are also producers are called *hyphenates*—writer-producers.

It's not unusual for television writers who have completed many successful freelance assignments to be asked to join the staff of a series. If they are productive and reliable, then they may be asked to develop a new series concept. If the series is sold, they'll be the show runners. These people are worth their weight in gold.

Register and Copyright Your Script

Before sending your script anywhere, register it with the Writers Guild of America (WGA) and the U.S. Copyright Office. You can also use online registration services to protect your script at any stage of development. For details, see "Register and Copyright Your Script" in Chapter 18.

How to Get an Agent

It is important to get an agent who will submit your project to the right places. Read over the strategies of finding agents in Chapter 18, including "Writing A Query Letter," "The Synopsis," and "How to Get an Agent."

The Writers Guild of America, west, publishes the *WGAw Agency List*, which lists Guild signatory agencies. That list is available on the WGAw Website at www.wga.org.

Analyzing the Marketplace

Each project requires its own marketing strategy, so marketing a script requires time. Ascertain which agents, producers, television production companies, and studios would be interested in the type of project you've developed.

Read the trade papers such as *Daily Variety, Hollywood Reporter*, and weekly *Variety. Written By* regularly offers a "TV Market List," which is now online at www.wga.org, in the "Members Only" section. It identifies shows that are open for submission and key contacts for those series. Also read *Scr(i)pt, Creative Screenwriting, Hollywood Scriptwriter: The Trade Paper for Screenwriters, The New York Screenwriter*, and *Broadcasting & Cable*. These publications provide clues about current and future activities of key people in film and television.

You can find film and television contacts in the *Hollywood Creative Directory - Producers (HCD)* (Vol. 39, Spring 2000). *HCD* publishes more than 1,700 companies, 7,700 names, as well as producers, production companies, and television executives with sample credits. They also have a subscriber Website service (www.hcdonline.com) for the most current contacts in the industry. Other excellent Websites that list motion picture and television production companies are Done Deal at www.scriptsales.com and In Hollywood.com at www.inhollywood.com.

Marketing Trends in Television, January 2000

To give you an idea of television marketplace trends that you might find on the Web, see the following list, which includes sample television deals and projects sold for the first two weeks in January 2000. This information is reprinted with permission of Done Deal, at www.scriptsales.com.

TITLE: GORILLA WORLD

Logline: Show will explore a post-apocalyptic world where gorillas rule the earth and humans are the endangered species.

Writer: Todd McFarlane

Agent: n/a

Buyer: UPN

Price: n/a

Genre: Science Fiction

Logged: 1/15/00

More: UPN has ordered a premium script of the project.

TITLE: YOUNG AMERICANS

Logline: Follows the lives of a group of rich teenagers who attend an elite boys' boarding school in a small New England town.

Writer: Steven Austin

Agent: n/a

Buyer: WB

Price: n/a

Genre: Teenage Drama

Logged: 1/7/00

More: WB picked up this Columbia TriStar one-hour show with an eight-episode commitment, premiering in late June or July. To promote this new series, one or two of the characters may appear this season on "Dawson's Creek."

TITLE: FAIL-SAFE

Logline: Restaging of the live 1964 nuclear thriller.

Writer: Walter Bernstein (original and this new remake)

Agent: n/a

Buyer: CBS

Price: n/a

Genre: Drama

Logged: 1/15/00

More: George Clooney has resurrected this project and will executive produce with Noah Wyle starring. Stephen Frears may direct the live broadcast, which will be filmed on two stages on the Warner Bros. lot. John Frankenheimer will consult on this black-and-white production, which was originally adapted from the novel by Harvey Wheeler and Eugene Burdick. Scheduled for April 9.

TITLE: UNTITLED CRIME DRAMA

Logline: Crime drama set in Miami and centers on a crime boss who is being pursued by a female FBI agent.

Writer: Tom Fontana and Julie Martin

Agent: UTA

Buyer: NBC

Price: n/a

Genre: Drama

Logged: 1/5/00

More: From the same writing team who brought us "Homicide," this will be shot in March.

TITLE: THE TIE THAT BINDS

Logline: Story of how a town covers up a murder that was committed by a woman who happens to be the pillar of that community.

Writer: Ken Haruf (novel)

Agent: n/a

Buyer: CBS

Price: Six-figure option deal

Genre: Mystery

Logged: 1/5/00

More: Book was in the out-of-print category until Haruf's latest novel, *Plainsong*, brought attention back to the author's first novel. This will be turned into a TV movie.

TITLE: KISS AND XENA: WARRIOR PRINCESS

Logline: Rock band Kiss and female adventurer Xena will be in 3-D, multipath Webisodes, in which audiences can interactively choose how a plot develops.

Writer: n/a

Agent: n/a

Buyer: Time Warner Digital Media and Brillian Digital Entertainment

Price: n/a

Genre: Internet site/multipath Webisodes

Logged: 1/4/00

More: To be shown on Entertaindom.com. Univeral is also involved.

Disclaimer: All data provided by Done Deal is provided on an "as-is" basis and any or all warranties of any kind or character whatsoever, whether express or implied, including, without limitation, any warranty of merchantability or fitness for a particular purpose, are hereby expressly disclaimed. Done Deal does not guarantee or warrant the sequence, accuracy, timeliness, or completeness of any such data/material. Done Deal shall not be responsible or liable to any person or entity whomsoever, injury, claim, liability, or other cause of any kind or character whatsoever based upon or resulting from any data/material provided.

The Television Writer's Marketplace

A visual model of the writer's marketplace in television is shown in Figure 19-1.

Network, Cable Channels, and Pay TV

In network television, there is a network oligarchy. At the top of the network submission ladder are ABC, CBS, NBC, Fox, UPN, and the WB. If a project is submitted and "passed" (i.e., turned down), it's too late to move back down the ladder to producers. Their goal is to bring it back up to the networks. The same is true of the competitive cable channels and Pay TV marketplace, where producers want to sell to a few key financially viable buyers such as HBO or Showtime. Smaller companies can't compete with the deals offered by those larger companies and are more likely to structure a modest licensing agreement for the rights to the show. For a list of networks and cable channels, see "Television Production Companies" in Appendix B, available on website at www.focalpress.com/companions.

As Figure 19-1 shows, the closer a project comes to the top, the more limited the number of buyers. It faces stiffer competition and fewer alternatives. The marketplace is highly competitive, but not totally impenetrable.

Independent Producers

Independent producers represent the widest marketing potential for writers in television and motion pictures. If one producer turns down an idea, there are hundreds of others who might still find it fresh and interesting; however, the smaller independent producer is not likely to have the financial resources to compete with the development monies available at production companies and major studios.

THE WRITER'S MARKETPLACE IN TELEVISION

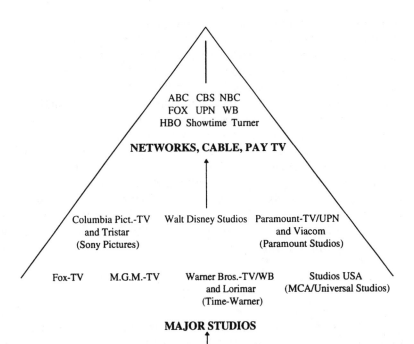

ABC CBS NBC
FOX UPN WB
HBO Showtime Turner

NETWORKS, CABLE, PAY TV

Columbia Pict.-TV   Walt Disney Studios   Paramount-TV/UPN
and Tristar   and Viacom
(Sony Pictures)   (Paramount Studios)

Fox-TV   M.G.M.-TV   Warner Bros.-TV/WB   Studios USA
                               and Lorimar   (MCA/Universal Studios)
                               (Time-Warner)

MAJOR STUDIOS

PRODUCTION COMPANIES

INDEPENDENT PRODUCERS

FREELANCE WRITERS

Figure 19-1
The Television Writer's Marketplace

Production Companies

Production companies do have that bargaining power, and they represent the strongest marketing resource for new scripts. The distinction between independents and larger production companies is their relative financial stability and current competitive strength at the box office or on television. Production companies form and dissolve according to the financial ebbs and flows of the industry. The more successful production companies have become mini-studios in their own right, with features in development and triumphant track records.

Examples of current successful television production companies include these powerhouses: Carsey-Werner Prods. ("Cosby," "That 70s Show," "3rd Rock From The Sun"), David E. Kelley Prods. ("Ally McBeal," "The Practice"), Spelling Television ("7th Heaven," "Beverly Hills 90210," "Safe Harbor"), Steven Bochco Prods. ("NYPD Blue"). For a more complete list, see "Television Production Companies" in Appendix B, available on website at www.focalpress.com/companions.

Major Studios

Major studios have the largest financial resources for development, production, and distribution. But with skyrocketing production costs and a rough-edged economy, some studios have been forced to merge with other companies. Development deals are now rare. The studios remain committed to finding those elusive new box office hits and actively seek co-production ventures to share the costs of production. They also have aggressive television divisions.

Corporate mergers may have clouded the logos of the studios, but these entities are currently the most identifiable: Sony Pictures (includes Columbia and Tristar), Walt Disney Studios, Paramount (includes merger with Viacom), Fox, MGM, Time-Warner (includes merger with Warner Bros. and Lorimar), StudiosUSA (MCA/Universal Studios, owned by Matsushita).

In major studios, the television division that is responsible for developing new shows is called *program development*. Executives in charge of comedy development and dramatic development head it. Another division, *current programming*, is responsible for maintaining the creative energy of current series. For a list of television divisions of major studios, see "Television Production Companies" in Appendix B, available on website at www.focalpress.com.companions.

Writing Professionally for Television Series

Writing for television involves meeting incredible deadlines, and writing and rewriting scripts according to disparate notes from producers, studios, and networks about making the script good. The industry is also rampant with "ageism"—a bias against any writer over the age of 30. The advertisers and networks mistakenly believe that younger writers will automatically appeal to younger audiences.

How do successful television writers deal with creative problems and script deadline pressures, and how do they know the script is good? What advice would they offer to other writers? *Written By* published profiles of some of the Emmy-nominated writers for the 51st annual nighttime awards for the Academy of Television Arts and Sciences. Those writers offered revealing advice (September 1999).

David E. Kelley (nominated for Outstanding Writing in a Comedy Series, "Ally McBeal," "Sideshow") is creator of "Chicago Hope," "Ally McBeal," "The Practice," the ABC series "Snoops," and a reconfigured half-hour version of "Ally McBeal" for Fox simply called "Ally." *Written By* calls him the most prolific writer in the business. Last season he wrote 17 episodes of "The Practice," all 22 episodes of "Ally McBeal," and the closing episode of "Chicago Hope." Both "The Practice" and "Ally McBeal" won 13 Emmy nominations each.

Kelley explains how he handles all the pressure of script deadlines, and how succinctness is important in television writing:

I work on one thing at a time. . . . Usually it takes four or five days to write a script. When I have a week or more, the scripts usually aren't as good. The only explanation I have is that without the adrenaline of a deadline, there's a resulting lack of adrenaline in some of the scenes. . . . One advantage of starting out as a lawyer is that I had three years writing motions or briefs. . . . Pay attention to what you can do with your camera. Because if you can tell a story with the camera, do it. If I can say something in four words as opposed to five, I'll choose four. That kind of economy over the course of a 60-page script really adds up. You get to tell more story, get to the center scenes faster. Succinctness is very important to storytelling and especially to the medium of television, where you only have an hour.[1]

Kelley also discloses the importance of work habits he learned from Steven Bochco:

> *I think the luckiest break I got in this business out here was working for Steven Bochco. The habits I got working for him I still hold very dearly because Steven never, never writes down to an audience, never assumes that people won't be there asking hard questions or demanding that you do better. Really respect the audience; that's the first rule and best that any writer/producer can adhere to when starting to do a television series.²*

How can Kelley tell if a writer is good? He explains it this way:

> *I'll look at the script first because it's not just a function of being smart. There's a lot of hugely intelligent people who are much smarter than I am. . . . Writing is as much an ear as it is anything else. It certainly helps to be intelligent, as well as probably educated, but to me it's the ear, it's the rhythms of how people speak, whether there's a flow in scenes, whether the writer is able to find conflict in scenes, and a general story guide. When you finish one scene, are you anxious to get to the next scene to see what happens? These are very inexact, unscientific talents, and the only way you can tell if someone can do it is really to read the script. So that's the ticket. If the script is impressive, then the meeting would follow.³*

Aaron Sorkin (who was Emmy-nominated for Outstanding Writing for a Comedy Series, "SportsNight," "The Apology") was also interviewed. He created and serves as executive producer and writer for 23 episodes of "SportsNight," and "The West Wing," for which he wrote the pilot. He also wrote his first screenplay, A FEW GOOD MEN, adapted from his play. As *Written By* notes, "In a feat that few have successfully managed, he will attempt to write most of the scripts for and executive-produce both "The West Wing" and "SportsNight" during the 1999–2000 season."

Aaron Sorkin's advice for new writers is this:

> *Don't write two television shows at the same time. That's something you don't want to try at home until you have a certain*

number of flying hours. My second suggestion is this: Write what you want to write, what you're good at. Don't try and bend yourself into what you think television is supposed to be. Television needs writers, not executives, to be the leaders. . . . Certainly the biggest challenge of TV is you have to do it every week. The scripts have got to be on the table every Monday at "SportsNight," and the show airs two weeks later. We did 23 this year; that's bigtime, relentless pressure. You need discipline. On the other hand, I would take two years to write many, many drafts of the screenplay of "A Few Good Men" or "The American President." I didn't think so at the time, but it's positively luxurious doing it that way, as if I had two years at Club Med.[4]

David Chase (who was Emmy-nominated twice for Best Drama Series for writing HBO's "The Sopranos," for the pilot and "College," which was co-written with James Manos, Jr.) was interviewed about writing for "The Sopranos." The interview was compiled from the Writers Guild Foundation's presentation, "Anatomy of a TV Drama: The Sopranos" at Words Into Pictures, 1999.[5]

Chase divulges that he created the idea of a mobster in therapy, who had problems with his mother, as a movie idea. He wrote the pilot script, and the studios and networks passed on it. He recounts how "I never heard from the chief executive at the studio. Almost all the networks roundly passed. Somebody said along the way. . . . 'Does he have to be in therapy?' I had said originally . . . 'Can't we go to HBO? . . . Most of their [HBO] notes are about making it smarter or just keeping it consistent. . . . They really are interested in making sure that it's smart."[6]

As for the process of developing stories for "The Sopranos" series, and writing for the characters, Chase discloses the following:

The writers and I meet and beat out the stories together. We're all in a room, just talking for days, and then finally maybe some story takes shape, and then we all beat it out together and write it on a board. We do an A-story, B-story, C-story. We marry those stories together, and then somebody usually has an affinity for one for logistical reasons and will say, "Why don't you do this one?" . . . In scenes there's always antagonism going on. Even the tender moments are antagonist and sarcastic. . . . That's one of the keys. They are always attacking each other, even just little love taps. . . . Every character is always blaming other people for their problems. No one takes responsibility for anything.[7]

Nicholas Wootton (who was Emmy-nominated for Best Teleplay, "NYPD Blue," "Hearts and Souls," with Steven Bochco, David Milch, and Bill Clark for the story) was interviewed about writing for "NYPD Blue." He reveals how he handled the delicate last episode of the season in which Jimmy Smit's character (Bobby Simone) would perish from a heart transplant that wouldn't take.

Wootton also reveals how he changed his writing process:

> *It was such an incredible idea and very fraught emotionally. . . . I worked in different ways. My process changed. I tried to get a little more internal. Whenever possible, I worked in darker rooms. I put myself in emotional situations. I generally work in my office, but I stayed in a little bit later, I took work home more than usual. . . . This was one writing experience I really wanted to make personal.*[8]

Pitching

If your spec script is good enough to impress a producer of caliber, then you might be invited to a pitch meeting. When your agent calls to say a producer is interested, it's time to write out *springboards* for the series. Springboards are three- to five-sentence episode ideas. Work up about half a dozen. Flesh out the story beats for each. Rehearse the pitches at home, with your friends, family, spouse, or by yourself. If you're writing comedy, be funny.

Pitch meetings usually last 30 to 45 minutes. Take a notepad for notes. Evan Smith, in his book, *Writing Television Sitcoms* offers these reminders when preparing for a pitch: "Remember your goal is to sell, not educate. . . . Because producers sometimes mull over a pitch, before deciding on an assignment, some writers like to leave them with *'leave-behinds.'* These are simply copies of the springboards . . . that were pitched, each neatly typed on a separate page, with the writer's name at the top."

There is helpful advice from major sitcom producers in Smith's book. Irma Kalish advises: "The main thing is enthusiasm."[10] Matt Williams cautions: "When pitching, there's a saying—pitch the sizzle, not the steak. I think the biggest mistake with pitching is [that some writers] get too bogged down in details."[11] Lawrence Konner counsels: "I always feel like I want to tell stories when I pitch and I want to hear stories when I'm listening to pitches. . . . Show the producers that you're smart enough and entertaining enough, and that you understand their show enough, and they will want to be in business with you."[12]

Before any pitch meeting, read over "The Art of Pitching Ideas" and "Personal Ingredients for Successful Pitching" in Chapter 17. Remember the key ingredients necessary for a successful presentation of a television concept are the same: *honest enthusiasm, abundance of detail, humor, conviction,* and *adaptability.*

TV Series Concepts

If you've written a new television series concept, then submit it to a producer or a production company that has been successful in developing those kinds of shows. You can also submit it to the head of development for a major studio because they have established track records with the networks that will greatly enhance your credibility. For details about series development and strategies, see "How To Create Marketable Television Series Concepts," in Chapter 17.

Long-Form Television

For a project that is a television film, movie of the week, or miniseries, get your agent to submit it to the head of TV film development at a major production company or major studio. Work closely with them in development because they know all the ins and outs of the TV film industry. If the network is too timid to handle a project, then submit it directly to a company like HBO Productions, which is more open to creative ideas.

The contract will adhere to the terms of the schedule of minimums negotiated by the Writers Guild of America. See the relevant "Portions of the WGA 1998 Theatrical and Television Basic Agreement Schedule of Minimums" in Appendix A.

As mentioned in Chapter 18, when a script for a theatrical motion picture or long-form television motion picture is under option, the company is obligated to employ the writer of the original material for the first rewrite of the material at not less than WGA minimum. In long-form television, it is important to determine whether the company is signed to Network MBA or the AMPTA MBA. (Call the WGA signatories department for this determination.) Both agreements provide for the first rewrite to the writer who sells or options original material, as time permits; however, note the following differences.

The Network MBA signed by the traditional networks (and many independent production companies) also provides that, for both long-form employment and sales, if the company contemplates replacing the writer, then a senior production executive who has read the material and has decision-making authority shall meet with the writer to discuss the company's view and give the writer reasonable opportunity to discuss continuing services on the project.

Business Deals and Contracts for Television

If a producer wants to purchase your television project, then get an agent to close the deal. He or she will take a standard 10 percent commission. An entertainment attorney would be equally effective. If you're dealing with a signatory producer or production company, then the terms for employment will adhere to the terms of the schedule of minimums negotiated by the Writers Guild of America.

For television, the Minimum Basic Agreement (MBA) covers fees and rights for network primetime (story, teleplay, story and teleplay), made-for-pay television or videocassette/videodisc, made-for-basic cable, informational programming, high-budget other than primetime, rewrite and polish, plot outline (narrative synopsis of story), backup script, format, bible, narration, rerun compensation, foreign telecast compensation, week-to-week and term employment, noncommercial opening and closing, purchase of literary material, optioned material, sequel payment, character payment, and low-budget minimum. It also covers comedy-variety, quiz and audience participation, serials (other than primetime), nonprimetime nondramatic strip programs, documentary programs, and news programs.

Portions of the WGA 1998 Theatrical and Television Basic Agreement Schedule of Minimums, applicable during the period 5/2/00–5/1/01, are reprinted with permission of the Writers Guild of America, west, Inc. (see Appendix A). If you have any questions regarding the application of these provisions or minimums, or relating to categories of minimums not included in the schedule, or if you have a question about interpretation of the Basic Agreement, then contact the Guild. Be sure to review the information in the "Rules of Spec Contracts" section in Chapter 18.

Credits and Arbitration

Television writing credits are based on your professional creative contribution to the project, and they mean money in the bank. If you receive sole credit—STORY AND TELEPLAY BY—then you are entitled to 100 percent payment for story and teleplay, as well as full residual payment.

If a producer hires another television writer to revise a project—which happens more often than not—then the credit problem is automatically referred to the WGA for arbitration. All material is reviewed by WGA members, anonymously. It's their job to decide who is entitled to what credit. If the final credit is sole story or teleplay (STORY BY or TELEPLAY BY), then the residuals will be based on that contribution alone. If a credit is shared with another writer (TELEPLAY BY "A" AND "B"), then so are the residual checks.

If you create a new series, the CREATED BY credit entitles you to 100 percent of the royalties every time a television show airs. That translates to thousands of dollars each week for a television series.

Many pages of legal definitions and regulations are included in the MBA concerning screen credits. In an effort to stay on top of credit problems, the Guild requires the production company to send a "Notice of Tentative Writing Credits" to Writers Guild headquarters and to all participating writers. If a writer protests the credits for any reason, then the project automatically goes into the arbitration process.

ENDNOTES

1. "Miracle Worker: David E. Kelley," *Written By,* September 1999, 20.
2. Ibid., 48.
3. Ibid., 49.
4. "Sports Knight: Aaron Sorkin," *Written By,* September 1999, p. 23.
5. "Chasing Emmy: David Chase," *Written By*, September, 1999, 24–25.
6. Ibid., 25.
7. Ibid.
8. "Heartbreak Kid: Nicholas Wootton," *Written By,* September 1999, 27.
9. Evan Smith, *Writing Television Sitcoms,* New York, Perigee, 1999, 217.
10. Ibid., 220.
11. Ibid.
12. Ibid., 221.

National and State Funding Sources

If you write high-quality drama or documentary projects, this chapter will help you wade through the maze of grant opportunities. Years ago, I served as senior program officer for the National Endowment for the Humanities (NEH), so I know the intricacies of grant support for film and television projects. The bureaucracy is dreadful, and the financial rewards are relatively limited, but there is something notable about having your project supported by the NEA, NEH, CPB, or a prestigious grant.

Note that the government bureaucracy constantly fluctuates, according to changing political winds. So be sure to check this information carefully. Investigate the mission of each agency.

National Funding Sources

The Corporation for Public Broadcasting

The Corporation for Public Broadcasting (CPB) is located at 401 9th Street NW, Washington, D.C. 20004-2129; phone: 202/879-9600; fax: 202/879-9700; Website: www.cpb.org. The Website provides general information on the agency's budget and television programming and includes a directory of public broadcasting stations, advice on how to write and apply for grants, and job listings.

The CPB is a major source of funding for programming on public broadcasting. Operating within congressionally prescribed guidelines, the CPB awards grants for the production of innovative, educational, and informational radio and television programs for national distribution. The CPB also helps fund television productions by and about minorities through its support of the Minority Consortia.

In addition, the CPB provides the Public Broadcasting Service (PBS) with annual funding for its national program service. Through the Radio Program Fund, the CPB invests in an array of public radio projects that use new media technologies, create new partnerships, and bring about high-quality radio programming.

Independent producers, writers, and public TV stations can submit program proposals, and the CPB encourages co-productions between independents and PBS stations. They also encourage submissions by women and minorities.

If you have an idea for development, write to them directly, or, more practically, set up a meeting with the head of programming at your local PBS station. Local stations are likely to know the program proposal requirements of the CPB, and they can help you put together a more competitive proposal if you mutually decide to pursue the idea.

When you apply for funding, you fill out a basic information sheet, which is supplied with the program guidelines. That is the face sheet of the application, which describes the content of the show, costs, and key personnel involved. In addition, you'll need to write a short synopsis that shows how you plan to handle the subject matter for television. It's written in precisely the same way you would write a storyline for the networks. If you have completed a detailed treatment, that can be attached as well.

A budget is required for CPB applications, indicating how much money is needed for development or production of the television show. The budget is something a writer must deal with in grant applications. The funding agency needs to know where you plan to spend its money. For script development grants, the budget is usually very simple: writer's fees, research fees, travel, and administrative costs. The writer's fees can be based on the Writers Guild of America's Minimum Basic Agreement. (For portions of the latest WGA Theatrical and Television Basic Agreement Schedule of Minimums, see Appendix A.)

The CPB is an approachable agency. Whether your project is dramatic, cultural, special, children's, news, or public affairs, contact them to find out how it fits in. You can also submit your project to the executive producer of a series that is currently funded by the CPB.

Annenberg/CPB Project

The Annenberg/CPB Project received $15 million over a 10-year period to support innovative projects that use new technologies—including television and film—to improve higher education. It's a very different and intriguing opportunity for writers and producers who want to collaborate with institutions of higher learning (and vice versa). For guidelines and more information about the program, write to the Annenberg/CPB project.

Public Broadcasting Service

The Public Broadcasting Service (PBS) is primarily concerned with the acquisition of programs already produced, and functions as a distributor of public TV programs. Still, they get involved, peripherally, in the development of new shows for the system, and they have been involved with interactive programming initiatives.

As explained in the PBS Website (www.pbs.org), PBS is a private, non-profit corporation whose members are America's public TV stations. Founded in 1969, PBS provides quality TV programming and related services to 348 noncommercial stations serving all 50 states, Puerto Rico, the U.S. Virgin Islands, Guam, and American Samoa.

Staff members in Alexandria, Virginia, and New York City oversee program acquisition, distribution, and promotion; education services; new media ventures; fundraising support; engineering and technology development; and video marketing.

PBS can be helpful in offering some backing for projects that might be of interest to their stations. That support usually comes in the form of a letter of endorsement rather than a banker's check. They will, however, help secure interest from appropriate funding sources, and, in some cases, will put up some seed money for development. The reality, though, is that PBS funds are scarce.

Some years ago, given the mandate to move PBS into a more aggressive program stance, Jennifer Lawson, former Chief Program Executive, negotiated the rights to a high-quality NBC drama series, "I'll Fly Away," when it was canceled by NBC. In discussions I had with her, Jennifer Lawson said she wanted to build a sense of quality drama that will bring new audiences to the network. The biggest problem was that PBS budgets can't compete with the big networks. The series was too expensive to produce, so she approved the purchase of reruns and the development of a new final episode.

In addition to targeting minority audiences, Jennifer Lawson wanted to bring in younger audiences, like those targeted with documentaries on Paul Simon, Gloria Estefan, and Billy Joel. With respect to development, PBS initiated a groundbreaking comedy produced by former NBC network president, Brandon Tartikoff, with WYES in New Orleans ("The Steven Banks Show"). That half-hour series broke a one-hour programming stranglehold that blocked half-hour shows from being developed at PBS. Lawson sought to break away from the notion that PBS is a "humor-impaired network." Lawson added: "We take the stewardship of public funds seriously. . . . It is perfectly within the realm of what public television should explore. Humor and satire can be a way of looking at ourselves."[1]

Because of unending political challenges from politicians and local stations, in the late 1990s, Jennifer Lawson stepped down as Chief Program Executive. So, investigate the PBS mission carefully. It is for the benefit of the station membership, and appears in their Website.

When you develop a script or film project for public television, try to elicit interest from a local PBS station. They know the landscape and the players. You can find a list of local stations at their Website. And remember that PBS has very little money to award to projects. They are the place to help find funding, and to award a primetime spot to air your project.

National Endowment for the Arts

The National Endowment for the Arts (NEA) is located at 1100 Pennsylvania Avenue NW, Washington, D.C. 20506; phone: 202/682-5400. It was created by Congress to encourage and support the Arts in America. Its fundamental role is to support creativity at the highest level, and to stimulate the enjoyment of the arts in our country. The agency fulfills its mission through various grant-making programs, including one called The Arts in Radio and Television. It also has a Literary Fellowships category. Contact them for applications and deadlines. You can also get the latest from the NEA Website (http://arts.endow.gov), which offers information about the programs.

The Arts in Radio and Television

Through this category, the NEA seeks to make the excellence and diversity of the arts widely available to the American public through nationally distributed television and radio programs. Grants are available to support the development, production, and national distribution of significant radio and television programs on the arts. Priority will be given to artistically excellent programs that have the potential to reach a significant national audience. Only projects of artistic excellence and merit, in terms of both the content and the use of the medium, will be funded.

Projects may include high-profile multipart television and radio series, single documentaries, performance programs, or arts segments for use within an existing series. Programs may deal with any art form (e.g., music, dance, literature, design, theater, musical theater, opera, visual arts, film/video/audio art, folk and traditional arts).

Literature Fellowships

Through fellowships to published creative writers and translators of exceptional talent in the areas of prose and poetry, the NEA advances its goal of expanding the opportunities for artists to interpret, explore, and create work. This program operates on a two-year cycle, with fellowships in prose available one year and fellowships in poetry available the next.

Fellowships for Creative Writers

Fellowships in prose (fiction and creative nonfiction) or poetry are available to published creative writers of exceptional talent. Fellowships enable recipients to set aside time for writing, research, travel, and general career advancement.

Panelists for the NEA give very serious consideration to the level of artistic and professional achievement exhibited in your sample project. Most of the film and video production grants are made to nonprofit organizations and are limited to a requirement for matching funds.

Cultural Programming: Federal, State, and Local Opportunities

The NEA has a new online resource of Federal funding available for arts initiatives through national, state, and local funding programs. It is available at http://arts.endow.gov/federal.html.

In the past, film and video artists could apply for fellowships through a regional program set up by the NEA and state arts agencies. You can contact the state agency nearest you to determine eligibility requirements. There is a list of state arts and humanities agencies in Appendix C, available on website at www.focalpress.com/companions.

The National Endowment for the Humanities

The National Endowment for the Humanities (NEH) is located at 1100 Pennsylvania Avenue NW, Washington D.C. 20506; phone: 202/606-8400. The mission of the NEH is to encourage and support important works in the humanities, and to disseminate that information to the widest possible audience. The media program at the NEH has been one of the largest and most important funding sources for public radio, television, and film.

The media program is particularly relevant to freelance writers and independent producers. It supports the development and production of new television, film, and radio projects. The NEH has an informative listing of projects funded at the NEH Humanities Media Log on its Website, at www.neh.fed.us. You will find a brief description of more than 800 radio, television, and film productions, each produced with substantial support from the NEH. These productions include such acclaimed documentaries as "The Civil War," "The Great Depression," and "FDR," literary biographies on James Baldwin, Edgar Allen Poe, and 13 American Poets (Voices and Visions), as well as such family programming as "Long Ago and Far Away" and "Booker."

The general themes that are relevant to the NEH shift with the incumbent administration's interpretation of the humanities. In the past, the NEH supported socially relevant projects tied to humanities themes, then shifted to a more conservative stance, supporting classical, scholarly subjects, such as "Masterworks of Civilization." You can keep up with the current trends by reading the media guidelines carefully and by contacting staff members to determine eligibility.

A project that is submitted to the NEH for consideration should meet one or more of these basic NEH goals: (1) provide an interpretation and appreciation of significant cultural works; (2) help illuminate historical ideas, figures, and events; or (3) provide an understanding of the disciplines of the humanities. Those disciplines have been defined by Congress and are listed by academic fields in the guidelines.

The NEH media program encourages professional writers and producers to work in cooperation with scholars in particular program areas. The meeting of the minds between professionals and scholars creates a challenging atmosphere and contributes to some mutually rewarding ideas about program development in the humanities. Contact them for applications and deadlines. You can also get the latest information from their Website.

Typically, the NEH offers *challenge grants*, which help media centers, and the makers of films and radio programs, to incorporate new technology and expand humanities programming. In the past, they supported the following other types of grants:

- *Planning grants* to support writers, producers, and scholars seeking to develop innovative media humanities projects.
- *Script development* to support the writing of scripts and series outlines. They cover appropriate research costs for treatment and scripts (travel, consultants) as well as other development costs (writer's fees, story conferences, typing, and duplicating).

- *Production grants* for single programs, pilots, or series episodes. Because production costs are so high, they usually require additional gifts and matching funds from other sources.

As for submission of proposals, the NEH strongly recommends a preliminary inquiry before each deadline. The staff can help determine the appropriateness of the project, and can help you prepare a more competitive proposal for submission. In addition, they can guide your project through formal evaluation procedures.

For a complete description of grants, write to them for guidelines and applications. You can also get that information from their Website at www.neh.fed.us.

State Funding Sources

State Arts and Humanities Agencies

One of the most practical places to look for seed money for the development of original scripts is the state arts and humanities agencies. Each state has money appropriated by the legislature for support of artistic and cultural work relevant to that state. In the past, the NEA and NEH also contributed block grants for regranting purposes to the state agencies.

The Arts and Humanities agencies are usually separate and distinct from each other, operating within the same general mandate as their national counterparts. Because each agency has different guidelines, you should contact the staff to determine whether script development grants are possible. For a list of state arts and humanities agencies, see Appendix C, available on website at www.focalpress.com/companions.

State Film and Television Commissions

State film and television commissions are another resource for discussing your ideas and projects. Although they have no funding capabilities, these agencies are committed to the idea of nurturing new productions, and they can be helpful in the pragmatics of preproduction contacts. They know who is doing what in your state and can often provide interesting leads. For a list of state arts and humanities agencies, see Appendix C, available on website at www.focalpress.com/companions.

Private Foundations and Corporate Sources

Relatively few foundations are waiting to fund scriptwriters; however, several have been active in funding film and television projects, including the Ford Foundation, Guggenheim Foundation, Lilly, Mellon Foundation, Markle, Exxon, Sears Roebuck Foundation, and the Jerome Foundation (which funds screenwriters living in New York). One very helpful place to begin your search for appropriate funding is The Foundation Center, which has offices in New York City and Washington, D.C. They also have field offices and repository libraries in several parts of the country. The Center is the only nonprofit organization in the country designed to analyze and disseminate information about foundations.

One of its publications, *The Foundation Directory*, profiles thousands of foundations and can help identify those organizations that support projects similar to your own. The directory identifies foundations that have supported film and video projects, as well as those interested in a vast array of catalogued subjects. For other opportunities, be sure to investigate resources such as *Grants and Awards Available to American Writers* and *Gadney's Guide to International Contests, Festivals, and Grants in Film, Video.*

After determining the most appropriate possible contacts, tailor a letter to the specific interests of each foundation. You can define how your project relates to the mission of that organization, how you plan to carry out the project, what the television project might look like, and how your background fits in to guarantee the success of the project.

With respect to corporations, you can learn a great deal about their interests, objectives, and philosophies from their annual reports. You can also delve into several research directories that are available at your local library to determine which ones support similar kinds of projects.

How to Write Grant Proposals

If you're planning to submit a project to any public agency, first write for their guidelines and application forms. The guidelines will give you a broad idea of the agency's needs, and your proposal will have to address those needs. A grant proposal generally consists of three parts:

1. the application form (called the *face sheet)*
2. the narrative proposal, which details your objectives and program format
3. the budget

In addition, a timetable and the curriculum vitae (résumés) of all key personnel are included.

The Face Sheet

The first page of the application is called a face sheet. It asks for identifying information about the applicant and the proposal. Most face sheets require an abstract, to be written in a paragraph or two, outlining the objectives and format of the show. They also ask for information about key personnel. A carefully worded synopsis is especially important when you consider the fact that some evaluators might see only that first-page abstract.

Let's create a face sheet to identify some terms and to answer some questions about filling it out.

- *Item #1.* Asks for the name of the individual applicant or project director. The project director is equivalent to an executive producer. This is the person responsible for creating the show and overseeing the total creative and administrative activities.
- *Item #2.* Asks whether the proposal is new or was submitted in some other form. The application is considered new if it was never submitted to that agency. It is a revision if it was submitted and was rejected previously. It is a renewal if it is based on work done on an earlier grant (e.g., a request for production based on a script development grant). A supplemental request is one that is an extension of current grant activities.
- *Item #3.* Asks the name of the program. This refers to the name of the division within the agency as it appears on the program announcement.
- *Item #4.* Asks whether the applicant is an individual or an organization. If you are applying as a freelance writer or independent producer, you would specify "individual." If you are applying as a production entity or joint venture, you would check "institution" and specify the type of company (e.g., Television Production) as well as private or nonprofit status. Unless an agency specifically requests evidence of nonprofit status in advance, you can generally incorporate after a grant is awarded.
- *Item #5.* Asks for the grant period (i.e., when the project will start and finish). As a rule, the start date should be several weeks after you expect to hear about the award decision. That assures you that your time won't be wasted waiting for a letter of confirmation while the grant period is already in effect. Similarly, the completion date ought to provide you ample time to finish the project. It is not unusual for script development

requests to be six months long. That length of time serves as a contingency because federal agencies are reluctant to authorize extensions later on.

- *Item #6.* Asks you to define the intended audience. You can take your cue from the stated objectives of the agency. One agency might be primarily interested in reaching general adult audiences, whereas others might be targeted for minority, handicapped, bilingual, or elderly audiences, or children.
- *Item #7.* Asks for the amount of funds required to accomplish the project. Money requested directly from the agency is called an *outright grant.* The *gifts and matching* category refers to money that might be forthcoming from other sources. Some agencies require a gifts and matching situation. They will offer money contingent on your ability to raise a matching sum from another source. *Cost sharing* refers to the contributions received in the form of service, facilities, and similar donations from your own production company.
- *Item #8.* Asks for the field of the project. This refers to the specific subject category as it relates to the agency's announcement.
- *Item #9.* Asks for the chief location in which most of the work will be accomplished during the grant period. It is a curious category for freelance writers and can generally be listed as your home state. The purpose of this type of question is to provide the agency with a broad base of data to determine how effectively they serve their constituencies.
- *Item #10.* Asks for the public issues of the project. This refers to the thematic issues of relevance to the agency.
- *Item #11.* Asks for the topic title. This is the complete working title of the project.
- *Item #12.* Asks for a description of the proposed project. This is an extremely important item because it defines the objectives and approach in a paragraph or two. The synopsis should clearly and succinctly define the intentions, the film approach, the proposed content, and the key personnel involved. You'll be able to flesh out all that information later in the attached narrative proposal.

The Narrative Proposal

The *narrative* is the body of your request. It fully details the concept and film approach of the show. The narrative may run 20 to 100 pages or more, depending on the nature of the project. The narrative section expands on the ideas proposed in the abstract. Objectives are clarified, approaches are defined, and sample visual treatments are provided. In a request for script development funds, a fully detailed pilot story or treatment may also be included. If a production grant is sought, then the full script is needed, and a budget breakdown is required.

A well-written narrative generally covers each of these areas in depth:

1. the nature and scope of the project
2. the importance of the project to target audiences and general audiences
3. the selected format and visual approach for television or film
4. the timetable for research, development, and/or production
5. the background and expertise of key personnel
6. the budget

Some applications ask for a detailed synopsis of the project on a continuation sheet. This is the time to address the aforementioned points in a condensed version of the entire proposal. A continuation sheet provides significant background information on the nature and scope of the project, the personnel, and the relevance of the project to specific agency goals.

For example, if this project were for the NEH to support a film script based on a book, then the description of the book would be minimal, compared to a larger discussion of issues and themes relevant to the humanities. The treatment would appear in the narrative section of the proposal.

If this project were designed for another agency (e.g., the CPB), then this page would offer a straightforward synopsis of the dramatic storyline, instead of focusing exclusively on the historical and cultural background.

The narrative section of the proposal begins after the application forms are completed. This is the heart of the grant proposal. Objectives need to be stated clearly, and the program content should be relevant to those goals.

A well-written treatment is particularly important because it gives the reader a specific sense of the program you have in mind. It's the basis for determining how you intend to script the project. Treatments for grants are written in precisely the same way as those for network television or features. The format and structure are identical, as is the dramatic storytelling technique.

The Budget

A budget is an integral part of a grant proposal. It demonstrates the creator's ability to plan accurately, realistically, and professionally. Moreover, it assures the funding agency that the money will be spent reasonably.

"But wait!" you say, "I'm a writer! What do I know about budgets?" That's a reasonable, plaintive cry, but the fact is, in grantsmanship, the creator must be equipped to think like a hyphenate (writer-producer).

The budgetary needs of projects differ considerably; however, certain elements do tend to appear regularly. For example, in script development, the budget generally includes costs for scriptwriting, research, travel, consultant fees, typing and duplicating, administrative overhead, and so on. The actual cost for each item depends on the development needs of a particular show.

This is not to suggest that there are no budget guidelines for research and development. You can refer to the Writers Guild of America MBA for appropriate fees for writing services (see Appendix A.) You may need to budget consultants into your project. These are academic or technical advisors who are experts in their fields. You may find that one or two will be sufficient for the project, or that a full-fledged 10-member advisory board is necessary. Consultants usually receive a per diem honorarium. The number of days must be clarified in the budget and their responsibilities clarified in the narrative.

As for travel costs incurred in researching or developing a script, it's necessary to know who must travel where, and for how long. Funding agencies will support travel, but the costs must be justified in the budget. Airplane trips should be coach fare, and per diem costs should be within standard federal guidelines. The funding agency itself can offer per diem guidelines for travel in both domestic and foreign cities.

Production budgets are much more difficult to determine than script costs. If you are seeking funds for production on the basis of a completed script, then it is essential to get some professional help. At the local level, a production manager at a station or production house can supply you with rate sheets (i.e., the established costs for using facilities and personnel).

If the script to be produced is more complex, then an independent producer or production manager can help break down costs for above-the-line (talent and creative staff) and below-the-line items (technical services and facilities).

The Directors Guild of America might help you locate specific people for the purpose of budgeting the show. In addition, other key guilds and unions can provide you with up-to-date information concerning going rates.

How Projects Are Evaluated

Every agency has a different review system, but the general process remains the same. PBS and the CPB review projects in cooperation with each other and will try to find support and distribution for projects of the highest merit. The CPB usually preselects projects for review by an advisory panel of experts. They base their evaluation on the relevance of the project to the priorities of the CPB and PBS, the credentials of the production team, and the innovation and diversity the project offers to the PBS schedule. It is likely that your local PBS station has a similar evaluation process or can initiate that process with your project ideas.

One of the most rigorous evaluation systems is set up by the NEH. The NEH might select outside reviewers who are scholarly experts in various fields to look at the proposal and comment on its intellectual soundness. Whether or not the proposal receives this outside review, it is submitted to a specially convened panel of experts who represent a wide range of experience and interests in academics and television or film. The panel might consist of a Hollywood writer, a studio executive, a philosopher, an anthropologist, a cultural historian, an archaeologist, and a documentary filmmaker. The panel meets for two days, much like a sequestered jury, discussing each proposal on its own merits and in comparison with other projects submitted in that cycle.

The NEH staff forwards the recommendations of reviewers and panelists to the National Council on the Humanities. The Council consists of presidential appointees who generally endorse the recommendations of reviewers, panelists, and staff. The Council then recommends action to the Chairman of the Endowment, who has sole legislative authority to make final decisions about funding. Most often, those decisions are consistent with the advice received from the evaluation process.

The process sounds terribly cumbersome, but in fact the applicant gets a definitive word three or four months after the submission deadline. In addition, if you request the information, the staff will provide you with complete copies of the reviews and a summary of the panelists' comments.

The NEA has a similar, although less complicated, review process. The staff reviews the applications and refers them to the appropriate advisory panel. The panel's comments are reviewed by members of the National Council on the Arts, and they in turn recommend approval or disapproval to the Chairman of the Endowment. Once again, the Chairman has sole legislative authority to make final decisions but will most often act on the advice and recommendations of the Council. The applicant is notified of acceptance or rejection by the Chairman's office.

Rights, Profits, and Royalties

If a project is funded, the writer or project director usually retains creative rights; however, the question of rights should be fully investigated—and negotiated—before signing any agreement. As a reference, keep the Writers Guild's MBA by your side.

Try to get complete information about a particular agency's stance on royalties, profits, and rights. The NEH, for example, gives the grantee total control over the project and total ownership of creative rights. That's a very critical and important right for any creative writer. If the policies seem carved in stone, there's probably no room for negotiation; however, if there is some latitude, it can't hurt to negotiate.

ENDNOTES

1. Stuart Miller, "New Sked Stance Spurs Comeback," *Variety*, March 14–20, 1994, 32.

APPENDIX A

PORTIONS OF THE WGA 1998 THEATRICAL AND TELEVISION BASIC AGREEMENT THEATRICAL COMPENSATION

This material is being reprinted with permission of the Writers Guild of America, west, Inc. This schedule covers the third period of the 1998 Basic Agreement, but is not the total contract. If there is any inconsistency between this schedule and the Basic Agreement, the Basic Agreement shall prevail.

If you have any questions regarding the application of these provisions or minimums, or relating to categories of minimums not included in this schedule, or if you have questions about interpretation of the Basic Agreement, contact the Guild.

		Second Period Effective 5/2/99–5/1/00	
		LOW	HIGH
A.	Original Screenplay, IncludingTreatment		
	Installments:	$45,490	$85,330
	Delivery of Original Treatment	$20,614	$34,134
	Delivery of First Draft Screenplay	$17,916	$34,134
	Delivery of Final Draft Screenplay	$6,960	$17,062
B.	Non-Original Screenplay, Including Treatment Installments:	$39,812	$74,035
	Delivery of Treatment	$14,928	$22,758
	Delivery of First Draft Screenplay	$17,916	$34,134
	Delivery of Final Draft Screenplay	$6,968	$17,143

		Second Period Effective 5/2/99–5/1/00	
		LOW	HIGH
C.	Original Screenplay, Excluding Treatment or Sale of Original Screenplay	$30,570	$62,571
	Installments for Employment:		
	Delivery of First Draft Screenplay	$23,608	$45,511
	Delivery of Final Draft Screenplay	$6,962	$17,060
D.	Non-Original Screenplay Excluding Treatment or Sale of Non-Original Screenplay	$24,877	$51,195
	Installments for Employment:		
	Delivery of First Draft Screenplay	$17,916	$34,134
	Delivery of Final Draft Screenplay	$6,961	$17,061
E.	Additional Compensation for Story included in Screenplay	$5,692	$11,377
F.	Story or Treatment	$14,928	$22,758
G.	Original Story or Treatment	$20,614	$34,134
H.	First Draft Screenplay, with or without Option for Final Draft Screenplay (non-original)		
	First Draft Screenplay	$17,916	$34,134
	Final Draft Screenplay	$11,940	$22,758
I.	Rewrite of Screenplay	$14,928	$22,758
J.	Polish of Screenplay	$7,468	$11,377

The MBA provides for a discount with respect to employment on a flat-deal basis of a writer who has not been previously employed under a Guild MBA in television, theatrical films, or dramatic radio, subject to an adjustment to full minimum if a photoplay is produced and the writer receives any writing credit. For details, contact the Guild Contracts Department.

		Third Period Effective 5/2/99–5/1/00	
		LOW	**HIGH**
A.	Original Screenplay, Including Treatment Installments:	$47,082	$88,317
	Delivery of Original Treatment	$21,335	$35,329
	Delivery of First Draft Screenplay	$18,543	$35,329
	Delivery of Final Draft Screenplay	$7,204	$17,659
B.	Non-Original Screenplay, Including Treatment Installments:	$41,205	$76,626
	Delivery of Treatment	$15,450	$23,555
	Delivery of First Draft Screenplay	$18,543	$35,329
	Delivery of Final Draft Screenplay	$7,212	$17,742
C.	Original Screenplay, Excluding Treatment or Sale of Original Screenplay Installments for Employment:	$31,640	$64,761
	Delivery of First Draft Screenplay	$24,434	$47,104
	Delivery of Final Draft Screenplay	$7,206	$17,657
D.	Non-Original Screenplay, Excluding Treatment or Sale of Non-Original Screenplay Installments for Employment:	$25,748	$52,987
	Delivery of First Draft Screenplay	$18,543	$35,329
	Delivery of Final Draft Screenplay	$7,205	$17,658
E.	Additional Compensation for Story included in Screenplay	$5,891	$11,775
F.	Story or Treatment	$15,450	$23,555
G.	Original Story or Treatment	$21,335	$35,329
H.	First Draft Screenplay, with or without Option for Final Draft Screenplay (non-original)		
	First Draft Screenplay	$18,543	$35,329
	Final Draft Screenplay	$12,358	$23,555
I.	Rewrite of Screenplay	$15,450	$23,555
J.	Polish of Screenplay	$7,729	$11,775

THEATRICAL BUDGET THRESHOLDS

LOW BUDGET: Photoplay costing less than $2,500,000
HIGH BUDGET: Photoplay costing $2,500,000 or more

ISSUANCE OF DEAL MEMO

The MBA requires timely delivery, generally 10 to 12 days, of a deal memo to the writer or the writer's representative after agreement on the major deal points. Contact the Guild Contracts Department for details.

PAYMENT SCHEDULE

Upon commencement of writing services, the writer is to receive **the greater of:**

(a) 10% of the agreed compensation for delivery of first material;
   or
(b) $3,321 (effective 5/2/98–5/1/99);
   $3,437 (effective 5/2/99–5/1/00);
   $3,557 (effective 5/2/00–5/1/01).

In addition, Company will make its best efforts to pay writer within 48 hours of delivery but in no event more than seven (7) days after delivery.

Payment shall not be contingent upon the acceptance or approval by the Company of the literary material so delivered, or upon any other contingency such as obtaining financing.

PURCHASES FROM A PROFESSIONAL WRITER

The Flat Deal minimums shall apply to purchases of literary material from a "professional writer" as that term is specifically defined in the Basic Agreement.

OPTIONED MATERIAL (THEATRICAL)

Company may option literary material from a "professional writer" for a period of up to 18 months upon payment of 10% of minimum. Each renewal period of up to 18 months requires an additional 10% of minimum.

WEEK-TO-WEEK AND TERM EMPLOYMENT

Compensation Per Week++	Effective 5/2/98–5/1/99	Effective 5/2/99–5/1/00	Effective 5/2/00–5/1/01
Week-to-week	$3,577	$3,702	$3,832
14 out of 14 weeks	$3,321	$3,437	$3,557
20 out of 26 weeks	$3,068	$3,175	$3,286
40 out of 52 weeks	$2,820	$2,919	$3,021

++The MBA provides for a discount for a limited period of time with respect to employment on a week-to-week or term basis of a writer who has not been previously employed under a Guild MBA in television, theatrical films, or dramatic radio. For details, contact the Guild Contracts Department.

NARRATION (written by a writer other than writer of Screenplay or Story & Screenplay)

Minimums for narration are based on status of film assembly and nature of previously written material as follows:

Nature of Material Written prior to employment of narration writer	Film Assembled in Story Sequence	Film Footage Not Assembled in Story Sequence
None	Applicable Screenplay excluding Treatment Minimum	Applicable Screenplay including Treatment Minimum
Story Only	Applicable Screenplay excluding Treatment Minimum	Applicable Screenplay excluding Treatment Minimum
Story and Screenplay	Per Rate Schedule A	Per Rate Schedule A

Rate Schedule A	Effective 5/2/98–5/1/99	Effective 5/2/99–5/1/00	Effective 5/2/00–5/1/01
Two minutes or less	$673	$697	$721
Over two minutes to five minutes	$2,378	$2,461	$2,547
Over five minutes of narration	Applicable Polish Minimum		

THEATRICAL AND TELEVISION PENSION PLAN AND HEALTH FUND

All employment under the WGA 1998 Theatrical and Television Basic Agreement is subject to employer contributions of:

- 6% to the PRODUCER-WRITERS GUILD OF AMERICA PENSION PLAN
- 6 1/2% to the WRITERS GUILD-INDUSTRY HEALTH FUND.

Effective 5/2/99 and 5/2/00, Health Fund contribution may be increased or decreased by up to 1/2%. In this event, minimums for that period will be reduced or increased by the same percentage. Contact the Guild in the second and third periods to ensure that the minimums and contribution rates have not changed.

Employer reporting forms and information regarding benefits are available from the Pension Plan and Health Fund offices:

Producer-Writers Guild of America Pension Plan
Writers Guild-Industry Health Fund
1015 N. Hollywood Way
Burbank, California 91505
Telephone: 818/846-1015

WGA 1998 THEATRICAL AND TELEVISION BASIC
AGREEMENT TELEVISION COMPENSATION

NETWORK PRIMETIME (ABC, CBS, NBC, and FBC)

Applicable minimums

Length of Program: 15 minutes or less	Effective 5/2/98–5/1/99	Effective 5/2/99–5/1/00	Effective 5/2/00–5/1/01
STORY+	$3,106	$3,199	$3,295
TELEPLAY	$7,542	$7,768	$8,001

Installments:
+First Draft: 90% of minimum or 60% of Agreed Compensation, whichever is greater

Final Draft: Balance of Agreed Compensation

Length of Program: 15 minutes or less	Effective 5/2/98–5/1/99	Effective 5/2/99–5/1/00	Effective 5/2/00–5/1/01
STORY & TELEPLAY	$9,331	$9,611	$9,899

Installments:
+Story: 30% of Agreed Compensation

First Draft Teleplay: The difference between the Story Installment and 90% of minimum, or 40% of Agreed Compensation, whichever is greater

Final Draft Teleplay: Balance of Agreed Compensation

Length of Program: 30 minutes or less (but more than 15 minutes)	Effective 5/2/98–5/1/99	Effective 5/2/99–5/1/00	Effective 5/2/00–5/1/01
STORY+	$5,692	$5,863	$6,039
TELEPLAY	$12,248	$12,615	$12,993

Installments:
+First Draft: 90% of minimum or 60% of Agreed Compensation, whichever is greater

Final Draft: Balance of Agreed Compensation

Length of Program: 30 minutes or less (but more than 15 minutes)	**Effective 5/2/98–5/1/99**	**Effective 5/2/99–5/1/00**	**Effective 5/2/00–5/1/01**
STORY & TELEPLAY	$17,076	$17,588	$18,116

Installments:
⁺Story: 30% of Agreed Compensation

First Draft Teleplay: The difference between the Story Installment and 90% of minimum, or 40% of Agreed Compensation, whichever is greater

Final Draft Teleplay: Balance of Agreed Compensation

⁺On pilots only, the writer is to be paid 10% of the first installment (as an advance against such first installment) upon commencement of services. The applicable minimum for a pilot is 150% of the applicable minimum set forth above.

Length of Program: 60 minutes or less (but more than 45 minutes)	**Effective 5/2/98–5/1/99**	**Effective 5/2/99–5/1/00**	**Effective 5/2/00–5/1/01**
STORY+	$10,019	$10,320	$10,630
TELEPLAY	$16,522	$17,018	$17,529

Installments:
+First Draft: 90% of minimum or 60% of Agreed Compensation, whichever is greater

Final Draft: Balance of Agreed Compensation

STORY & TELEPLAY	$25,116	$25,869	$26,645

Installments:
+Story: 30% of Agreed Compensation

First Draft Teleplay: The difference between the Story Installment and 90% of minimum, or 40% of Agreed Compensation, whichever is greater.

Final Draft Teleplay: Balance of Agreed Compensation

Length of Program:
  90 minutes or less

(but more than 60 minutes)	Effective 5/2/98–5/1/99	Effective 5/2/99–5/1/00	Effective 5/2/00–5/1/01
STORY+	$13,387	$13,789	$14,203
TELEPLAY	$23,805	$24,519	$25,255

Installments:
+First Draft: 90% of minimum or 60% of Agreed Compensation, whichever is greater

Final Draft: Balance of Agreed Compensation

STORY & TELEPLAY	$35,336	$36,396	$37,488

Installments:
+Story: 30% of Agreed Compensation

First Draft Teleplay: The difference between the Story Installment and 90% of minimum, or 40% of Agreed Compensation, whichever is greater

Final Draft Teleplay: Balance of Agreed Compensation

+On pilots only and one-time programs 90 minutes or longer, the writer is to be paid 10% of the first installment (as an advance against such first installment) upon commencement of services. The applicable minimum for a pilot is 150% of the applicable minimum set forth above.

Length of Program:
  120 minutes or less

(but more than 90 minutes)	Effective 5/2/98–5/1/99	Effective 5/2/99–5/1/00	Effective 5/2/00–5/1/01
NON-EPISODIC			
STORY+	$17,880	$18,146	$20,701
TELEPLAY	$33,332	$34,332	$35,362

Installments:
+First Draft: 90% of minimum or 60% of Agreed Compensation, whichever is greater

Final Draft: Balance of Agreed Compensation

Length of Program: 120 minutes or less (but more than 90 minutes)	**Effective 5/2/98–5/1/99**	**Effective 5/2/99–5/1/00**	**Effective 5/2/00–5/1/01**
STORY & TELEPLAY	$50,817	$52,342	$53,912

Installments:
+Story: 30% of Agreed Compensation

First Draft Teleplay: The difference between the Story Installment and 90% of minimum, or 40% of Agreed Compensation, whichever is greater.

Final Draft Teleplay: Balance of Agreed Compensation

Length of Program: 120 minutes or less (but more than 90 minutes)	**Effective 5/2/98–5/1/99**	**Effective 5/2/99–5/1/00**	**Effective 5/2/00–5/1/01**
EPISODIC			
STORY+	$17,880	$18,416	$18,968
TELEPLAY	$30,546	$31,462	$32,406

Installments:
+First Draft: 90% of minimum or 60% of Agreed Compensation, whichever is greater

Final Draft: Balance of Agreed Compensation

STORY & TELEPLAY	$46,491	$47,886	$49,323

Installments:
+Story: 30% of Agreed Compensation

First Draft Teleplay: The difference between the Story Installment and 90% of minimum, or 40% of Agreed Compensation, whichever is greater

Final Draft Teleplay: Balance of Agreed Compensation

+On pilots only and one-time programs 90 minutes or longer, the writer is to be paid 10% of the first installment (as an advance against such first installment) upon commencement of services. The applicable minimum for a pilot is 150% of the applicable minimum set forth above.

PAYMENT SCHEDULE

Company will make its best efforts to pay writer within 48 hours of delivery but in no event more than seven (7) days after delivery.

Payment shall not be contingent upon the acceptance or approval by the Company of the literary material so delivered, or upon any other contingency such as obtaining financing.

In certain instances on long-form television movies, the network (or other licensee) has agreed to reimburse the Company for a "producer's draft," even when such draft is not delivered to the network (or other licensee). Please call the Contracts Department for further information.

MADE-FOR-PAY TELEVISION OR VIDEOCASSETTE/VIDEODISC

The minimum initial compensation for a writer shall be the same as the applicable minimum initial compensation for a "free" television program. Where the program is of a type generally produced for network primetime, the network primetime rates are to be utilized.

MADE-FOR-BASIC CABLE

For high-budget dramatic programs, the provisions of the MBA apply. For all other types of programs, the terms of the MBA may be used to employ writers. Producers wishing to negotiate modified provisions may contact the Guild Contracts Department.

INTERACTIVE/MULTIMEDIA PROGRAMMING (DISC, CARTRIDGE, CD-ROM, TELEVISION, THEATRICAL, ETC.)

The Guild is currently offering a modified contract for Interactive/ Multimedia writing. Contact the Industry Alliances Department at WGAW or the Signatories Department at WGAE for information on applicable provisions.

INFORMATIONAL PROGRAMMING

For informational programming, the Guild offers a special contract. Contact the Industry Alliances Department at WGAW or the Signatories Department at WGAE for details,

ANIMATION

The Guild negotiates terms and conditions for animated projects. Contact the Industry Alliances Department at WGAW or the Signatories Department at WGAE for details.

OTHER THAN NETWORK PRIMETIME

Length of Program: 15 minutes or less	Effective 5/2/98–5/1/99	Effective 5/2/99–5/1/00	Effective 5/2/00–5/1/01

HIGH-BUDGET MINIMUMS ($150,000 & over to $60,000 & over in the case of non-primetime network films)

STORY+	$1,972	$2,041	$2,112

TELEPLAY	$3,611	$3,737	$3,868

Installments:
+First Draft: 90% of minimum or 60% of Agreed Compensation, whichever is greater

Final Draft: Balance of Agreed Compensation

STORY & TELEPLAY	$4,926	$5,098	$5,276

Installments:
+Story: 30% of Agreed Compensation

First Draft Teleplay: The difference between the Story Installment and 90% of minimum, or 40% of Agreed Compensation, whichever is greater.

Final Draft Teleplay: Balance of Agreed Compensation

Length of Program: 30 minutes or less (but more than 15 minutes)	Effective 5/2/98–5/1/99	Effective 5/2/99–5/1/00	Effective 5/2/00–5/1/01

STORY+	$3,611	$3,737	$3,868

TELEPLAY	$5,862	$6,067	$6,279

Installments:
+First Draft: 90% of minimum or 60% of Agreed Compensation, whichever is greater

Final Draft: Balance of Agreed Compensation

STORY & TELEPLAY	$9,022	$9,338	$9,665

Installments:
+Story: 30% of Agreed Compensation

First Draft Teleplay: The difference between the Story Installment and 90% of minimum, or 40% of Agreed Compensation, whichever is greater

Final Draft Teleplay: Balance of Agreed Compensation

+On pilots only, the writer is to be paid 10% of the first installment (as an advance against such first installment) upon commencement of services. The applicable minimum for a pilot is 150% of the applicable minimum set forth above.

Length of Program: **120 minutes or less (but more than 90 minutes)**	**Effective 5/2/98–5/1/99**	**Effective 5/2/99–5/1/00**	**Effective 5/2/00–5/1/01**
NON-EPISODIC			
HIGH-BUDGET MINIMUMS ($300,000 & over to $200,000 & over in the case of non-primetime network films)			
STORY+	$6,559	$6,789	$7,027
TELEPLAY	$11,360	$11,758	$12,170

Installments:
+First Draft: 90% of minimum or 60% of Agreed Compensation, whichever is greater

Final Draft: Balance of Agreed Compensation

STORY & TELEPLAY	$16,399	$16,973	$17,567

Installments:
+Story: 30% of Agreed Compensation

First Draft Teleplay: The difference between the Story Installment and 90% of minimum, or 40% of Agreed Compensation, whichever is greater.

Final Draft Teleplay: Balance of Agreed Compensation
Length of Program: 90 minutes or less (but more than 75 minutes)

STORY+	$9,858	$10,203	$10,560
TELEPLAY	$17,473	$18,085	$18,718

Installments:
+First Draft: 90% of minimum or 60% of Agreed Compensation, whichever is greater

Final Draft: Balance of Agreed Compensation

STORY & TELEPLAY	$24,644	$25,507	$26,400

Installments:
+Story: 30% of Agreed Compensation

First Draft Teleplay: The difference between the Story Installment and 90% of minimum, or 40% of Agreed Compensation, whichever is greater.

Final Draft Teleplay: Balance of Agreed Compensation

+On pilots only and one-time programs 90 minutes or longer, the writer is to be paid 10% of the first installment (as an advance against such first installment) upon commencement of services. The applicable minimum for a pilot is 150% of the applicable minimum set forth above.

Length of Program: 120 minutes or less (but more than 90 minutes)	Effective 5/2/98–5/1/99	Effective 5/2/99–5/1/00	Effective 5/2/00–5/1/01

HIGH-BUDGET MINIMUMS ($900,000 & over to $450,000 & over in the case of non-primetime network films)

STORY+	$12,917	$13,369	$13,837

TELEPLAY	$23,176	$23,987	$24,827

Installments:
+First Draft: 90% of minimum or 60% of Agreed Compensation, whichever is greater

Final Draft: Balance of Agreed Compensation

STORY & TELEPLAY	$32,298	$33,428	$34,598

Installments:
+Story: 30% of Agreed Compensation

First Draft Teleplay: The difference between the Story Installment and 90% of minimum, or 40% of Agreed Compensation, whichever is greater.

Final Draft Teleplay: Balance of Agreed Compensation

+On pilots only and one-time programs 90 minutes or longer, the writer is to be paid 10% of the first installment (as an advance against such first installment) upon commencement of services. The applicable minimum for a pilot is 150% of the applicable minimum set forth above.

HIGH-BUDGET MINIMUMS

Rewrite – Applicable Minimum	Effective 5/2/98–5/1/99	Effective 5/2/99–5/1/00	Effective 5/2/00–5/1/01
15 min. or less	$2,127	$2,201	$2,278
30 min. or less (over 15)	$3,552	$3,676	$3,805
60 min. or less (over 45)	$6,719	$6,954	$7,197
90 min. or less (over 75)	$9,897	$10,243	$10,602
120 min. or less (over 90)	$13,073	$13,531	$14,005

Polish – Applicable Minimum			
15 min. or less	$1,064	$1,101	$1,140
30 min. or less (over 15)	$1,773	$1,835	$1,899
60 min. or less (over 45)	$3,364	$3,482	$3,604
90 min. or less (over 75)	$4,945	$5,118	$5,297
120 min. or less (over 90)	$6,535	$6,764	$7,001

PLOT OUTLINE – NARRATIVE SYNOPSIS OF STORY

Company may request writer to prepare a narrative synopsis of plot outline of a story owned by a writer to determine the suitability of the story for teleplay purposes. Company has 14 days from delivery to elect to acquire the outline and to employ the writer. If Company does not proceed, then the outline and all right, title, and interest therein is retained by writer.

APPLICABLE MINIMUMS

	Effective 5/2/98–5/1/99	Effective 5/2/99–5/1/00	Effective 5/2/00–5/1/01
15 min. or less	$986	$1,021	$1,057
30 min. or less (over 15)	$1,643	$1,701	$1,761
60 min. or less (over 45)	$3,116	$3,225	$3,338
90 min. or less (over 75)	$4,606	$4,767	$4,934
120 min. or less (over 90)	$6,072	$6,285	$6,505

BACK-UP SCRIPTS

Applicable minimum compensation for a "Back-Up Script" (story and/or teleplay) is 115% of the compensation set forth herein for story and/or teleplay.

	Effective 5/2/98–5/1/99	Effective 5/2/99–5/1/00	Effective 5/2/00–5/1/01
Format	$6,825	$7,064	$7,311
Bible for Multipart Series	$34,507	$35,715	$36,965
Plus, for each story line			
In excess of six (6)	$3,451	$3,572	$3,697

(A discount of 20% is applicable if "bible" is intended for Non-Network or Non-Primetime.)

LOW-BUDGET MINIMUMS

Story	Effective 5/2/98–5/1/99	Effective 5/2/99–5/1/00	Effective 5/2/00–5/1/01
15 min. or less	$1,678	$1,737	$1,798
30 min. or less (over 15)	$2,791	$2,889	$2,990
60 min. or less (over 30)	$5,279	$5,464	$5,655
90 min. or less (over 75)	$8,048	$8,330	$8,622
120 min. or less (over 90)	$10,633	$11,005	$11,390

Teleplay

	Effective 5/2/98–5/1/99	Effective 5/2/99–5/1/00	Effective 5/2/00–5/1/01
15 min. or less	$2,629	$2,721	$2,816
30 min. or less (over 15)	$4,519	$4,677	$4,841
60 min. or less (over 30)	$8,615	$8,917	$9,229
90 min. or less (over 75)	$13,191	$13,653	$14,131
120 min. or less (over 90)	$17,457	$18,068	$18,700

Story and Teleplay

	Effective 5/2/98–5/1/99	Effective 5/2/99–5/1/00	Effective 5/2/00–5/1/01
15 min. or less	$4,183	$4,329	$4,481
30 min. or less (over 15)	$6,972	$7,216	$7,469
60 min. or less (over 30)	$13,207	$13,669	$14,147
90 min. or less (over 75)	$20,126	$20,830	$21,559
120 min. or less (over 90)	$26,584	$27,514	$28,477

Rewrite	Effective 5/2/98–5/1/99	Effective 5/2/99–5/1/00	Effective 5/2/00–5/1/01
15 min. or less	$1,558	$1,613	$1,669
30 min. or less (over 15)	$2,667	$2,760	$2,857
60 min. or less (over 30)	$5,085	$5,263	$5,447
90 min. or less (over 75)	$7,507	$7,770	$8,042
120 min. or less (over 90)	$9,920	$10,267	$10,626

Polish

15 min. or less	$775	$802	$830
30 min. or less (over 15)	$1,329	$1,376	$1,424
60 min. or less (over 30)	$2,540	$2,629	$2,721
90 min. or less (over 75)	$3,756	$3,887	$4,023
120 min. or less (over 90)	$4,963	$5,137	$5,317

NARRATION (written by a writer other than writer of Teleplay or Story & Teleplay)

Minimums for narration are based on status of film assembly and nature of previously written material as follows:

Nature of Material Written prior to employment of narration writer	Film Assembled in Story Sequence	Film Footage Not Assembled in Story Sequence
None	Rate Schedule A	Rate Schedule B

Story Only	Rate Schedule A	Rate Schedule B
Story and Screenplay	Rate Schedule C	Rate Schedule C

RATE SCHEDULE A	**Effective 5/2/98–5/1/99**	**Effective 5/2/99–5/1/00**	**Effective 5/2/00–5/1/01**
15 min. or less	$4,266	$4,415	$4,570
30 min. or less (over 15)	$7,093	$7,341	$7,598
60 min. or less (over 30)	$13,452	$13,923	$14,410
90 min. or less (over 75)	$19,816	$20,510	$21,228
120 min. or less (over 90)	$26,173	$27,089	$28,037
Plus, for each additional 1/2 hour or fraction thereof	$6,359	$6,582	$6,812

RATE SCHEDULE B

Program Length			
15 min. or less	$4,926	$5,098	$5,276
30 min. or less (over 15)	$9,014	$9,329	$9,656
60 min. or less (over 30)	$16,399	$16,973	$17,567
90 min. or less (over 75)	$23,776	$24,608	$25,469
120 min. or less (over 90)	$31,152	$32,242	$33,370
Plus, for each additional 1/2 hour or fraction thereof	$7,388	$7,647	$7,915

RATE SCHEDULE C

Two minutes or less	$683	$707	$732
Over two minutes to five minutes	$2,392	$2,476	$2,563

Over five minutes of narration: Rewrite minimum for applicable program length

WEEK-TO-WEEK AND TERM EMPLOYMENT

WRITER Compensation per week+	Effective 5/2/98–5/1/99	Effective 5/2/99–5/1/00	Effective 5/2/00–5/1/01
Week-to-Week	$2,871	$2,971	$3,075
6 out of 6 weeks	$2,871	$2,971	$3,075
14 out of 14 wks guarantee	$2,667	$2,760	$2,857
20 out of 26 wks guarantee	$2,460	$2,546	$2,635
40 out of 52 wks guarantee	$2,249	$2,328	$2,409

WRITER EMPLOYED IN ADDITIONAL CAPACITIES

Compensation Per Week Week-to-Week & Term Employment up to & including 9 weeks guarantee	$5,352	$5,539	$5,733
10 to 19 weeks guarantee	$4,461	$4,617	$4,779
20 weeks or more guarantee	$4,013	$4,153	$4,298
Program Fees			
30-minute program	$671	$694	$718
60-minute program	$891	$922	$954
90-minute program or longer	$1,114	$1,153	$1,193

Program fees apply only to network (ABC, CBS, NBC) primetime episodic series. Unless one or more writers has negotiated an irreducible program fee, there is a limit of 3 fees in total per episode produced, which is split among the eligible writers if there are more than 3 eligible writers.

PURCHASES OF LITERARY MATERIAL

The minimums are applicable to purchases of previously unexploited material from a "professional writer" (as defined in the Basic Agreement).

OPTIONED MATERIAL (TELEVISION)

Company may option literary material from a "professional writer" for an initial period of up to 180 days upon payment of 5% of minimum and 10% for each period of up to 180 days thereafter.

+The MBA provides for a discount for a limited period of time with respect to employment on a week-to-week or term basis of a writer who has not been previously employed in television, theatrical films, or dramatic radio. For details, contact the Guild Contracts Department.

SERIALS AND OTHER DRAMATIC FIVE-PER-WEEK (STRIP) PROGRAMS, OTHER THAN PRIMETIME

Aggregate Minimum for Each Weekly Unit of Five (5) Programs (Head Writer)	Effective 5/2/98–5/1/99	Effective 5/2/99–5/1/00	Effective 5/2/00–5/1/01
15 minutes	$8,043	$8,325	$8,616
30 minutes	$13,408	$13,877	$14,363
45 minutes	$19,440	$20,120	$20,824
60 minutes	$24,803	$25,671	$26,569
90 minutes	$37,204	$38,506	$39,854

SCRIPT FEE

For each script on which a writer, other than the Head Writer, performs writing services, such writer will be paid not less than:

	Effective 5/2/98–5/1/99	Effective 5/2/99–5/1/00	Effective 5/2/00–5/1/01
15 minutes	$793	$821	$850
30 minutes	$1,329	$1,376	$1,424
45 minutes	$1,923	$1,990	$2,060
60 minutes	$2,455	$2,541	$2,630
90 minutes	$3,692	$3,821	$3,955

LONG-TERM STORY PROJECTION

The minimum for a long-term story projection (when written by a writer other than the Head Writer) for a non-primetime serial is:

	Effective 5/2/98–5/1/99	Effective 5/2/99–5/1/00	Effective 5/2/00–5/1/01
3 months or less	$11,502	$11,905	$12,322
6 months or less, but more than 3 months or unspecified	$17,254	$17,858	$18,483
12 months or less, but more than 6 months	$23,004	$23,809	$24,642

BREAKDOWNS

The minimum for a daily breakdown of a network non-primetime serial (when written by a writer other than the Head Writer) is:

	Effective 5/2/98–5/1/99	Effective 5/2/99–5/1/00	Effective 5/2/00–5/1/01
15 or less	$336	$349	$363
30 or less (but more than 15)	$655	$681	$708
45 or less (but more than 30)	$802	$834	$867
60 or less (but more than 45)	$1,249	$1,299	$1,351
90 or less (but more than 60)	$1,545	$1,607	$1,671

SCRIPT AND BREAKDOWN EDITING

The minimum for rewriting or polishing a non-primetime serial script or breakdown (when done by a writer other than the Head Writer) is 30% of the script fee.

*The Head Writer aggregate may be reduced by payments of up to five (5) minimum script fees.

QUIZ AND AUDIENCE PARTICIPATION – NETWORK

	Effective 5/2/98–5/1/99	Effective 5/2/99–5/1/00	Effective 5/2/00–5/1/01
APPLICABLE MINIMUM PER WEEKLY UNIT OF NOT MORE THAN FIVE (5) PROGRAMS			
Guarantee			
13 weekly units	$1,944	$2,012	$2,082
14, but less than 20 weekly units	$1,805	$1,868	$1,933
20, but less than 39 weekly units	$1,659	$1,717	$1,777
39 or more weekly units	$1,522	$1,575	$1,630
WRITERS OF QUESTIONS, ANSWERS, AND/OR IDEAS FOR STUNTS WHERE SUCH WRITER SUPPLIES NO OTHER MATERIAL			
Guarantee			
13 weekly units	$1,031	$1,067	$1,104
14, but less than 20 weekly units	$954	$987	$1,022
20 or more weekly units	$882	$913	$945

For syndicated series in production prior to August 8, 1988, the applicable minimum compensation shall be two-thirds (2/3) of the above compensation applicable to network programs.

For series produced for syndication which begin production on or after August 8, 1988, the following formula will apply:

- Two-thirds (2/3) of the above for the first fifty-two (52) weeks of production, and
- Five-sixths (5/6) of the above for the next fifty-two (52) weeks of production.
- Thereafter, the above rates will apply to that series.

If any one program per weekly unit is on a network, then the network rates shall apply to the entire weekly unit. For services on six (6) programs per weekly unit, the applicable minimum shall be increased by 80%. For services on seven (7) programs per weekly unit, minimum shall be increased by 100%.

COMEDY-VARIETY PROGRAMS

APPLICABLE PROGRAM MINIMUMS – Per Program

Length or Time Bracket	Effective 5/2/98–5/1/99	Effective 5/2/99–5/1/00	Effective 5/2/00–5/1/01
5 minutes	$1,172	$1,213	$1,255
10 minutes	$2,329	$2,411	$2,495
15 minutes	$3,286	$3,401	$3,520
30 minutes	$7,131	$7,381	$7,639
45 minutes	$7,736	$8,007	$8,287
60 minutes	$9,810	$10,153	$10,508
75 minutes	$11,421	$11,821	$12,235
90 minutes	$13,374	$13,842	$14,326
120 minutes	$16,939	$17,532	$18,146

ONE PROGRAM PER WEEK, MINIMUM VARIETY SHOW COMMITMENT

If *all* writers on a once-per-week variety series are employed under a contract providing for guaranteed employment in cycles of thirteen (13) or more weeks, then the applicable weekly minimum for each such writer is:

Effective	
5/2/98–5/1/99	$2,590
5/2/99–5/1/00	2,681
5/2/00–5/1/01	2,775

and the aggregate minimum compensation for each program is:

Number of Writers	Percentage of Applicable Program Minimums
1	100%
2	150%
3	175%
4	200%

plus 25% for each additional writer.

FIVE PROGRAMS PER WEEK, MINIMUM VARIETY SHOW COMMITMENT

If all writers on a five-per-week variety series are employed under a contract providing for guaranteed employment in cycles of thirteen (13) or more weeks, then the aggregate minimum compensation for each weekly unit of programs is as follows:

First Period **Effective 5/2/98–5/1/99** **Length or Time Bracket**	**1**	**Number of Writers** **2–3**	**4–5**
10 minutes (Primetime)	$9,022	$9,837	$11,484
(Non-Primetime)	$7,215	$7,869	$9,188
15 minutes (Primetime)	$12,626	$14,266	$15,910
(Non-Primetime)	$10,101	$11,413	$12,731
30 minutes (Primetime)	$21,323	$23,368	$25,429

(Non-Primetime)	$17,060	$18,701	$20,347
60 minutes (Primetime)		$40,182	$42,228
(Non-Primetime)		$32,145	$33,783

Second Period
Effective 5/2/98–5/1/99

Length or Time Bracket	1	Number of Writers 2–3	4–5
10 minutes (Primetime)	$9,338	$10,181	$11,886
(Non-Primetime)	$7,468	$8,144	$9,510
15 minutes (Primetime)	$13,068	$14,765	$16,467
(Non-Primetime)	$10,455	$11,812	$13,177
30 minutes (Primetime)	$22,069	$24,186	$26,319
(Non-Primetime)	$17,657	$19,356	$21,059
60 minutes (Primetime)		$41,588	$43,706
(Non-Primetime)		$33,270	$34,965

Third Period
Effective 5/2/98–5/1/99

Length or Time Bracket	1	Number of Writers 2–3	4–5
10 minutes (Primetime)	$9,665	$10,537	$12,302
(Non-Primetime)	$7,729	$8,429	$9,843
15 minutes (Primetime)	$13,525	$15,282	$17,043
(Non-Primetime)	$10,821	$12,225	$13,638
30 minutes (Primetime)	$22,841	$25,033	$25,429

Third Period Effective 5/2/98–5/1/99 Length or Time Bracket	1	Number of Writers 2–3	4–5
(Non-Primetime)	$18,275	$20,033	$20,347
60 minutes (Primetime)		$43,044	$45,236
(Non-Primetime)		$34,434	$36,189

The applicable weekly minimum for each writer is:

Effective	
5/2/98–5/1/99	$2,590
5/2/99–5/1/00	2,681
5/2/00–5/1/01	2,775

DISCOUNTS FOR NON-CANCELLABLE CONTRACTS

For any writer who is employed under a term contract non-cancellable for thirteen (13) or more weeks, the applicable weekly minimum is subject to a ten percent (10%) discount. For any writer who is employed under a term contract non-cancellable for twenty-six (26) or more weeks, the applicable weekly minimum is subject to a twenty percent (20%) discount. If all of the writers on a variety series are employed under term contracts non-cancellable for thirteen (13) or more weeks, the applicable program minimums are subject to a ten percent (10%) discount. If all of the writers on a variety series are employed under term contracts non-cancellable for twenty-six (26) or more weeks, the applicable program minimums are subject to a twenty percent (20%) discount. Discounts are not applicable to pre-production periods.

COMPENSATION PER WEEK

Length or Time Bracket	Effective 5/2/98–5/1/99	Effective 5/2/99–5/1/00	Effective 5/2/00–5/1/01
MINIMUMS FOR PRE-PRODUCTION PERIODS FOR WRITERS EMPLOYED UNDER MINIMUM VARIETY SHOW COMMITMENT			
First and Second Weeks	$1,811	$1,874	$1,940
Third and Fourth Weeks	$2,072	$2,145	$2,220
Fifth and Sixth Weeks	$2,331	$2,413	$2,497
Thereafter	$2,590	$2,681	$2,775
SKETCH MINIMUMS			
Primetime	$2,416	$2,501	$2,589
Non-Primetime	$1,929	$1,997	$2,067
LYRICS UNACCOMPANIED BY MUSIC	$1,903	$1,970	$2,039

DOCUMENTARY PROGRAMS

For the purpose of documentary programs, "high budget" (HB) refers to programs whose negative cost equals or exceeds the amounts set forth below. Low budget (LB) refers to programs whose negative cost is less than the amounts set forth below:

15 minutes or less	$50,000
30 minutes or less (more than 15)	100,000
60 minutes or less (more than 30)	200,000
90 minutes or less (more than 60)	300,000
For each additional 30 minutes	100,000

STORY AND TELECAST

Program Length in Minutes	Effective 5/2/98–5/1/99		Effective 5/2/99–5/1/00	
	LB	**HB**	**LB**	**HB**
10 or less	$2,582	$3,034	$2,672	$3,140
15 or less	$3,769	$4,433	$3,901	$4,588
30 or less	$6,271	$8,116	$6,490	$8,400
60 or less	$11,897	$14,765	$12,313	$15,282
90 or less	$17,473	$21,398	$18,085	$22,147
120 or less	$23,074	$28,036	$23,882	$29,017

Program Length In Minutes	Effective 5/2/00–5/1/01	
	LB	**HB**
10 or less	$2,766	$3,250
15 or less	$4,038	$4,749
30 or less	$6,717	$8,694
60 or less	$12,744	$15,817
90 or less	$18,718	$22,922
120 or less	$24,718	$30,033

STORY ONLY

Program Length In Minutes	Effective 5/2/98–5/1/99		Effective 5/2/99–5/1/00	
	LB	**HB**	**LB**	**HB**
10 or less	$750	$835	$776	$864
15 or less	$1,105	$1,218	$1,144	$1,261
30 or less	$1,827	$2,206	$1,891	$2,283
60 or less	$3,459	$4,142	$3,580	$4,287
90 or less	$5,094	$6,076	$5,272	$6,289
120 or less	$6,731	$8,007	$6,967	$8,287

Program Length In Minutes	Effective 5/2/00–5/1/01	
	LB	**HB**
10 or less	$803	$ 894
15 or less	$1,184	$1,305
30 or less	$1,957	$2,363
60 or less	$3,705	$4,437
90 or less	$5,457	$6,509
120 or less	$7,211	$8,577

TELEVISION COMPENSATION

Program Length in Minutes	Effective 5/2/98–5/1/99		Effective 5/2/99–5/1/00	
	LB	HB	LB	HB
10 or less	$1,910	$2,608	$1,977	$2,699
15 or less	$2,790	$3,811	$2,888	$3,944
30 or less	$4,754	$6,324	$4,920	$6,545
60 or less	$9,069	$12,006	$9,386	$12,426
90 or less	$13,392	$17,670	$13,861	$18,288
120 or less	$17,717	$23,335	$18,337	$24,152

Program Length In Minutes	Effective 5/2/00–5/1/01	
	LB	HB
10 or less	$2,046	$2,793
15 or less	$2,989	$4,082
30 or less	$5,092	$6,774
60 or less	$9,715	$12,861
90 or less	$14,346	$18,928
120 or less	$18,979	$24,997

PLOT OUTLINE – NARRATIVE SYNOPSIS OF STORY

Company may request writer to prepare a narrative synopsis of plot out-line of a story owned by a writer to determine the suitability of the story for telescript purposes. Company has 14 days from delivery to elect to acquire the outline and to employ the writer. If Company does not proceed, then the outline and all right, title, and interest therein is retained by writer.

Applicable Minimums

Program Length in Minutes	Effective 5/2/98–5/1/99	Effective 5/2/99–5/1/00	Effective 5/2/00–5/1/01
15 minutes	$884	$915	$947
30 minutes	$1,469	$1,520	$1,573
60 minutes	$2,790	$2,888	$2,989
90 minutes	$4,101	$4,245	$4,394

Rewrite or Polish Minimum

Program Length in Minutes	Effective 5/2/98–5/1/99	Effective 5/2/99–5/1/00	Effective 5/2/00–5/1/01
Low Budget			
15 minutes or less	$1,394	$1,443	$1,494
30 minutes or less	$2,381	$2,464	$2,550
60 minutes or less	$4,387	$4,541	$4,700
90 minutes or less	$6,700	$6,935	$7,178
120 minutes or less	$9,017	$9,333	$9,660

High Budget

Program Length in Minutes	Effective 5/2/98–5/1/99	Effective 5/2/99–5/1/00	Effective 5/2/00–5/1/01
15 minutes or less	$1,903	$1,970	$2,039
30 minutes or less	$3,168	$3,279	$3,394
60 minutes or less	$5,997	$6,207	$6,424
90 minutes or less	$8,838	$9,147	$9,467
120 minutes or less	$11,675	$12,084	$12,507

NEWS PROGRAM

Minimum for a single news program script:

Program Length in Minutes	Effective 5/2/98–5/1/99	Effective 5/2/99–5/1/00	Effective 5/2/00–5/1/01
5 minutes	$1,021	$1,057	$1,094
10 minutes	$2,037	$2,108	$2,182
15 minutes	$2,879	$2,980	$3,084
30 minutes	$5,755	$5,956	$6,164
45 minutes	$6,771	$7,008	$7,253
60 minutes	$8,633	$8,935	$9,248
75 minutes	$9,989	$10,339	$10,701
90 minutes	$12,194	$12,621	$13,063

Minimum for News Programs broadcast as a strip five (5) times per week: (Column 1 refers to one telecast per day; column 2 refers to two telecasts per day.)

Program Length in Minutes	Effective 5/2/98–5/1/99			Effective 5/2/99–5/1/00		
	(1)	**Strip**	**(2)**	**(1)**	**Strip**	**(2)**
5 or less	$1,025		$1,676	$1,061		$1,735
10 or less	$1,355		$2,249	$1,402		$2,328
15 or less	$1,706		$2,707	$1,766		$2,802
30 or less	$2,136		$3,094	$2,211		$3,202
60 or less	$2,601		$3,734	$2,692		$3,865
90 or less	$3,063		$4,375	$3,170		$4,528
120 or less	$3,526		$5,015	$3,649		$5,191

Program Length in Minutes	Effective 5/2/00–5/1/01		
	(1)	**Strip**	**(2)**
5 or less	$1,098		$1,796
10 or less	$1,451		$2,409
15 or less	$1,828		$2,900
30 or less	$2,288		$3,314
60 or less	$2,786		$4,000
90 or less	$3,281		$4,686
120 or less	$3,777		$5,373

ONCE-PER-WEEK NON-DRAMATIC PROGRAMS (INCLUDING NON-DRAMATIC CHILDREN'S PROGRAMS)+*

Primetime	Effective 5/2/98–5/1/99	Effective 5/2/99–5/1/00	Effective 5/2/00–5/1/01
5 minutes	$1,023	$1,059	$1,096
10 minutes	$2,037	$2,108	$2,182
15 minutes	$2,885	$2,986	$3,091
30 minutes	$5,762	$5,964	$6,173
45 minutes	$6,776	$7,013	$7,258
60 minutes	$8,638	$8,940	$9,253
75 minutes	$9,999	$10,349	$10,711
90 minutes	$12,194	$12,621	$13,063

Non-Primetime

	Effective 5/2/98–5/1/99	Effective 5/2/99–5/1/00	Effective 5/2/00–5/1/01
5 minutes	$815	$844	$874
10 minutes	$1,537	$1,591	$1,647
15 minutes	$2,304	$2,385	$2,468
30 minutes	$4,070	$4,212	$4,359
45 minutes	$4,984	$5,158	$5,339
60 minutes	$6,439	$6,664	$6,897
75 minutes	$7,121	$7,370	$7,628
90 minutes	$8,982	$9,296	$9,621

PRIMETIME FIVE-PER-WEEK (STRIP) NON-DRAMATIC PROGRAMS (INCLUDING NON-DRAMATIC CHILDREN'S PROGRAMS WHETHER OR NOT PRIMETIME)+*

	Effective 5/2/98–5/1/99	Effective 5/2/99–5/1/00	Effective 5/2/00–5/1/01
5 minutes	$2,104	$2,178	$2,254
10 minutes	$2,979	$3,083	$3,191
15 minutes	$3,388	$3,507	$3,630
30 minutes	$4,381	$4,534	$4,693
60 minutes	$5,009	$5,184	$5,365
90 minutes	$5,941	$6,149	$6,364

NON-PRIMETIME FIVE-PER-WEEK (STRIP) NON-DRAMATIC PROGRAMS+*

	Effective 5/2/98–5/1/99	Effective 5/2/99–5/1/00	Effective 5/2/00–5/1/01
5 minutes	$1,676	$1,735	$1,796
10 minutes	$2,249	$2,328	$2,409
15 minutes	$2,707	$2,802	$2,900
30 minutes	$3,094	$3,202	$3,314
60 minutes	$3,734	$3,865	$4,000
90 minutes	$4,375	$4,528	$4,686

+Use of this category requires notice to the Guild. Contact the Guild Contracts Department for details.

*These rates also apply to dramatic religious programs.

NON-COMMERCIAL OPENINGS & CLOSINGS

Aggregate Running Time of Material	Effective 5/2/98–5/1/99	Effective 5/2/99–5/1/00	Effective 5/2/00–5/1/01
3 minutes or less	$1,773	$1,835	$1,899
More than 3 minutes	$2,490	$2,577	$2,667

COMEDY-VARIETY, DOCUMENTARY, AND NEWS PROGRAMS

Minimal Writing+

Where there is minimal writing and the only literary material written for a program is for openings, closings, introductions, questions, and/or bridging, the minimums for non-dramatic programs on page 25 may be utilized in lieu of the otherwise applicable minimums.

DOCUMENTARY, NEWS, AND ONCE-PER-WEEK NON-DRAMATIC PROGRAMS

Segment Formula+

Different writers may be employed to write self-contained segments of programs under a segment formula subject to certain conditions. Contact the Guild Contracts Department for details.

Minimum Series Commitment

If *all* writers are employed under a contract providing for guaranteed employment in cycles of thirteen (13) or more weeks, then the applicable weekly minimum for each such writer is:

Effective	
5/2/98–5/1/99	$2,030
5/2/99–5/1/00	2,101
5/2/00–5/1/01	2,175

and the aggregate minimum compensation for each program (or weekly unit) is:

Percentage of Applicable
Number of Writers	Program Minimums
1	100%
2	150%
3	175%
4	200%

plus 25% for each additional writer.

+Use of this provision requires notice to the Guild. Contact the Guild Contracts Department for details.

Discounts For Non-Cancellable Contracts

For any writer who is employed under a term contract non-cancellable for thirteen (13) or more weeks, the applicable weekly minimum is subject to a ten percent (10%) discount. For any writer who is employed under a term contract non-cancellable for twenty-six (26) or more weeks, the applicable weekly minimum is subject to a twenty percent (20%) discount. If all of the writers on a series are employed under term contracts non-cancellable for thirteen (13) or more weeks, the applicable program minimums are subject to a ten percent (10%) discount. If all of the writers on a series are employed under term contracts non-cancellable for twenty-six (26) or more weeks, the applicable program minimums are subject to a twenty percent (20%) discount.

GRANDFATHERING OF PROVISIONS

Certain provisions in this section may not be applied to series in production prior to May 2, 1995. Call the Guild Contracts Department for details.

APPLICABLE TIME PERIOD

Where fifty percent (50%) or less of a television program covered by Appendix A is intended to consist of material written by a writer or writers, the applicable minimum compensation shall be the minimum basic compensation applicable to the time period actually consumed by the material but no less than the minimum time bracket indicated:

(1) Primetime Comedy-Variety, One Per Week or Less

Length of Program	Minimum Time Bracket
15 minutes or less	10 minutes
Over 15 minutes but less than 60 minutes	15 minutes
60 minutes or over	30 minutes

(2) Documentary and News Programs

Length of Program	Minimum Time Bracket
15 minutes or less	length of entire film
Over 15 minutes but not over 60 minutes	15 minutes
Over 60 minutes	30 minutes

However, if a writer writes the story and telescript for a one-hour documentary film, the minimum time bracket shall be 30 minutes.

(3) Comedy-variety (other than those specified in (1) above) and Non-Dramatic Programs (other than those specified in (2) above and Quiz and Audience Participation programs)

Length of Program	Minimum Time Bracket
15 minutes or less	10 minutes
Over 15 minutes but not over 60 minutes	15 minutes
Over 60 minutes	30 minutes

PRIMETIME RERUNS ON ABC, CBS, AND NBC

All reruns on ABC, CBS, and NBC in primetime are payable at 100% of the applicable minimums. However, the applicable minimum for the purpose of calculating all rerun compensation is the minimum applicable to "Other Than Network Primetime" television films.

PRIMETIME RERUNS ON FOX BROADCASTING COMPANY (FBC)

	5/2/98–5/1/99	5/2/99–5/1/01
2nd Run	60.5%	66.6%
3rd Run	45.4%	49.9%
4th–6th Run	37.8% each run	41.6% each run
7th–10th Run	22.7% each run	25.0% each run
11th–12th Run	15.1% each run	16.6% each run
13th Run and each run thereafter	7.6%	8.4%

OTHER RERUN COMPENSATION+

The minimum compensation payable with respect to reruns in the United States and Canada (other than in primetime on ABC, CBS, NBC, or FBC) is as follows:

	Percent of Applicable Minimum
2nd Run	40%; 50% if on ABC, CBS or NBC
3rd Run	30%; 40% if on ABC, CBS or NBC
4th–6th Run	25% each run
7th–10th Run	15% each run
11th–12th Run	10% each run
13th Run and each run thereafter	5%

PRIMETIME VARIETY RERUN COMPENSATION, ONCE PER WEEK OR LESS

Compensation for reruns is allocated among the credited writers and shall be computed as follows:

2nd Run	100% of applicable aggregate minimum

3rd Run
    Primetime
    Other Than
    Primetime
	100% of applicable aggregate minimum
	
	75% of applicable aggregate minimum

4th–5th Run	50% of applicable aggregate min. for each such run
6th Run	25% of applicable aggregate minimum
7th Run	10% of applicable aggregate minimum
Each subsequent run	5% of applicable aggregate min. for each such run

+There is a limited waiver based on a ratio of "revenues contracted for" covering syndication reruns of one-hour network (ABC, CBS, NBC) prime-time dramatic series which were not broadcast in syndication before March 1, 1988. For details, contact the Guild Residuals Department.

FOREIGN TELECAST COMPENSATION

Initial Foreign Telecast	15% of applicable minimum

When foreign gross exceeds:
    $7,000 on 30-minute film
    $13,000 on 60-minute film
    $18,000 on longer film
	Additional 10% of applicable minimum

When foreign gross exceeds:
    $10,000 on 30-minute film
    $18,000 on 60-minute film
    $24,000 on longer film
	Additional 10% of applicable minimum

NOTE: For one-hour network (ABC, CBS, NBC) primetime series covered by the limited waiver (see footnote on page 396 for details), the 15%, 10%, and 10% payments are to be collapsed into a single payment of 35%, which is payable upon initial foreign telecast. In addition, the Guild may elect an alternative foreign residuals formula for these series. Contact the Guild Residuals Department for details.

COMEDY/VARIETY FOREIGN TELECAST COMPENSATION

When calculating foreign telecast compensation for primetime variety programs originally broadcast once per week or less, the applicable story and teleplay minimums are to be substituted for the applicable comedy/variety minimums.

RERUN COMPENSATION FOR MADE-FOR-BASIC CABLE PROGRAMS ON BASIC CABLE – "SANCHEZ" FORMULA

The minimum compensation payable with respect to reruns on basic cable of made-for-basic cable programs is as follows:

Percent of Applicable Minimums		
2nd Run	14.4%	
3rd Run	10.8%	
4th Run	9.0%	43.2% (2nd through 5th)
5th Run	9.0%	
6th Run	5.0%	
7th–10th Run	3.0% each run	
11th–12th Run	2.0% each run	
13th Run and each run thereafter	1.0%	

Payments for the second through fifth runs shall be made when the residual payment is due for the second run.

RERUN COMPENSATION FOR MADE-FOR-BASIC CABLE. PROGRAMS ON BASIC CABLE – "HITCHCOCK" FORMULA

For dramatic programs, the difference between the corresponding Network Primetime minimum and the applicable minimum for the program is payable as a reuse fee covering 12 runs over 5 years on the basic cable service. For other types of programs, the reuse fee is 70% of the applicable minimum. The reuse fee is payable upon the initial exhibition of the program.

MADE-FOR-PAY TELEVISION, VIDEOCASSETTE/VIDEODISC RESIDUALS

A 2% residual is payable after certain thresholds are met, depending on the type of program. For details, contact the Guild Residuals Department.

FREE TELEVISION PRODUCT RELEASED ON BASIC CABLE

A 2.5% residual is payable for free television product produced prior to July 1, 1984, released on Basic Cable. For free television product produced after July 1, 1984, a 2% residual is payable. For details, contact the Guild Residuals Department.

USE OF EXCERPTS

The use of excerpts (clips) from a theatrical motion picture or television program in another theatrical motion picture or television program requires payment to the Guild for distribution to the credited writers. For details, contact the Guild.

INTERACTIVE REUSE COMPENSATION

The MBA contains provisions governing additional compensation for reuse of MBA-covered writing in interactive programs. Contact the Guild Contracts Department for information.

SERIES SEQUEL PAYMENTS

If a Company commences exploitation of the television series sequel rights in connection with material to which separation of rights applies, the writer or writers entitled to separation of rights must be paid not less than the following series sequel payments for each sequel episode:

Series of:	Effective 5/2/98–5/1/99	Effective 5/2/99–5/1/00	Effective 5/2/00–5/1/01
15-minute episodes	$766	$795	$823
30-minute episodes	$1,280	$1,325	$1,371
60-minute episodes	$2,432	$2,517	$2,605
90-minute episodes or longer	$3,201	$3,313	$3,429

MOVIE-OF-THE-WEEK (MOW) SEQUEL PAYMENTS

The writers entitled to separation of rights in the first MOW must be paid not less than the following MOW sequel payment for each MOW sequel:

Effective:
5/2/98–5/1/99	$12,805
5/2/99–5/1/00	$13,253
5/2/00–5/1/01	$13,717

Under certain circumstances, twice the above payment applies. Contact the Guild Contracts Department for details.

CHARACTER "SPIN-OFF" PAYMENTS

Character "spin-off" payments equal to the above sequel payments are payable to the writer who introduces a new character in a serial, episodic, anthology, or one-time show if such character becomes the central character in a new serial or episodic series.

RECURRING CHARACTER PAYMENTS

Recurring character payments are payable to the writer who introduces a new character in an episodic series for each episode in which such character appears in the following amounts:

Effective:

5/2/98–5/1/99	$365
5/2/99–5/1/00	$378
5/2/00–5/1/01	$391

Index